The Chicken Came First

T0094876

Friday Prayer

At Hillcrest's Damgoode Pies, Randall's playing
the Beatles' Revolver CD. Yuba City,
CA, my teen grandniece can sing
all lyrics to Elvis gold. A tuba
haloes Tronzo's slide guitar on Spanish
Fly's '94 **Fly By Night** flowing from
my Internet. Spirit, please grant my wish:
Fill our great globe with Bill Asti's wisdom.
Let fearful eyes see what he sees—vast breath
of human song, a single song's lyric
in every action, each chord joining death
and life as one dance linking our mystic
selves to our earth selves—a city divine,
meeting this inspired architect's design.

Roger Armbrust
JANUARY 11, 2008

The Chicken Came First

A PRIMER FOR RENEWING AND SUSTAINING OUR COMMUNITIES

William Henry Asti, AIA

Parkhurst Brothers, Inc., Publishers

LITTLE ROCK

Our National Conversation
Raising the level of public discourse

© Copyright 2011 by William Henry Asti. All rights reserved. No part of this book may be reproduced in any form, except for brief passages quoted within reviews, without the express prior written consent of Permissions Director, Parkhurst Brothers, Inc., Publishers.

www.pbros.net

Parkhurst Brothers books are distributed to the trade through the Chicago Distribution Center, a unit of the University of Chicago Press, and may be ordered through Ingram Book Company, Baker & Taylor, Follett Library Resources and other book industry wholesalers. To order from the University of Chicago's Chicago Distribution Center, phone 1-800-621-2736 or send a fax to 1-800-621-8476. Copies of this and other Parkhurst Brothers, Inc., Publishers titles are available to organizations and corporations for purchase in quantity by contacting Special Sales Department at our home office location, listed on our website. Manuscript submission guidelines for this publishing company are available at our website.

Printed in Canada

First Edition 2011

2011 2012 2013 2014 2015 2016 2017 2018   16 15 14 13 12 11 10 9 8 7 6 5 4 3 2 1

Library of Congress Control Number: 2009942593

ISBN: Hardcover: 978-1-935166-40-5   [10 digit: 1-935166-40-9] $29.95
ISBN: Trade Paperback: 978-1-935166-20-7   [10-digit: 1-935166-20-4] $19.95

An e-book edition of this title is available.

This book is printed on archival-quality paper that meets requirements of the American National Standard for Information Sciences, Permanence of Paper, Printed Library Materials, ANSI Z39.48-1984.

Design Director and Dustjacket/cover design:
Wendell E. Hall

Page design:
Shelly Culbertson

Acquired for Parkhurst Brothers, Inc., Publishers by:
Ted Parkhurst

Editor:
Roger Armbrust

Proofreader:
Drew Glover

Contents

In memory of
Granddaddy Boo

Acknowledgments

I would like to acknowledge a bunch of people. First, the ones I have never met; both from the past and from the present, and secondly, the individuals that I have met, known, loved, and engaged with. The composite writings, discourse and diatribes of all have helped to shape my life experiences and have given rise to my thoughts and my thought processes; thoughts that I address throughout this book, and a thought process which has ceded me a stimulated, fulfilled, wonderful life.

You'll note when reading this book, one of the major themes that runs throughout: the topic of how we can all work together; not how we can call each other names, and not how we can be degrading, but how working together actually accomplishes more than working at odds with each other. Having said that, I recognize that I have, at times, slipped and said things that I shouldn't have said, or maybe in ways that I shouldn't have said them. In light of that, the first guy that I have never met, but should thank, is *Jay Leno* for helping to make what was a terribly negative word—Idiot—into a colloquial term that has become somewhat caustically endearing rather than abusive. I may have used the word a few times in this book, hopefully without coming across as being too mean. You know … in a good way.

Following up on that point, by definition I believe that all of us may act like idiots at one time or another, although some may have greater occasion than others to do so. There are many wonderful well-meaning individuals who seem to have periodic bouts of lunacy, individuals and situations which we will discuss throughout this book; they make this world a fun, crazy, wonderful place, and at times frustrating and seemingly oppressive.

My great enjoyment has been due to the musings of the great thinkers, writers, and philosophers past and present who have influenced me: Aristotle, Spinoza, Francis Bacon, Rene Descartes, John Locke, Thomas Jefferson and his contemporaries, Adam Smith, John Maynard Keynes,

Milton Friedman, Albert Borgmann, and Michael Crichton ... just to name the ones that come immediately to mind.

At 16 years old, my 12th grade civics teacher, Mrs. McKim, required us to read *The Worldly Philosophers* by Robert Heilbroner. That year my quest began in earnest. Forty plus years later I still thank her. As a kid that planned to major in music when I went away to college, that high school class was cause for me to decide to major in economics; eventually deciding to do so at the J. William Fulbright School of Arts and Sciences at the University of Arkansas. This experience unveiled a new world to a boy from Miami, Florida.

My economic education was highlighted by a bunch of great professors. After the obligatory macroeconomic and microeconomic classes, as well as various and sundry pricing policy and transportation classes, I took a class called Current Economic Problems from one of the most engaging professors of my nine years of college, Chuck Britton. If you want to know what the class was like, read *Freakonomics* by Steven D. Levitt and Stephen J. Dubner. That was my class. After you read Levitt and Dubner, then imagine an entire semester of that, graphing everything from the legalization of drugs to the impact of abortion on the future workforce. The purpose was to get us to think and evaluate everything that goes on in the world from the perspective of an economist. It was a turning point for me in looking at the world.

I know that I will leave someone out, but being taught by some of the greatest architects that have ever graced the face of the earth was the best treat of all. Cyrus Sutherland was a brilliant professor and friend, not to mention the first architect that I worked for. Ernest Jacks was at one time head designer at Edward Durrell Stone's office in New York. This guy was one of the most astute, gifted architects in the world. The buildings that he worked on, the stories he told, and the discussions pertaining to the philosophical underpinnings of the great architecture from around the world was invaluable. I must admit that Ernie taught like the great Greek masters. Some of our best discussions were either on his Chris-Craft cogitating the ages on Beaver Lake in Northwest Arkansas, or drinking beer at the Fayetteville Elks Club while awaiting the opening of a tennis court. Sometimes we never got a court. This is where I acquired the excitement and passion for my profession. Education doesn't get much better than that.

Finally ... Fay Jones. Wow! What a beautiful man: the decency, the brilliance, the kindness. For those who don't know, Fay was the most successful disciple of Frank Lloyd Wright, and in some ways, he out-Wrighted Wright. There will be a chapter dedicated to the Wright/Jones philosophy and the implication of that philosophy on creating sustainable communities and a sustainable world. Fay's philosophical prodding over many years is why I do what I do.

With all of this education in hand, there were a couple of situations which proved the catalysts for me designing the first-in-history "Third Wave City of the Future." The oil embargo was one, which I address in the Preface, and the other was due to my lifelong pal, Rod Glaubman. It was while sitting on the beach near the Miami Marine Stadium after sailing for half a day and talking with Rod: We began building a structure in the sand that would eventually become the model for a Sustainable City of the Future.

A special thanks to David Barlow, the guy that has been my *discussitour* and sounding board for the past 25 years—a guy that would pick up the phone and call the likes of Albert Borgmann to ask why we should read his book—and Joe Glass, a dear friend who was cause for me to begin what eventually became one of the largest and most prestigious documentary film festivals in the world.

I am indebted to my local political cronies who developed the neighborhood movement in central Arkansas, and who have involved me over the past 20 years in the most intimate aspects and functioning of a community. Jim Lynch, the most brilliant political organizer along with Annie Abrams and Kathy Wells, and my most special thanks to Ethel Ambrose and the wonderful individuals who make up the Central High Neighborhood Association. Working with that association for the past 15 years has been not just fun, but terribly enriching, developing friendships through our hard work to better the neighborhood. Chapter 32 of this book is to a great degree about these wonderful individuals and the work that we have done.

Thanks to former Little Rock Mayor Jim Dailey who allowed me to chair the first ICE Commission in the United States, and worked with me in addressing educational and telecommunications issues with the Federal Communications Commission and the Office of the President—issues which are vitally important to the evolution of our civilization.

Over an eight- or 10-year period I had the opportunity to spend time thinking out loud with a guy that pushed me beyond what others had. No matter how big the dream I was dreaming, he pushed me to dream bigger and to think in more complex terms. God rest his soul, I miss the push from this man that wasn't afraid to dream big. He was given opportunities beyond most people's wildest imaginations, and he dealt with those opportunities in the most gracious way. Winthrop Paul Rockefeller understood the global implications of what I was doing. He supported me with the political clout of his office as Lt. Governor and as a friend. Win helped to implement some of these dreams behind the scenes in a way that very few people will ever know.

Most important are the guys that I hang out with and their families. I have always held in highest regard the Thomas Jefferson type of farmers. The ones with an intimate understanding of independence, and whose brilliance and work ethic possess a direct philosophical lineage from Columbus and Copernicus; a realization of our place on earth and in the universe; a profound understanding of the freedoms which are the foundations of modernity. Those are the types of farmers and friends with whom I run. That might sound kind of heady for a bunch of farmers, but I guarantee the discussions around a kitchen table on the Grand Prairie can be as good as they get. Believe me, there are lots of Jeffersonian farmers that exist around this great nation of ours.

My most profound thanks to Ed and Rosemary Hooks and all of their kids for making me part of their family when I moved to Arkansas, and a special thanks to Dan and Paul Hooks, Jim Limbird, Steve Adams, Ken Kaufman, Dave Rohlman, and Bill Denton the industrial engineer I run everything past. I don't want to dispel the myth or burst anyone's bubble, but the discussions at our hunting camp aren't always about guns, girls and liquor. I would surmise that our talks about the functioning of our civil society are better, and at times more in depth, than what goes on in the halls of Congress. As we age, we tend to talk more about health care, or should I say our aches and pains, than about guns, girls and liquor—all of which can cause aches and pains.

Finally, to my family: My deepest thanks to Martha Kay, my wife of 32 years, who has supported me in all that I do; in spite of my idiosyncrasies, she seems to have loved me; and to my daughter Lauren, the little girl that caused me to unconditionally love, and gave me reason for putting into motion a process that hopefully one day might help develop our world so that it will sustain itself and become more civil.

Last, I should acknowledge my brothers Jeff, Russell, and Pierre, and my mom, and my dad Helen and Robert. My brothers and I were required to engage in discussions about every subject imaginable around the dinner table every night. You had to have a thought, you had to express it, you had to allow for others to critique it; and you had to defend it against the greatest devil's advocate imaginable ... Dad. We were taught the spectrum of human passion and human endeavor. My mom gave the consent to explore the world at that critical time of life, knowing that I was awkwardly seeking approval. At age 15, having discussions with Mom about inflation, the money supply, and valuation of currency—in the car on the way to Sears—I thought was normal.

My dad was a brilliant attorney who laid the foundation for the constant inquisition of everything, and was cause for my own inquisition throughout my life. He'd send a continuous stream of articles and notes for me to ponder, as well as share hours and hours of discussions and calls about any variety of subjects. This, along with his good counsel and salient advice throughout my life gave me great joy, and he knew it. For 25 years after I got out of college, my dad would buy any book that I was interested in. Dave Barlow and I shared most of them. Sometimes Dad would read it first and then send it on. As he got older and his eyesight diminished, he got to a point that he would say, "Just buy the book and tell me how much it cost." He would then ask for a synopsis.

Dad, this book is my synopsis.

Preface

How many times and how often have you said to others, "How can we be so stupid?" Or "How did we get to the point where we allow ourselves to do such dumb things?"

In 1974 I was working in a restaurant at a North Carolina ski resort when the oil embargo hit. This may not have been the ideal job for a young economist fresh out of college, but it's the type of job that I would recommend to any kid, college or not. It was great fun!

The oil embargo was cause for me as a young economist to begin evaluating how we got into the crisis. It was also the catalyst for me to begin addressing our world's future along with institutional changes necessary to maintain and create civil societies along with efficient economies. Cerebral stuff for a 22 year old? I didn't know any different. That's how my brothers and I were raised: Identifying problems and trying to figure out how to solve them. The difference between me and the majority of everyone else out there in TVland was my relative ability. That is to say, I had relatives that were supportive both morally and financially.

Having studied economics at the University of Arkansas gave this native Miamian the foundational understanding of globalization; but the Oil Embargo of 1974 brought home to me a real-world understanding of what I had learned in the classroom. Living in North Carolina at the worst time of the embargo, there were times when I had to get up at three in the morning—on odd days according to my license tag—to sit in my car, waiting in a long line till the gas station opened, so they could pump their minimal gas allocation within an hour of opening. This made me question a lot more than the availability of fuel. The question wasn't if there were adequate supplies, but how did we get into this situation, and what could we do to make sure it didn't happen again?

The politics and the economics of the crisis were somewhat understandable. The question for me, at that ripe old age, was how to counter the effects of the radical fluctuations in the energy markets, and how to address the micro issues which affect the macro trends and cycles. I wanted to understand better the multiplicity of issues, and how to actually implement micro solutions which could affect our economy's efficiency. I began to focus on the physical environment, the creation of the built environment, and the function of the natural environment. How each of these could become a solution to our collective problems rather than *being* the problem.

My short-term personal solution was to sell my six-cylinder, three-speed, stick-shift, '68 Mustang that averaged 22 miles a gallon, and buy a four-cylinder, four-speed, stick-shift, '72 Subaru station wagon that got an average of 32 miles a gallon. Thirty-five years later, we're not doing any better. People get excited if they get 32 miles to a gallon, if they even care.

My mid-range personal solution was to study Architecture and Planning under some of the worlds finest architects. My long-term solutions will be discussed in some of the following Chapters.

My mid-range solution to become better-educated resulted in being exposed to some of the greatest minds in the world: Buckminster Fuller, Paulo Soleri, Willie Peña from CRS, Ed Stone, Morris Lapidus and more. The professors at the University of Arkansas' Fay Jones College of Architecture allowed us to critically analyze the world. They didn't try to have us think like them, but attempted to expose us to various concepts in hopes that such exposure would catalyze new thought. These were not just brilliant individuals in their own right, but they were great educators. The likes of E. Fay Jones, the protégé of Frank Lloyd Wright; Ernie Jacks, one of the great designers from the heyday of Edward Durrell Stone; Cy Sutherland, Frank "Applepan" Doughty, Dick Kellogg, Mort Carp, Murray Smart, and one of the early pioneers of passive solar design, Jim Lambeth.

Ernie Jacks and Fay Jones brought to the table an international reputation and a level of discussion on global issues that surpassed most architectural schools. Having participated with Mr. Stone on the development of the International Style, Ernie focused on the foundations of modernity and Fay brought to the table Frank Lloyd Wright's philosophy. Embodied within these two individuals were two of the dominant schools of thought in architecture's modern movement.

Fay taught a process which linked all that happens in the world around us into a comprehensive philosophy: invaluable in understanding the complex systems we are discussing in this book.

This comprehensive approach to problem solving, coupled with a detailed approach to programming and implementation, gave the necessary tools to conceive and implement broad, sweeping changes for our society, our economy, and more so, for our institutions.

Still concerned with energy crisis's effects, I began to focus my attention on writing about how to alter our built environment to create greater efficiency, and to lessen our dependence on fossil fuels over the long run. In 1977, while still in school, I started the nation's first private foundation dedicated to educating individuals about the issues of energy-efficient buildings and sustainable communities. Had the world listened to me in 1978, we wouldn't be in the mess we are in today. Those early writings linked energy prices with our national security, our institutional propensity for war, our capital markets, our balance of payments, the productivity of our workforce, and more. Doesn't that sound familiar today?

After nine years of higher education, I was ready to start changing the world, but how and where? I lit in Little Rock, Arkansas because I married a girl from Little Rock. Changing the world from Little Rock would probably not be easy, but Bill Clinton eventually proved it to be doable.

By 1980, I had designed Prodigy, the first third-wave sustainable city of the future. By 1986, I had designed a more complex model for the redevelopment of existing communities for a third-wave economy. That brings us to the present and this book. It's my attempt at presenting much of the rationale for these development and redevelopment models. It's also an explanation of the actual process used in implementing the 1986 model I termed, years later, as the Centennial Model.

Introduction

Ever since I was a little kid growing up at the far tip-end of Florida, I always wanted to know, when my parents were planning a vacation, where we were going, and when we would get there? Having kinfolk in the Midwest and the Northeast, our vacations involved a lot of driving … DAYS of driving, mainly because we had to get from one end of Florida to the other end before the trip really began. Of course, like any group of kids, my brothers and I always wanted to know, once we got on the road: How much farther?

When traveling, our first major question involved how far we'd have to travel until we could eat lunch. Of course, my Mom always had packed a picnic lunch and plenty of snacks. We also wanted to know how far we'd drive on the first day. I mention all of this because it's like a universal truth. I assume that most everybody is the same and, you might be asking where we are going with this book, and how we're going to get there. This book discusses where we are going and how to get there … a road map to creating sustainable communities. There are lots of ways to get there. This book offers a guide to just one of the ways. It is hopefully a discussion that allows you to follow my train of thought. (Notice how I worked in another form of transportation there.) Following this Introduction is a chapter on definitions. Hopefully it will show where we are, (what this book is about) relative to the myriad of categories contained within the subject matter called sustainability.

You may note throughout this book, passages which are marginally inflammatory. This is intentional; sometimes to get things off my chest, and sometimes to get us to think together about an important issue. I make the assumption that we, at times, have screwed up the world, and have degraded it possibly beyond our ability to salvage it. One of the most recent examples is the 2010 oil spill in the Gulf of Mexico. Don't get me wrong, we've faced various forms of degradation since the beginning of time. We as humans do good things, and we do bad things … and we learn from them and then we alter our definitions and sometimes our behaviors accordingly. Throughout history people have rebelled against social degradation, political degradation, and the physical degradation to others and to our environment.

The whole world isn't degraded or ugly. Unabashed beauty and good exist in the world, as well as an interesting level of degradation caused by humans doing things without either looking into the future or understanding the implications. In this book, we will talk about some of these implications: what we should be doing to develop sustainable and civil societies.

We are in a constant tug-of-war, back and forth, to determine everything from our forms of governance, to our forms of conflict, our art forms, our culture and even our language. This will be part of our discussion as it relates to developing sustainable communities, and hopefully a sustainable world. We will discuss the validity of the lineal thought process in which we constantly engage. That discussion will be at the core of HOW WE CONNECT DOTS. Why? Because it is the reason we make so many poor decisions, and sits at the heart of the organizational form of many institutions here in our United States. The assumption that, somewhere in between the extremes, we will find truth or the answers is a false assumption. The lineal processes and corresponding institutions which created our problems and our solutions is just one of this book's components to consider.

I believe we need a certain foundational understanding as we begin to talk about futures. NOT *the* future, but futures ... plural. This is why I have organized the book as it sits before you.

When we travel as individuals, we want to know where we are going and when and how we are going to get there. This also applies to the public at large and to society in general. I contend that this notion is why, here in the United States and in other parts of the world, we have the types of elections where people are concerned about where we're going—the big picture and what our future holds. These elections many times don't concern themselves with the details. Not until we figure where we are going do we need to know the size and color of the car, or the type of tires on which we will be riding, or if we should fill up with gas. Not that these things aren't important, they are! They are very important. However, many times we tend to focus on the big things to the exclusion of the small things, and vice versa. Sometimes we address one aspect to the detriment of the other. This dialogue will lead us to discuss differences among us as humans, and the divisions of labor resulting from our differences, and how we can use these differences to create sustainable communities.

Some folks deal better with the big stuff and some better with the minutiae. This type of specialization and division of labor has been institutionalized for good reason, and many times to our collective detriment. The big picture to small picture tug-of-war is another critical component we will discuss. The adage "The whole is to the part as the part is to the whole," made famous by Frank Lloyd Wright, is a key component to developing the processes necessary to create truly sustainable communities. There will be a chapter on these philosophical underpinnings, and we will explore ways we can do both big and small at the same time.

The objective of this book is to help us think about where we want to go, and how we want to get there. In Section I we will discuss some concepts and establish some premises important in developing a sustainable future. Sections II thru IV focus us on where we have been, how we got to where we are, where we are, and where we want to go. The last segment, Section V, shows a way to get where we want to go, a model that we actually have been implementing.

Think of it this way, we are starting at the southern tip of Florida with Section I. The real trip, Section V, doesn't begin until we cross the state line into Georgia. We have a long trip ahead, but there is a lot to see and do along the way. Maybe we can even stop for a nice picnic. Load up.

Definitions

There are hundreds, if not thousands of books, articles, pamphlets, magazines, and Internet-based publications dealing with the issue of sustainability and the sub-category of "Green." No telling how many documentaries have been made on the multitude of subjects analogous to sustainability. Most of the writings, publications, broadcasts and narrow-casts focus on how we as humans can do our part in making the world less dependent upon depletable resources. The intent is to educate us to the importance of becoming more reliant on resources which are recyclable or can be replenished in a short period of time, that is to say, the average life span of a human being.

> *Sustainability—To meet the needs of the present without compromising the ability of future generations to meet their own needs.*
> —BRUNDTLAND COMMISSION

In the last 40 years or so, sustainability has been most commonly used in relationship to biological and human systems. Having said that, always keep in mind that sustainability is really about how we live as humans. It isn't about mosquitoes or whales or ivory-billed woodpeckers or any number of animals. We define sustainability in human terms. I hope it's apparent that, if we as humans weren't here on earth, we wouldn't be having this discussion. I'm not trying to be coy, but it is important that we keep this whole issue in proper context. Over the past 40 years we have defined humans as the problem; that which has become the aberration to the natural world. We're the one animal on earth that is screwing it up: the organism polluting the Petri dish.For the most part, this assessment is correct. Are we in fact an aberration to the natural world? That subject would be a lot of fun to discuss, but probably not necessary for this book.

We can pigeonhole every aspect of life on Earth into some category of sustainability. That's good, because it helps us to understand the subject's complexity, especially the umpteen varied degrees of biological groupings, like oceans, rainforests, wetlands, prairies and the like. Sustainable biological and human systems come together in an ecological context where we define sustainability as the ability of an ecosystem (of which we have an ecosystem unique to humans) to maintain ecological processes, functions, biodiversity and productivity into the future. This can be expressed in human organization concepts, human activities, and human disciplines, which we will discuss throughout this book.

We are going to define certain human behaviors as problematic. Behaviors which run counter to our ability to sustain ourselves and the biological systems that surround us. Subject to that, we can then define the alteration of some of these behaviors as solutions to the problems that we have created. So this book is also about ... problems and solutions.

It is to the long-term benefit of human civilization to live sustainably. This mandates that we use the Earth's resources at a rate at no faster than the ability for the resources to be replenished. With the projected increase in global population for the next 50-100 years, along with the supposition that sufficient scientific evidence exists that humanity is living unsustainably, we have but a few courses of action available to alter that trend. One action is to alter the amount of depletable resources we consume, or we can alter the numbers of people consuming depletable resources ... or some permeation of the two's combinations. Which way you lean on that subject may be a function of your politics or form of government. or the business sectors which dominate your local or regional economy. Worse case: your leanings may be determined for you as the problem of over-population gets worse and individuals and countries begin to fight for scarce resources ... It's already beginning to happen. Look at the struggle for fresh-water resources in the western U.S.

As for our definition's time frame, if we define replenishable resources in mosquito years, then there wouldn't be any resources to extract for human consumption. On the other extreme, if we define the extraction of materials to be anything replenishable, then even fossil fuels would qualify. There may be more petroleum available in say ... a million years or so. Some believe it is being replenished, but just realllllll sloooowly.

As for the wonderful animals inhabiting earth: sorry, we can only project from a human perspective what we believe to be best for them. I'm not saying that dolphins and whales and other animals aren't important, and I'm not saying that, out of the kindness of our hearts, we shouldn't save all the wonderful animals on earth (the biodiversity). What I am saying is that these are but canaries in the mine shaft. Remember, we are defining from a human point of view. If problems exist in the animal world's survivability, we can infer that there may be some serious problems coming down the pike for humans. As the good humans we are, we try to constantly be aware of impending problems, and we try to solve them.

Since we're considering how to create sustainable communities—part dependent upon outside systems and part independent from outside systems—throughout this book we will categorize in five parts our definition of sustainability. This way we have recognizable components when we get to the *solutions* in Section V. These "Fundamental Five," are Economic, Educational, Legal, Political, and the Built and Natural Environment. We will see a lot more of these five in the following chapters.

As we focus on those issues which most strongly relate to our subject, it is important to understand the myriad of terms we'll use, and where they fit in the big scheme of things.

This book isn't about the eight things you can do to preserve the environment when disposing of waste in your home ... which is important. Nor is it about the various green bio-fuels, or how to buy locally, or cleaning your furnace, or caulking around windows, or changing incandescent bulbs with compact fluorescent bulbs, or using solar concepts and products in the design and construction of your home. It's about a bigger picture. It's about ... **Sustainable Communities**; communities which are a part of a local environment, and which have unique physical, social and economic attributes.

Many of the various related subjects pertaining to sustainability are also important to the development of sustainable communities; however, we're going to focus on those areas most important to the development and redevelopment of the physical environment in which we reside.

The subject of Sustainable Communities is one of the many categories of Sustainability. It's one of the most important areas of systems analysis because it is where the greatest amount of energy savings can take place. It is also where the political structure's rubber meets the road. Where the implementation of goals required to alter the future can take place with dramatic physical results and behavioral results.

I've noted below some of the general categories of sustainability, green things and lists of subjects which one might encounter. These lists are intended to show us where this book fits in the overall scheme of the subject matter. Hopefully, from this you will begin to connect some of the interrelated dots and the not-so-interrelated dots that we will discuss throughout this book.

These categories also include sustainable and green subjects which you might encounter on the news, on the web, in newspapers and so forth. I have highlighted in bold letters those areas which we will discuss in some form.

Some Sustainable Subjects

Sustainable World; Sustainable Life; Sustainable Environment; Sustainable Ecosystems; Sustainable Global Economy; *Sustainable Nations;* Sustainable National Economy; Sustainable Regions; *Sustainable Communities; Sustainable Land Use Policies;* Sustainable Agriculture; Sustainable Global Economy; Sustainable Forest Management; Sustainable National Economy; *Sustainable Transportation; Sustainability Use of Energy;* Sustainable Waste Management; *Sustainable Development;* Sustainable Property Transactions; Sustainable Buildings; Sustainable Building Materials; Sustainable Products; *Sustainable Social Systems; Sustainable Governance;* Sustainable Fisheries; Sustainable Air; *Sustainability and Health;* Sustainable Agriculture; *Sustainable Consumption; Sustainable Production; Sustainable Tourism;* Sustainable Travel; Rural Sustainability; *Sustainable Investment Strategies*

Some Green Subjects

Green Buildings; Green Business; Green Economic Development; Green Economics; Green Accounting; Green Philosophy & Politics; Green Design; Green Architecture; Green Infrastructure; Green Cars; Green Transit; Green Building Materials; Green Clothing; Solar Design; Solar Homes; Solar cars; Geothermal; LEED; more and more.

Section I
Basics
Chapters 1 thru 7

SECTION I of this book includes things that I believe are important; important for a variety of reasons, not least of which is laying the foundation for us to think about issues in context to other issues. It is important for us to develop the ability to, not just think of issues and concepts by themselves, but ALWAYS try to link everything to everything else. Is it tough to do that? You bet. Is it always necessary or appropriate to link everything with everything else? No. I didn't say it is always right or necessary, I just said that we should always try.

Knowing when to link things and when not to link things is the question. The Chapters in this Section will hopefully give some salient arguments as to why we should try. We'll get into the problems that this process creates later in the book.

For years I've observed how we as humans try so desperately hard to do the right thing. Most times we actually believe we are doing the right thing, and sometimes we actually *are* doing the right thing. Believing that we are solving problems we set out to solve is basic to our nature. It seems, however, that recognizing the actual effects of our actions squarely conflict with our psyche when anything goes wrong or seems to go wrong, especially in the political arena. It has always amazed me to see how bright individuals are so capable of justifying poor results, or results which may be marginal at best. They explain how the institution they're working with can only function one way. It's as if some mystical force created the institution—that we as humans actually created—and it can only function separate from human intervention. Let me ask you: Did the institution create us, or did we humans create the institution? Which came first? We'll get real about institutions right away, in Chapter 1.

This book is intended to be a primer on connecting dots … that means thinking about issues in context to other issues. Section I will begin to establish some simple concepts which we'll carry through to the final section describing a model for actually creating a sustainable community.

There will be both positive and negative examples throughout this book. We will hopefully learn lessons from these, and establish the rationale for the models we will showcase in SECTION V.

A little bit of advice for those who are actually interested in creating a sustainable world. We humans have the ability to shape our future. Our task is to determine which future we want, and how we go about implementing that future.

1

Chickens & Eggs

For purposes of this book, eggs are ... concepts, and institutions, and businesses, and governments, and laws, and all the things that surround us and their effects on our lives. We humans are the chickens. The Chickens Came First ... we came first. We are the ones that create the concepts and the institutions. We are the ones that create the businesses and governments and the multitudes of laws. We're the ones in charge. We're the grown-ups. This is the fundamental premise of this book: Understanding that we as humans create the institutions, and can change them or create new ones that are functional for today's society. Without this critical understanding, our ability to shape our collective futures is severely hampered.

Here's what happens over generations: time-honored beliefs develop that these institutions that have served us for so long are there because ... they are there. In most cases, they were there before we were born, and even before our grandparents were born. We become the slaves to these institutions rather than the other way around. Understanding this and embracing this stands at the core of altering aggregate human behavior so we will be able to survive far into the future.

Along with this fundamental premise is a corresponding assumption: We have the ability as humans to shape our future. Some people honestly believe that humans don't have the ability to shape outcomes or control some aspects of the future. They envision only the mysterious hand of a divine being with that ability, a premise that is untenable, and by their own actions verifiably inaccurate. As an example, there's a basic societal understanding that, by educating people in the present, we shape the future. In most cases, we think this type of human behavior will create a future not so grim or hopeless. Even those with the most deep-seeded religious beliefs engage in this behavior supposing a better future.

I know this may sound a tad bit silly, but think about it. We humans have gone about our daily lives working within the constraints of our surrounding institutions, believing for the past 100 or 200 years, or even 1,000 years in some cases, that all our daily doings—along with the tens of thousands of laws which we have created—will, in fact, make a difference ... as we career toward sure oblivion through religious bickering, war, pestilence, super bugs, el Niño, food shortages, oil shortages, water shortages, and global warming.

I remember in high school chemistry how we conducted experiments with various small cultures of micro-organisms swiped across a food source in a Petri dish. In every case the molds would multiply to take up the entire dish, consuming the food and spreading until they had nothing left to consume. Then they would die off. I actually saw that experiment happen in real life during college: a house I lived in with some other guys. The Petri dish was a stew pot and the food source was the stew. After not washing the dishes for about a week, a mold began to grow. We kept an eye on it for two or three more weeks. It grew into one of the most beautiful fluffy, downy, sericeous molds you ever saw, then turned ugly and died. That was so cool. To Kenny Kaufman's girlfriend at the time, it was gross and infantile. She may have been right, but here's the point: We assume in some circles that, regardless of the machinations we put ourselves through as humans, no matter what forms of government we have, no matter what institutions we create, we are going to multiply and pollute and consume all that is in our Petri world. Then we'll die off. Even in a Petri world that is able to regenerate food.

Do the many wonderful accomplishments of mankind really make a difference? Or is all our activity a way for us to just feel good about ourselves? We engage in actions and talk, but are we solving the real problems that face our future?

Some believe the multitude of institutions function to keep us organized and categorized—a manifestation of a human need. But in the end, it won't make a bit of difference.

I'm not trying to make light of this. All of these things are serious. The question for us is: Are we merely delaying the inevitable, or do we in fact have the ability to alter the future outcomes by altering the course of human behavior?

This is the beating heart of our definition of sustainability. Are we able or not as humans to alter this supposed inexorable outcome. Can we look into the future at our Petri world, select an altered outcome and work toward that outcome by creating new businesses, and new institutions? And, as Alvin and Heidi Toffler discussed in *The Third Wave:* can we alter and democratize our institutions to facilitate these selected outcomes?

This mystique that surrounds certain foundational institutions is an outgrowth of their multi-generational nature. This facile, perfunctory acceptance of what has been, hovers at the center of our inability to change outcomes which would benefit humankind. We bow-down to institutions which have, in some cases, outlived their usefulness—institutions that have become entities working in direct conflict to our efforts to survive far into the future.

This philosophical premise isn't about our dominance over our domain, over the land and sea and all the animals on earth. It's about our ability to be creative. It's about our ability as humans to think. *Cogito, ergo sum.* I think, therefore I am ... basic Descartes. (My hope here is that if I throw in a little Latin, you might take me more seriously.)

The recognition of self stands as the foundation of our democracy, as well as the unalienable rights which we possess as individuals. It's the critical component which will allow us, as a civil society, to create institutions that will sustain us far into the future. Self-awareness allows us to recognize that we shouldn't pee upstream. Something unique to humans ... or I should say, to most humans.

Back to Chickens and Eggs. Sometimes eggs need to gestate. Sometimes we need to break an egg. Sometimes we need to poach an egg and sometimes we need to scramble an egg—damn I need to take a break, this is making me hungry.

I just popped a Lean Pocket in the microwave and ate it. I like to kid myself by believing that just because I'm *pretending* to eat healthy I actually am healthy. The fact is it was quicker and easier, and I am just like most of the other couch potatoes out there: give me a clicker and put me in front of the TV with some mindless entertainment.

This is just what we do as a civil society. We pretend or justify that we are doing the right thing because we have a system in place that teaches us and constantly reinforces this premise: We shape our future by working within the institutions that already exist. And did I mention ... it's easier that way.

I have to rely on others for specific information so I can make decisions about my eating habits, my clothing, my housing and so on. This is the foundation of a civil society; but it requires that we get reliable information—the truth.We'll look at this struggle for the truth as we move through the book.

We sense security and permanence in many of our business, social, and governing institutions. This holds true throughout the world for most societies. We love our institutions. We create behaviors to constantly shore up these institutions. After a while, our thinking and decision making flows from the authority of the institution or, in some cases, the rules and regulations of the institution itself. The individual defers. The individual relinquishes his or her ability to think and create ... the antithesis to a vibrant functioning democracy. Are there better ways to allow our institutions to facilitate communication up and down the line? To function in ways that will not constrict our collective futures? I think so..

Being the chicken or at least acknowledging that we need chickens and that chickens come first, meaning we have to have individuals who are constantly creating a new world or re-creating the existing world is a necessary component in the development of our civil society, if we want to move towards becoming a sustainable society. This means, don't get upset when people question the insanity around them, and even more so, don't get upset if someone questions the sanity. This questioning is important. Should it be institutionalized? Yes and No. We just need to be real careful to make sure that we don't turn everybody into eggs as we unwittingly tend to do. We do this by being supportive of and civil towards those who question, not by demonizing them.

This doesn't mean that we have to listen to every opinion that exists, it means that arguments based on facts and are part of our communal quest for truth should be facilitated and in some cases even institutionalized. We will eventually get around to discussing the creation of and need for institutions as a basic component of creating sustainable communities and a sustainable world.

I heard Bill Renfro one day say that Hope is the memory of the future. The question for us is, whether we are able to not just hope for a future which is projected within the memories of our minds, but can we set about a course to definitively take us to that future. That's what we will further explore in the ensuing pages ... helping to chart that course.

Rule 1 ... The chicken came first. We have the ability to shape our future.

2

Sustainability in a *Modern* Democracy

Before I am labeled as an Americentric ideologue I want to briefly give credit to some of our friends around the world. I am one of the first to admit that who we are in America and how we function as a society may seem unique to some, but our origins cover the corners of the globe. To some, we seem to function differently because we have merged the ideas, concepts and institutions from some of the world's great cultures into a functioning civil society which is admired, envied, despised and emulated. America is the melting pot. We aren't a melting pot because we've ever been homogeneous in our culture, national origins, or beliefs; but because our system is constantly melding and bastardizing the institutions, beliefs, behaviors, and other components of those who come here into new institutions uniquely ours.

I recognize that the origins of man are from Africa; the origins of the agriculture age and the Bronze Age from ancient Egypt; the beginnings of communal form in the built environment—what we will be talking about a lot throughout this book—came from Iraq; the Iron Age from Iran and India and, as a result of the end of feudalism in Britain, the Industrial Age. Rene Descartes was French. John Locke and Frances Bacon were both English, which brings me to the issue of modern democracy and a little side story about our democracy based on my personal experience during a trip to Great Britain.

A number of years ago I had to go to London on business. It was during an historic debate that the Brits were having about the future of the House of Lords. A member of that body explained to me that this was only the second time in Great Britain's history that such had taken place.

I didn't have the level of comfort that I needed or wanted with those I would meet on this business venture. I had not been successful at finding enough background information about them. To not be deterred, I called a friend to talk through the situation and see if he knew anyone in London I could rely on if I needed some political help. The friend I called was Dan Garner (god rest his soul), a guy with whom I worked for a number of years on a direct broadcast satellite (DBS) deal: The DBS that is now called DISH Network Corporation whose founder and chairman is Charlie Ergen. While we were still on the phone, Dan patched in a friend of his in London. After the pleasantries were exchanged and out of the way, the conversation was basically: "Ben, my friend Bill Asti is going to be in London next week and I need you to take care of him while he is there." Ben said, "Bill, I'm going to be quite busy but we will make a point to get together. My telephone numbers are, etc. ... Call me when you get settled and when you think you have time to get together." Well, that was easy enough. I now had my comfort level, somebody I could trust in a foreign land, and I was ready to go to London.

After arriving in London the following week, and after my first set of meetings and a nap, I called Ben at the number he gave me. Dan never told me much about Ben other than he was a wonderful friend that he would trust implicitly. To my surprise, the number I called was the House of Lords. This wasn't just Ben I was calling, it was Lord Benjamin Mancroft. You know ... a member of the House of Lords.

Ben, I mean the Honorable Lord Mancroft, told me that he was busy and if it was alright with me, would I mind coming over to the House of Lords for drinks and dinner that night. Alright with me? What a treat! He told me to take a cab to the peers entrance—the cab driver would know where that was—and let the fellow at the entrance know whom I was calling ... which I did.

After a few minutes, Lord Mancroft came down and greeted me. He then proceeded to take me on a tour of every significant and non-significant area of the British Parliament, from the House of Lords and the House of Commons to the coat room and everything in between. I realized later that there was a method to his madness, or should I say more properly, a reason for all that he was doing.

I had a really great scotch in the private bar where he introduced me to various individuals as a yank from America. I'm not sure that he said from America. That would actually be redundant. I think he just introduced me as Mr. Asti who was a yank. You may be asking, what does having scotch in a bar have to do with democracy and sustainability? I'm not sure. It just seemed to be an interesting part of the story that I should relay to you.

Dinner in Parliament's dining hall was wonderful. As we dined, introductions continued to various individuals from the House of Lords who never failed to ask what I thought about their current debate, the debate for which final arguments were scheduled later that evening, about 11 pm London time.

Because of my jet lag and time zone difference, my days and nights were mixed up. This was great for me in this particular instance, because at 11 pm I was wide awake. Due to my then current state of insomnia, I had earlier in the day watched the ongoing debate on their government channel What did I think about the debate they were having about the "future of the House of Lords?" I suppose that, due to my interest, or maybe to my expressed opinions, or maybe it was due to Lord Mancroft's interest in educating a yank about English democracy, he asked if I would like to stay after dinner for the final arguments. I couldn't wait.

After Ben talked to a couple of different individuals, I was ushered to one of the private small side balconies overlooking the House of Lords where I could watch the goings-on. How cool was this, a treat of a lifetime. The cap to one of the most wonderful evenings of my life ... But wait, it wasn't over. After the closing arguments everybody filed out to mingle and talk about the debate. I walked downstairs and mingled with all of the members, just like I was one of them. I was glad that I wore my best suit that evening. That might sound petty to some, but this wasn't a House of Blues event. This was a House of Lords event, and looking nice and being respectful to my host was something ingrained in me from the time I was a little kid.

While talking to various House members, a young documentary filmmaker walked up to me and asked; as an American, what did I think about this issue? I now found myself in the awkward position of talking for America. How weird was that? I heard a lot of issues discussed on TV, over drinks and dinner, and during the final arguments that evening. But the one issue that I had not heard was that of a parliamentary democracy versus a popular democracy ... both being representational. I asked this young documentarian to look around and tell me how many individuals in the room she thought could get elected in a popular election. And did she think that only those with the looks or oration skills should be allowed to opine and give counsel as to the future of Great Britain, the way America does. I told her that all democracies that I knew of, including America's, have a way of soliciting the sage advice of a broad spectrum of individuals;

but because of the evolution of the forms of governance that Great Britain had experienced, their form allowed the Queen to appoint those who's vested interest, their history and status could be advantageous to the country's future. Notice I said could be.

She asked if she could come to America and interview me for the documentary she was doing. My immediate response was no. I wasn't about to tell my host on film how I think they should govern themselves.

After we finished the evening of wonderful discussions, Lord Mancroft led me to Westminster Hall and had the guard turn on the lights. He positioned me at various locations within the hall where historical figures once stood, or had their heads cut off, and proceeded to give me a 45-minute private history lesson about Great Britain and the origins of my own American democracy. Now we're talking a treat of a lifetime for which I will forever be in his debt.

This leads me back to the issue of power and status giving the right to advise. It does make sense to solicit the opinions from those whose successes have added so greatly to a country's status and treasury. However, the status or dominance of the institutions created around this should be thoroughly questioned as to their long-term implications. We in America never think that anyone with wealth, power, or status has all of the answers. So we have a democratic system of governance that actually exacerbates change to the dismay of some, and constantly alters the status quo in an attempt to find truth relative to other democracies—a real attempt at expressing the foundations of Modernity. Let me explain.

Many of the institutions which function within modern democracies are fundamentally different from those that function within various authoritarian forms of governance. How sustainable concepts within these different forms are implemented is just as different.

The underlying conditions for the origins of modern democracy are important to understand ... at least they are to me. Without that basic understanding I have found that we tend to lose sight of the broad trends which keep us focused on how to create the new institutions which can guide us to a sustainable future. The models for creating sustainable communities that will be discussed in SECTION V are based on the origins of modern democracies, and on my understanding of Modernity.

Indulge me for a moment. I'd like to review a little history. M—O—D—O is the Latin origin for modern. MODO meant just now. It meant recent; the present; contemporary; the time frame of the present. MODERN in present-day usage arose from the desire to distinguish one's culture from one's predecessor's. Actually, to deviate a little, and to be more correct, in classical antiquity a time continuum, or more properly stated, a relationship existed between generations that possessed an historical consciousness. Meaning the kids did what the parents did, and there weren't a lot of questions asked. The way of the world was the way that it was supposed to be, and you pretty much accepted it.

During the first half of the 2nd Century B.C., a Greek grammarian named *Aristarchus* distinguished newer poets from the ancient *Homer*. This distinction of newer to ancient carried through until the late 5th Century A.D. when the Latin word modo appeared and left it to the Middle Ages which distinguished then from now. "That was then—this is now."

MODO-ernism as we think of it today is global. Originally it came from local circumstances of the Medieval Period. That's how our global movement on sustainability began, with the caveat of the communications technologies helping it become a global phenomenon faster than it would have otherwise.

The social institutions, the work related institutions and the human behaviors of the Middle Ages ... authority, chivalry, community, courtesy, celebration, and craft ... still exist in some forms within our society and other societies. In some societies these exist very meagerly, and in others somewhat more robust. Regardless of the machinations a society may put itself through, some of these behaviors are falling by the wayside, and many of the institutions created to support these behaviors are constantly being dissolved. This reshaping of behaviors, institutions, and the functioning of society remains a constant in the modern world, and it's very important that we understand this if we are to survive. It's a key to implementing sustainable solutions to our local and global problems.

The ancient cultures of Rome and Greece came to uncertain endings over a fairly long period of time. It was a slow, arduous process. Contrast that to the demise of medieval life in the late 15th Century which came to a grinding halt as the result of technology and ideas. Then contrast that to the rapid generational changes that that we accept today as if it's no big deal.

At the turn of the 15th Century, you saw the destroyers of medieval culture: Columbus, Copernicus, and Martin Luther. Medieval culture was locally bound, and you were geographically bound to your community. Columbus destroyed Middle Age geography. Medieval culture was cosmically centered, meaning the earth was at THE center of all that we knew. Copernicus de-centered the earth. This was scathing, not to mention being psychologically devastating, mainly because people were vested in the institutions which perpetuated the myths. Medieval culture was divinely constituted. The Roman Catholic church was the power structure and the mouthpiece for God. Martin Luther protested that, initiating the Protestant Reformation. He helped make the bible and the individual the final authority on Christianity and gutted the power of THE church.

The result was that overnight my little plot of land and my land lord were not my only world; and come to find out my world was not the center of the known cosmos or the center of divinity; and to beat all, I didn't have to do what the powers told me to do.

This is the origin of individual freedom, and the foundation of democracy. This is the origin of our Constitution. This is the reason why we have the right to be where we are and to do what we do. This begins the modern world as it exists today. And as I had discussed in a recent presentation that I made to a conference sponsored by the American Institute of Architects, this represents the origins of many of our social institutions today. This was the start of Social Activism, leading to future institutions required for us to create truly sustainable communities and a sustainable world.

Back to Columbus, Copernicus, and Martin Luther ... Think about it: There existed at that time a phenomenal vacuum in the power structure and in the day's form of governance. From that vacuum came the founders of MODERNITY, the French and English guys, Frances Bacon, Rene Descartes, and John Locke.

Bacon's *New Atlantis* helped us to find the proper foundation for modern research & technology. Descartes' *Discourse on Method* gave us rationality for starting from the beginning and for understanding our world, and Locke's *Second Treatise of Civil Government* derived from the origin of nature, of man, and of god, governance by reason ... the origins of our Constitution. This was the enlightenment, the dawn of human liberation. Man's conquest for THE truth began in earnest. At this point in time, it was inexorable; it was the movement; the revolution; the quest for that which democracy cannot do without ... TRUTH.

This end of one period and beginning of another yielded the institutions that today allow us to question what we do. It has allowed us a socially civil way of questioning our collective insanity of how and why we pollute our Petri world.

It was reason reigning over superstition and dogma. It was reason over oppression and authoritarianism. Does any of this sound vaguely familiar today? Could this be one of the reasons why we have the cultural wars today not just globally, but even within our own society? Modernity, the modern project, is that which some despise and want to do away with. It is the foundation for the philosophical incompatibility causing recent conflict and war—an incompatibility between medieval beliefs and the corresponding institutions and modern beliefs and their institutions.

Thomas Jefferson summed up these basic fundamental truths. He said that the superstructures of the physical and moral sciences have been realized in the **institutions** of science and democracy. These institutions, that Jefferson saw then, are established as norms or expectations today. Scientific perspective which resulted from the demise of medieval culture is pretty well accepted globally today, and remains for the most part unchallenged. This dictates that CHANGE will remain a constant in our lives until we find ultimate truth. Without the modern institutions which have emanated from the institutions of science and democracy, we would not have the freedom to explore for institutional, behavioral and technological solutions to the problems that we as humans are experiencing and will continue to experience. Solutions to issues like overpopulation and pollution in our Petri world.

Democracy is the institutional process which took hold in the western world and has spread as a result of a commitment to freedom and equality. This is why I truly believe that we will not just find solutions to our problems—which come from that quest for truth—but we will be able to actually implement the solutions due to our collective openness.

Back to Jefferson for a moment. He said, "It is incumbent on every generation to pay its own debts as it goes." Not leaving a burden to future generations is at the heart of the definition of sustainability. Polluting the environment so future generations will have to clean it up is, in fact, leaving a debt to the future. Spewing tons of particulates into the air which can affect the health of future generations is, in fact, leaving a debt to the future. Altering the environment which can cause global warming or a new ice age is, in fact, leaving a debt to the future. These things that we do, whether all verifiable in fact or not, run counter to the issue of sustainability; not to mention it is just wrong to do that to our kids. It is, in fact, anti-democratic and could potentially ruin our modern democracy.

3

The Day the Earth Stood Still
Politics & Economics in a Sustainable World

Gort! Klaatu barada nikto! ... means save these idiots from them-selves. Actually the quote comes from the film "The Day the Earth Stood Still." It was a statement to keep the robot Gort from destroying the sol-diers facing him, so he and the protagonist Klaatu could leave Earth and report back to their world that humans can't live in peace. The result would then be that the rest of the universe's inhabitants were going to destroy earth before earth destroyed the universe. Whew! Where are Klaatu and Gort when you need them? Even though the premise of the original 1951 movie was about war and peace, I like to think it could also be about our inability as humans to do what's necessary to coexist with each other both in the universe and in our Petri world.

The issue of sustainability, even with all of its many permutations and variations seems fairly simple and straight forward ... that is until politics and economics come into play. I'm not saying politicians and economists, I'm saying politics and economics: Two human institutions with the ability to alter future outcomes through the understanding and altering of human behaviors.

I met an old investment banker named Witt Stephens from Little Rock many years ago. He was one of the most affable and successful individu-als in the world. At that time, I guess it was 25 years ago or so, he had the largest Off-Wall-Street investment bank in the United States, and from what I understood, the best capitalized investment bank in the nation. There were some really wonderful stories that had circulated about his business dealings as well as his personal life, and equally wonderful adages attributed to both him and his brother Jack. The one maxim of Witt's that I found to be most insightful was how he defined politics. He said that politics wasn't the best game in town … it was the only game in town. As explained to me, politics wasn't about dealing with politicians and specific legislation (although it could also be about that), but it was having lunch with a friend or talking to an investor about opportunities, or visiting with a janitor about what was going on in his neighborhood, and on and on and on. It was understanding that what we did in our daily lives and how we engaged with others at all times was, in fact, important, very important. Important enough to constantly be aware of how you lived your life, and the impression you gave to others about yourself. Politics in this sense is the only game in town.

Mr. Stephens was old school, cut from the same cloth as the likes of Claude Pepper and Wilbur Mills, and the likes of my own dad, and the likes of Win Rockefeller and Jack Eckerd and Percy Malone, and I could go on and on. This wonderful group of people knew how to make things happen by being engaged as well as demanding—demanding extremely high standards from the people with whom they "politicked."

I mention this "politicking" and how we present ourselves because each of us has the ability to politic; and each of us needs to politic more if we are to create a sustainable world for future generations. When bunches of us politic together and we focus on the same subject, that's called a movement. And when we actually put our money where our mouth is, like Mr. Stephens did for many years, it's called something like … not just talking, but actually doing something. It's like the early pioneers in the green/sustainability movement that actually built solar homes and self-sufficient homes 40 years ago when most people thought they were crazy. They put their money where their mouths were. You have to credit them and admire them. They actually did something. They didn't just talk about it.

When we politic, we are engaging with others. We have to constantly educate others with our words and our deeds. We *show* the importance of doing what we can to individually bring about changes that will help take us into a future that allows us to survive more humanely … like the early pioneers in the green movement did.

The fun part of writing a book is that you get to give advice on things. So, here's my first bit of wisdom to everyone that wants to help create civil, sustainable societies: When we politic, it is important to not polarize each other or to require everyone to reside at one extreme of the opinion spectrum or the other. I say this because the purpose of polarization is to stifle debate, including legitimate debate. Remember that debate in our democracy is the process that we use in the public arena to find truth.

Now, a little caution … The lineal process of being for or against, and believing that through this process we find truth, isn't necessarily true. This "Crossfire Syndrome," as termed by Michael Crichton many years ago, is at times at the heart of our inability to solve many of our communal problems.

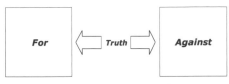

Figure 2.1 – The "Crossfire Syndrome"

Some of the most important institutions that we have created in our democracy are based on this model: our legal system, our media, and our political system. For those in media and in politics, exacerbating the extremes for ratings or for votes doesn't mean you are engaging in a quest for the truth. There ARE more than two sides to any number of issues. The extreme positions of the Crossfire Syndrome require distorted simplification, framing the debate in ways which many times ignores the real issues. Worse still, this type of characterization lies at the heart impulse to polarize every issue.

My next bit of advice … Don't do that!

Mr. Stephens wasn't successful because he was a jerk; he was successful because he was considerate and looked for common ground. He didn't try to polarize people. He was thoughtful and tough.

At some time in the future, we may need everyone to work together and trust each other to do what is best. That's not done by alienating each other or constantly attacking the motives or the personal lives of everybody that doesn't agree with you. We each should try this attitude: We are going to educate ourselves and others with our deeds and our words, and we are going to try to learn from each other. It doesn't mean that you will actually accomplish that, or in all cases that you actually should. It means you will allow for legitimate debate … all sides … to take place. This is the sophistication of Mr. Witt's politicking. My suggestion is that your next New Year's resolution could be that each of us will attempt to politic like Mr. Witt.

I repeat: The issue of sustainability is fairly simple until politics and economics come into play. The politics of debate can at times be restrictive, especially if done by using the crossfire syndrome. However, the stifling of debate isn't only done through the overt debate process. Sometimes the muzzling of discourse can be quite subtle. Depending upon your status or your wealth, it can be as simple as the raising of an eyebrow, the wink of an eye, or the shrug of the shoulder. For someone of wealth or power it can be a simple phrase which others may interpret as meaning to not engage with "those people." The net effect on those who are afraid to cross "the man" or even in today's world "the woman" is to ostracize individuals or groups that may, in fact, be doing good or have something to offer. These individuals and groups become outcasts … the closest thing to being a leper who others learn to avoid. These behaviors become reinforced and institutionalized over a period of time. That has been done to many in the green movement for the past 40 years. Think of where we would be today had we listened to some of those kooks and tree huggers. We don't need to be afraid. Just because we listen doesn't mean we have to adopt what the others might suggest. It just means listen. Find the truth, and if appropriate, adopt what's good and throw out what isn't.

I noted in one of the other chapters that I had a wonderful relationship with my former Lieutenant Governor, Winthrop Paul Rockefeller, who was extremely cognizant of how others could be tainted because of his position and wealth. He tried to make sure he always discussed issues with me, especially the issue of sustainability and its implications to developing communities of the future. He was always careful with his words and actions around others, knowing it could debase an issue and negatively affect both those who needed to be persuaded and those who were trying to persuade. He didn't want anyone to be afraid of discussing subjects important to our future. Again, a great example of the nuance of political action and leadership.

The use of the crossfire syndrome has been exacerbated over the years by the media, sometimes because they want debates to be seen and heard

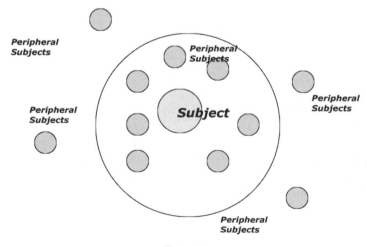

Figure 2.2

and they know that people will tune in if they dramatize the extremes ... their polls don't lie. They show that this type of "debating" is sellable. However, we've begun to notice that today's debates are being framed differently with today's technology. The hope is that we begin to see the debates and our politics shift from the lineal form (shown in earlier figure 2.1, page 39) to the spherical (figure 2.2, page 40).

Dave Barlow and I have been using this spherical form of discussion for 25+ years. We have found that we can actually keep track of issues better as they relate to other issues ... It's easier to connect complex issues over the long run. It's easier to connect dots.

Politics & Economics in a Sustainable World

In the preceding chapter we painted with a broad brush the important role that modern democracy plays in creating a sustainable world: A political movement which is important to our future. However, the lead-up to that discussion is as equally important to understand ... the relationship between politics and the functioning of an economy in a third-wave (communications-based) economy. This will be a fairly simple discussion about some complex relationships.

Local politics are integral to the development of creating sustainable communities. All movements start with small groups of people at a local level. That's the reality of politics and the nature of the beast. When you have an issue that needs to be addressed in a democracy, you do something about it. Remember, we are the chickens. We have the ability to do what we know to be right if we so decide. We don't need politicians or government to tell us what to do and how to do it.

As an example, the green movement started at the local level with a focus on greening homes and passive solar design and active solar systems for homes; this has grown to a worldwide social and economic movement. It was not a movement which emanated from any governing institution. However, once a movement gets started and the social and economic rationale becomes apparent, then governments tend to get involved, mostly as a cheerleader and—as we have seen in the green/sustainability movement and in more recent years—with real expertise and with some money, meaning *your* money. Once public money gets involved in the process, we begin to step into the complex issue of the economics of sustainability and the governing politics. We then tend to think we are actually doing something about an issue when in fact we may not be. It's amazing to me how brilliant people are capable of allowing governing institutions to function that way.

A few obvious components are required for third-wave (communications-based) communities to sustain themselves. First, as with any society and any type of economy, is the issue of survivability in a dysfunctional economy and the relationship to governance. The second is the issue of protection of capital and the security of your community and nation.

The UN has issued a report looking into the future based on current trends; and guess what? There will be more population growth and much more poverty as a percentage of population—crushing poverty that can affect the operations of our governments, the harmony of our populations, and the functioning of our economies. Survivability in a dysfunctional economy is many times overlooked in the discussions of creating sustainable communities. If your economy is in the tank, and your community is trying to survive, like many communities throughout the world are trying to do, it becomes extremely difficult. For example, how do you develop green-forest programs when the populace is using every piece of wood in sight for cooking? You have no ability to produce inexpensive housing components and housing alternatives locally, because your local environment has been decimated. Your community doesn't create any wealth, so you are not even able to purchase from outside your area the basic necessities to survive ... So you're in a world of hurt. And by the way, this has been going on in small communities throughout the U.S. for decades. Thousands of little towns have dried up and blown away over the past 150 years or so. In the big scheme of human history, that can be good in some respects and not so good in others.

Don't believe that people who live in abject poverty live in a sustainable world. Granted, tribes deep in the Amazon jungle live in a sustainable fashion. For them, the definition of poverty and wealth don't apply. That's a different world and a different model. Sorry to tell you, but that model is not sustainable for the number of people on the globe today, so don't think that's a viable alternative.

What does all this have to do with us creating sustainable third-wave communities? Everything! It matters not what type of economy you live in. If no one is producing anything, then you can't survive. If you believe that 12 million people in New York City are going to produce enough farm products on the land they inhabit to feed themselves, then I have a bridge in Brooklyn I want to sell you.

So how do you produce things? You use your elbow grease, your back, your wits, your mind and, in today's world, some investment capital ... money. Money will be invested in your community only if you can convince someone to either give you some or loan you some. Governments and nonprofit groups give money. Investors and banks loan money. The interesting dichotomy: Investment capital requires a level of government and societal stability where government money doesn't.

Ahh ... we now get to the second issue: the protection of capital and the security of a community and nation. For sustainable investments to take place, there must be some assurance—guarantee—that those who loaned you the money will get it back; and if you save your money, you will be able to get it out of the bank. This is where politics and economics collide. For sustainable investments to take place—not just investments, but sustainable investments—those with the money to loan prefer to deal with the individuals that will repay the money. If they don't repay the money, there is some legal recourse. This issue has been turned on its head to some degree recently with the 2008 economic meltdown, and the U.S. government's investing in a number of corporations.

A person (or company) that makes money, in say Senegal, either spends that money in the local economy, or goes outside the local economy and spends it somewhere else. If she doesn't spend it, she saves it. Depending upon the level of security of the institutions and the community, she either saves it under the mattress or an institution where she gets the highest most secured returns. This next statement may seem simple, but typically savings doesn't occur in a society that can't or won't protect the savings. In functional economies, savings equals investment. This means if you can't at minimum have savings and secure those savings, there is a great likelihood that there won't be much investment. How do you have a sustainable community without savings and investment? That's a tough one. Maybe you'll come to some of the same conclusions that I have by the time you finish the book. If you don't, call me and we can discuss it.

I hope it's becoming apparent why democracy and capitalism work so well together. Most investment capital prefers stable democracies and a viable, fair, honest legal system devoid of outside political control. That way, they aren't squeezed by some strong-arm man, or have to collect debts with guns. It is preferable for investors to work in democratic systems with a rule of law. It is actually easier to assess risks as well as project long-term returns in a democracy than in an authoritarian regime where you're at the mercy of the whim of one individual or a group of people. That's what scares capitalists about socialist systems when it comes to distribution of investment capital, especially when the governing institutions begin to border on being authoritarian. An individual's cash goes where it will be protected. An institution's investment funds will go where they will be protected and where they can expect to make a profit, and where decision making is not encumbered by outside institutions or individuals who are not concerned about profits. Why do you think a great deal of money derived from Arab-world petroleum is invested in those economies with democratic governments and a rule of law?

Government institutions are not established to create profits. If they are creating profits, they are competing against the private sector. They then can act like a monopoly or an oligopoly, two entities that tend to be detrimental to consumers by limiting competition. That's one of the reasons why democratic governments try to control monopolies legislatively.

Anyway, the democratic rule of law is vital to the development of sustainable communities. Without that you can't have a level of wealth creation and investments, including long-term investments which will affect the ability of your community, rich or poor, to sustain itself.

As an aside, a political conflict exists within the sustainability movement which we won't dwell on in this book, but it is helpful to know some of the issues and how they can be resolved over the long haul. It is the conflict between economic parity/equity on a global scale and the issue of producing the things you need locally. The former requires a greater focus on exporting goods to the rest of the world to create sustainable wealth versus producing the goods you need locally so that you are more sustainable. In the case of the latter, we would decrease our imports and exports as would China, and India and Korea and Botswana. You think the world has problems now ... what would be the net effect if Nigeria no longer exported their raw product of oil which creates wealth in their economy? You think they're poor now. Economic balkanization could take place. The opposite being free trade zones or open borders. These have a greater chance of creating wealth and sustainable investments for poor countries. It can be a foundation for savings and investment. If controlled by enlightened and educated individuals, and hopefully democratic governments, it would mean a foundation for developing sustainable initiatives ... just some food for thought.

In the run-up to the 2000 U.S. presidential election, Governor George W. Bush announced he would be visiting Central High School, in the Central High Neighborhood near the core of Little Rock. For those who aren't aware of the history, in 1957 nine black students integrated the all-white Central High School. Arkansas Governor Orval Faubus used the National Guard to try to keep the black students out. President Eisenhower used the 101st Airborne to guarantee the nine students' safety, affording them equal opportunity to education as guaranteed by our Constitution and affirmed by the U.S. Supreme Court in Brown versus Board of Education.

This represented a real showdown over civil rights and the power and rights of the states and of the federal government. (Betsy Jacoway's book on the subject is a great start if you want to know more about the "Crisis at Central High.")

The Central High neighborhood is the area where we have been working for the past 15 years, creating a model for redevelopment into a sustainable third-wave community. Lt. Governor Rockefeller, a Republican, had been brought up to speed about the project on numerous occasions, and was familiar with the grassroots players involved in the community redevelopment. Then it was announced that the Texas Republican governor would be visiting the site, doing a Q&A and a photo-op with students, teachers, and individuals within the neighborhood. So this question arose within the Republican circles: Who are these community people that have been invited?

Win, being the good Republican that he was, looked at the list and recognized some of the names. Knowing that I had been actively involved in the neighborhood on the sustainability project, he called to "visit" with me. (Mr. Witt's definition of politicking.) Some were concerned that one of our community activists might embarrass Governor Bush. Win wasn't concerned about that so much. He saw an opportunity for Ethel Ambrose, the president of the Central High Neighborhood Association, to let people in our community and our nation know about what was going on in the neighborhood. He saw a chance, not to exacerbate the polar extremes of politics in America, but to *educate* folks, including then Governor Bush, about the grassroots movement of a neighborhood taking possession of its own future, and not waiting for government to do something. For some it was a lost opportunity to nastily go at each other. For me, it was an opportunity to educate some of the rich and powerful about issues that affect us all in a non-confrontational way. That has led us here to this ... me writing a book that could spur some discussion, and hopefully help solve some of our communal problems. For me, that day of Ethel's educating Bush and the nation, with Win's blessing, was *"The Day the Earth Stood Still."*

4

It's the Stupid Economy, Stupid

I'm not calling you stupid. It's a reminder to myself to keep focused on how things really work. This chapter's title, for those too young to remember, is an enhanced offshoot of Bill Clinton's adage leading up to the 1994 presidential election. I just want to remind all of us that the economy is the driving force behind our ability to create sustainable communities. I wish it weren't so, but regional and local economies drive this issue. If the production of goods, the transporting of the things we make, and we humans didn't create various forms of pollution; if the need for efficiency wasn't necessary for us to be competitive and humanely survive in today's modern economy; if, because of the increasing numbers of people on earth, our modern global economy didn't require a constant flow of investment capital, then we wouldn't need to create sustainable communities. We would survive in our Petri world as we have since the beginning of time, oblivious to cause and effect. Descartes wouldn't be relevant.

I said that I wish regional and local economies didn't drive this issue. That's because the composite scale of these regional and local economies into the global economy and the fluctuations in the overall system, as we have recently experienced, cause us to act differently than we would have 50 or 100 years ago. Recessionary trends today impact a staggering number of our earth's people. I wish our governments didn't have to tinker so much with the economy, but I have to admit that the decisions made in Washington, and around the world, as this latest recession began, were brilliant. There will probably be some adverse effects to some of the follow-up actions, but none the less, the early decisions were appropriately measured, considering the options available. The beginnings of new institutions and altering of some existing institutions should address this shift in the paradigm which can, over the long run, be good or bad. I'm not sure that all the decisions have been brilliant, but this book isn't about all the decisions made for the current global recession. It's about how each of our individual and communal decisions affect the functioning of regional and local economies; these, in turn, affect our ability to be competitive and sustain our populations far into the future.

We noted in the one of the last chapters the United Nations' findings regarding population growth. As the world population expands, so does its needs and demands. So, depending upon the structure of the society, i.e. the composition of its institutions and the type of economy and functioning of the local and regional economies, someone or some institution will end up supplying those demands. They will fulfill those needs. I know this is pretty simple stuff, but it is important for us to keep this in mind as we lay the foundation for understanding why we haven't been able to create a sustainable world over the past ... let's say ... 60 years.

It doesn't take a lot to understand supply and demand in the simple form. It is the foundation of how communities are created, function, and evolve. Contrary to what some urban planners want you to believe, the built environment is the physical manifestation of the economy, not the other way around. When we went from a nomadic people to an agricultural-based economy over 15,000 years ago, the physical forms of our communities were established. These early communities were to a great degree sustainable. They are the foundations for our communities of today. When the industrialized economies began to develop and mature, the economic changes caused changes in the physical forms of our communities. That is to say, we began to regulate our use of land via laws and ordinances. This has grown into an entire body of law here in the United States and other parts of the world. We deal with land use and zoning, as well as lien laws: the legal rider to real property used for the protection of a person's labor. We will see the importance of each of these components during our additional discussions throughout this book. This is necessary because the rationale for those laws has changed radically with the coming of the post-industrial economy, and because these laws and ordinances have caused terrible inefficiencies resulting in the United States becoming uncompetitive. Changes must occur to these institutional eggs of land use and a person's toil if we are to sustain our civilization far into the future.

We will keep coming back to the issue of earth's population as we talk about our functional economies and creating sustainable communities. Population is a pivotal issue. It has everything to do with, not just the functioning of our present institutions, but the structure of our future institutions. We see the development of institutions at the U.N., in China and elsewhere beginning to deal more forthrightly with population growth, portent of civil societies' futures around the globe.

I mentioned in this book's acknowledgments my high-school teacher Mrs. McKim who had us read *The Worldly Philosophers* as part of our curriculum. Two of the individuals we studied were Malthus and Ricardo. Not Ricky Ricardo who was married to Lucy, but the British economist David Ricardo along with the Rev. Thomas Robert Malthus. Both lived around the late 1700s and early 1800s, and both were concerned with the potential dangers of population growth.

Malthus stated, "The power of population is indefinitely greater than the power in the earth to produce subsistence for man." Meaning, as animals, we think with parts of our anatomy other than our brains. We are going to overpopulate because we can't help it. We propagate because we are hard-wired to propagate. That's what we do as boys and girls. If you want to know the details of why Malthus said that, you need to read his papers. It really is neat stuff. He thought that ideas of social reform were overly optimistic and doomed to failure. He saw a disaster looming because of population growth outstripping our resources. Some say he influenced evolutionary biologists of the day, like Darwin, and that he provided the intellectual rationale for the survival of the fittest—an interesting theorem from a man of the cloth. Regardless, Malthus argued against what were existing welfare laws, called "Poor Laws." He also placed the longer-term stability of the economy above short-term expediency: a key component in creating programs, policies and expenditures for sustainability today and far into the future. He supported a system of taxes on imports to encourage domestic production, which he felt would have long-term benefit. His arguments were strong for the day and the type of social economy that existed in isolation. In some respects, his views are still relevant.

Ricardo also feared increasing population would cause problems, including a shortage of productive land which created wealth—something we have already experienced here in the United States. Florida is a good example of population squeezing out billions of dollars of first-wave agricultural production over the past 30 years. This is happening all over the world, but in Florida's defense, they have supplanted the first-wave economic loss with the production of third–wave, communications-based products and the massive peripheral components which followed.

I can't remember the junior high teacher's name, but I do remember the class that I was in when President Kennedy was shot. I was actually in the office when I heard the news. When I got back to class, I mentioned it to my teacher who warned me not to spread rumors like that. When the principal came over the loud speaker to tell us about the President being shot, this wonderful teacher had the decency to apologize to me. I remember the seventh-grade class because of President Kennedy's assassination, and because I learned a socioeconomic concept that has stuck with me for all these years. This teacher was discussing current events one day, and praised the United States' goodness, and the wonderful, laudable policies we and other civil societies had to save people from impending death: you know, war, pestilence and the environment's harshness, in this particular case, famine. I remember that he did not berate the practice of helping others, but explained it could have the unintended consequences of adding additional population to the earth, and potentially more misery and greater famine. That was quite an epiphany for me at the time. I've learned that we and others can be too kind-hearted, wanting to help so badly that we often focus on what will help immediately, yet we don't consider actions to make those struggling societies sustainable. We sometimes make the situation worse over the long run, much as we do when rebuilding disaster-prone communities here in the United States.

As an example, we try desperately to save indigenous peoples and their cultures throughout the world. Rightfully, we believe these cultures have as much right to exist on earth as any. Then, without regards to these people's ability to sustain themselves, we swoop in and "help" them increase their life spans. We help more babies survive and keep the elders from dying too early. The net effect: We stress the indigenous people's ability to sustain themselves in the ecosystem that has sustained them since the beginning of time. This doesn't happen in all cases. The U.S., the E.U., and the U.N. are actually beginning to link aid to broader initiatives that will, in fact, help communities in the long run.

Still, we should keep this issue in the back of our minds as we proceed in our discussion on sustainability.

Malthus. Ricardo. The Petri dish. These are all part of our same economic debate we've been having for the past 200+ years in the west and much longer in the east: the effects of population on our economies' and communities' sustainability and survivability. The economic model our and other western-developed societies are currently working under, along with the corresponding institutions we have created to support this economic model, make it necessary for continued massive population growth to support our social system ... our Social Security system, the ultimate Ponzi scheme. This model of requiring a proportional real number increase in population to pay for our final years on earth—our retirement—is anti-thetical to where we need to be in the next 50 to 100 years. The system is not sustainable under current conditions. Like what Malthus talked about.

If we could live in harmony with nature, our communal system in complete balance and sustaining itself, we wouldn't ever need to expand our domain due to increased population. Conflict with others might not ever occur, and maybe we could be sufficiently naive enough to believe that simple solutions are available. I wish we could believe that all we have to do is make our homes run on solar power. We could quit burning fossil fuels and pumping carbon particulates into the atmosphere. Then the world will function the way god and nature intended … But I don't believe I am dumb enough to assert such simple solutions for complex problems which exist in complex systems. Having said that, I am seasoned enough to know that solutions often are not as complex as we sometimes make them out.

Creating sustainable communities is a function of how and where we, the consumer, spend our dollars. In particular, it's how and where we spend our dollars on energy. It is also a function of various income levels' propensity for consumption and savings which alter significantly every time the energy markets fluctuate. That means when the price of oil goes up, we have less to spend on other stuff. Our dollars then are taken out of one system's circulation and sent elsewhere to circulate, currently overseas. This shouldn't be hard to figure out: When we take massive amounts of money out of a functioning economic system that is in equilibrium, some-thing is going to happen. A new equilibrium has to be established. Under this particular scenario, a constriction of the economy is one of the results. You know, recession.

In 1974 I noted, and will reiterate today, the oil crisis wasn't about the lack of supply; it was a crisis in the pocketbook. It's pretty simple, the real crisis is the impact that rapidly rising oil prices have on the individual consumer's consumption habits, as well as the increases it causes in pro-duction costs of goods and services dependent upon stable prices. If you don't believe it, just look at what the net effect was of taking trillions of dollars out of the consumers' pockets over many years and funneling it towards gas for our SUV's instead of on the things that we like to buy for ourselves and our kids. It's just finally catching up to us, or, as some say, the chickens have finally come home to roost.

Congress has reacted by putting the additional monies we spent on gas back into our pockets in the form of a stimulus package. That was a way for Washington to pay off the petroleum suppliers by proxy. Did it have any effect? Yes! Did it cause the price of oil to go down? No! The constriction of spending by the consumer caused the price to go down, and along with some other things, had forced us into this latest recession, further constricting the consumption of gas. Let me interject a little something here to chew on, which we'll take up later in more detail. Had we begun to alter our land-use patterns after the 1974 oil embargo, as was suggested then, we wouldn't be in this pickle today. Having sustainable communities with land-use patterns that create efficiency in the built environment would alleviate much of the excessive need for energy forms that have caused this latest crisis, and will cause the next crisis. The implementation of this land-use initiative would have eclipsed all the savings created with the combined building-efficiency standards and auto-efficiency standards implemented after the oil embargo. Why don't we focus on this? I think I know the answer. The question is: Will you and I come to the same conclusions after we have a chance to think through the issues in this book?

The real crisis isn't the available quantity of gas at the pump or petroleum in the marketplace. It's the short-term effects on spending patterns and the long-reaching economic repercussion on the health-care system from the burning of gas and oil that puts tons of particulates into the air we breathe.

The next to the last thing in this chapter we should talk about is the concept of sustainable investment strategies. The types of investing taking place in various areas of the world depend upon the type of existing economy and its relative wealth. If a community wants to attract sustainable investments, long-term investments, then they have to develop those strategies which will show their short-term and long-term initiatives for creating wealth, and their ability for repaying debt. That type of strategic vision is addressed in this book's last section.

Creating sustainable communities is not about being socially responsible, as laudable as that may be. It's about those sustainable investment strategies which correspond with the type and scope of economy which will attract capital. It's not about catering to the poor and creating laws that protect that segment of society. It's about strategies that capitalize on those individuals' current and future capabilities to create wealth. That's being done in poor third-world countries. The question is: When that type of investment capital comes to a community, is that community prepared to take the new-found wealth and develop programs, policies and expenditures that will create greater efficiency and greater greening of all facets in their community. Such is necessary in a world with heightened levels of competition for their community to sustain itself.

Now, let's address the issue of jobs and wealth creation in a third-wave economy. As you might be figuring out, my focus is developing sustainable communities based on third-wave sectors of the economy, the implications to creating new communities based on those third-wave sectors, and redeveloping existing communities by expanding third-wave sectors into the existing economy.

In our local and regional economies, we create wealth by being net exporters of product rather than net importers of product. This holds true with creatively based, communications-based products as well as with every other type of product. The difference: In the third-wave sectors, for the first time in human civilization, no physical constraints exist for developing product and creating wealth. The implications to developing efficiencies in the economy and on the physical environment are staggering. Basic to the discussion will be what this means in our ability to compete globally, and how we take advantage of this trend by prioritizing policies for our communities' economic prosperity and the economic well-being of present and future generations. Third-wave industries and technology-based companies will be a foundation for our communities' future economy. It must possess the ability to sustain itself and its built and natural environment far into the future.

The route to a sustainable future in a post-industrial economy depends on developing a sound third-wave, communications-based economy to augment the existing economy. Maybe we can call it the Green Egg Theory. Let's start hatching our plan!

5

Creating / Recreating Institutions

We're discussing institutions as a basic component to begin heightening your awareness and thinking about the subject, so when we get to Section V on implementation you will have allowed this egg to gestate. In that later section we will see how recreating old institutions and developing new institutions are critical in generating sustainable communities.

I find it is important to periodically remind myself that the ultimate goal for us, as humans, is to propagate the species. We do that, not just by having carnal knowledge and babies, but by developing other types of knowledge, the types that help us perpetuate those institutions which allow our species to sustain itself. When we create or maintain institutions which run counter to our collective goal of human survival, or when we develop human behaviors which put into question our species' long-term survival, this insults our being. It's considered an affront to god and nature or god or nature ... whichever one you believe in ... and you have to believe in one or the other. Anyway, it's a disgrace and an atrocity to us mortals.

When we talk about institutions, we're talking about a pattern of behavior or of relationships accepted as a fundamental part of a culture: the things familiar or long-established; those things that are fixtures in our minds. Like people or practices, laws and customs, organizations, establishments, foundations, societies—the things devoted to the advancement of particular causes or programs. Things like marriage or the family ... you know, according to our definition in this book, the eggs, not the chickens.

Why discuss creating and recreating institutions? Remember the old adage of the definition of insanity? Doing the same thing over and over and expecting a different result. That's where we are. That's what certain types of institutions do for us. They help us do the same thing over and over even though we are seeking different results. By definition, they help to prove that at times we are insane, or maybe just idiots. One of the main reasons why we seem to act like idiots is, not because we ARE idiots, but because we are constantly creating and maintaining institutions and organizations which function in ways that make us look and function like idiots.

Let's look at a few examples of maladjusted institutions in this chapter—those of which I am personally aware—to highlight the point that we can and must do better at developing new institutions; and we must severely adjust some of our existing ones. We will hold a couple of institutions up to the light to see how to ask questions which will aid us in critiquing and evaluating them, revealing how they are not working for our changing times. We should relentlessly hold our institutions, our eggs, up to the light to scrutinize them. For you younger folks reading this, putting an egg up to a candle and seeing a silhouette through the shell was like an early form of X-raying to determine if an egg had been fertilized or not. You did this because you didn't want to break an egg that held a fertilized embryo. It may have been an old wives tale or a line fed to gullible kids, but some said they could actually determine if an egg was rotten by putting it up to a candle. Anyway, let's hold these institutions up to the light to see which ones are rotten and which ones are ready to hatch.

It's interesting to look back at our lives as kids. From that perspective of youth, we would see some individuals and many or our institutions as bigger than life. There was a real mystique that surrounded those entities that we didn't fully understand. We were to respect these institutions and individuals. Our parents, the President, church leaders, General Motors, military personnel, elected officials, teachers, lawyers, newscasters, our water supply, and on and on. As grown-ups, we sometimes need to understand how we can or should alter institutions that impact our lives. To do this, we must understand the foibles of many of our institutions as well as the good parts. We have to recognize them for what they are, warts and all.

Most of our existing institutions have been created to do certain specific jobs, and it's normally not the nature of those existing institutions to change what they do. So to alter outcomes—you know, to change what's going on in the world around you—you either need to get other people to help you, which is the foundation for developing a new institution, *(creating an institution)* or you need to get an existing organization to help do what they haven't been doing. That's called changing an organization, *(recreating an institution)*.

Most civil societies have enough problems that keep their various governing institutions in the business of governing. It's not that most individuals in government want job security so they don't solve the myriad of problems that confront them, although there are some of those that do exist. But the individuals within most institutions and bureaucracies, both governing institutions, private-sector and other institutions, actually want to help solve problems. The problem is that the institutions in which they work may not have been *designed* to solve the problems that confront them.

You have to wonder sometimes if we as humans really have the ability to create an organization to function the way we wish. Actually, I'm pretty sure that we have that ability, but by design we tend to limit the functions of our institutions. We do this for a variety of reasons; sometimes due to the need to limit capacity, sometimes so that it is easier to evaluate performance and outcomes, and sometimes so that managers are able to confine their managerial tasks … so they don't go crazy. There are loads of reasons why we limit the functions and capacity of our institutions. Anthropologists would probably tell us that such is the nature of our being, and they would probably be right. The institutions which we create are merely expressions of who we are and our own human limitations.

Understanding the functions and limitations of various institutions is one of the major components in creating sustainable communities. Seems pretty simple, doesn't it!

Many years ago, Winthrop Paul Rockefeller gave me some great advice about working with institutions. If you want to make changes to the world around you, be careful not to waste your time trying to get existing institutions to help you make the changes. Start your own new institutions to accomplish the goals that you want to achieve. Win had suggested that it is critically important to determine an existing institution's real function; whether or not it is even allowed to change or help you bring about change. Then you determine the level of recalcitrance of the individuals that guide and operate the institution. He warned about three things: First, even though individuals within institutions want to be helpful, and even suggest that they will help, that doesn't make it so. Second, he warned that the bigger the institution, the harder it would be to enlist it to help make changes. And third, the smarter the people are within the institution the more difficult it can be to get them to change. The last one I thought was of particular interest.

He noted, as an example, that for the previous 40+ years we had been trying to alter our student educational outcomes all over the country by working within the existing institutions. His point was this: Some of the brightest people you will ever meet are educators who can justify why their actions are correct, regardless of the outcomes. If you are trying to bring about change, Win's bottom line advice was to be careful as to the organizations from which you solicit help. You don't want to wake up after 20 years and find you are still talking about making changes. That's the way most institutions work—the definition of insanity.

Some of our current problems and problematic institutions came about as a result of industrialization of our society and much of the world. I am not saying that industrialization was bad or evil. I personally think it was and is wonderful, but it is important to understand its inherent limitations. The foundations and purpose of many of our existing institutions today were borne out of the agricultural and industrial sectors. They came about as an outgrowth of those major waves in civilization. When the agricultural age began, our institutions and behaviors developed to sustain that way life; same thing with the industrial age. During the period of industrialization, we humans created more specialized institutions, which focused on very specific and narrow areas, as if little linkage existed between issues. We are seeing the same with the new post-industrial sectors. New institutions and behaviors are emerging to support and sustain the new post-industrial sector of the economy. This type of behavioral development is how we as humans sustain ourselves ... through our personal and collective behaviors and through the institutions we develop.

During the early parts of the industrial age, new companies developed certain behaviors and decision-making processes so that they would be able to sustain themselves. These companies made things. They manufactured as cheaply as they could. That was good from the perspective of the specialized company. If the company made money, it could continue. It had permanence. It could sustain itself, which would sustain the people that worked there. As these early companies became successful and became institutionalized, it was recognized that the company's function was not to worry about anything other than making the things that it was supposed to make, and making as much profit as it could, or try to minimize losses in a competitive economy. It was not the company's function to worry about anything but doing what it did. It didn't worry about the effects it had on the environment, or on the future health of the consumers who bought its products. This focused behavioral trend which emanated from industrializing our economy permeated much of human endeavor. Even our governing and educational institutions have attempted to adopt this industrial model. This narrow-scope functioning and limited decision making has become the norm in our governing institutions, even when it doesn't make sense. The vestiges of this industrial model remain strong in most of our institutions, both public and private.

As a result, today we go about our daily lives doing specific things because of the perceived efficiency that comes from the division of labor and specialization, outgrowths of industrializing our world with little regard to its effects on the world around us. We drive vehicles that spew particulates into the air we breathe because it's to our personal benefit to do so, with little or no regard to its effects on our environment or on those around us. For the past 100 years, we as individuals have lived like miniature industrialized companies, making what we thought were rational decisions. That is until we began to notice that our decisions as individuals and as institutions were counter to our individual and collective goal of human survival. Remember the idea of sustaining the species ... our expanded definition of the propagation of the species. So, what should we do? We change our institutions, and we change our behaviors. The question in this book is: Which institutions and behaviors should we change to create sustainable communities?

Many years ago, some individuals described the behaviors and decisions emanating from institutions based on an industrialized model as stand-alone institutions. They termed these institutions with little or no connection to others as being akin to silos. To counter this institutionalized process, in 1993 Dave Barlow and I decided to create some new institutional behaviors. We came up with the "Networked Community" concept in which all of our decisions are interconnected. We will see an example of this in practice in Section V: an initiative matrix.

Just like decisions we make individually, which at times may be detrimental to our survival, the siloed behaviors of our governing institutions fall into the same trap. I fear this next example of institutional decision making is more common than not. It shows how a governing institution can make what seems like rational focused decisions within their own silo, when in fact, their decisions are a determent to our society. It may have you shaking your head in dismay, but not to worry ... just know there are a million more just like it. I hope this and other examples will help us to agree on the need for institutional and behavioral change.

A number of years ago I was closely involved with Advanced Communications Corporation (ACC). Dan Garner, the founder of the private company, was one of the pioneers of the Direct Broadcast Satellite industry. You know, small dish antennas ... Direct TV and DISH. Anyway, the founder along with some of his cohorts, were determined to use the broadcast technology for the public good. Pretty simple so far.

Under its own initiative, ACC voluntarily obligated, by contract, to the American public through the Federal Communications Commission nearly 20% of its satellite transponders' broadcast capacity—to an educational trust. The trust could deliver educational programming free of charge to kids and parents all over America. *Some estimates put it at potentially 200 channels dedicated to educating American kids and their parents.* This programming was to be made available to teachers as well, free of charge, to augment and enhance the teachers' curriculum. It was the most comprehensive educational reform initiative in the history of our civilization. Through utilizing advanced technology, it could have saved our federal, state and local educational systems hundreds of billions of dollars. The guy behind the voluntary commitment to our nation was the retired former congressman who had been the longest serving chairman in history of the House Committee on Ways and Means, the honorable Wilbur D. Mills. The guy that conceived the whole educational initiative was actually a lowly bureaucrat at a state agency in Arkansas. He was also a Peabody Award recipient for creating the first all children's radio station in the nation: Joe Glass.

This contract obligation to the American public was terribly problematic. The agency (institution) overseeing the licensing of satellites for television distribution didn't have anything to do with the education of our children, nor did it have anything to do with helping develop a competitive workforce of the future. Nor did it have anything to do with saving the taxpayers billions of dollars, nor with the security of our economy and therefore the security of our nation, nor with the ultimate ability of our nation to sustain itself. By a 4 to 3 vote of the institution's governing board, the Federal Communications Commission disallowed the initiative to go forward because it was not part of their institutional domain. My Congressman's chief of staff called that vote "the biggest scandal since Watergate." I suspect that it wasn't reported on other than in some internal industry journals and in Barron's, because it involved the biggest (institutional) players in the media. Go figure!

But let's get past what could have been, and the non-scandal scandal where everyone from the President, the Vice President, Congress, and all the way down to the legal staff of the FCC knew about the huge implications of the initiative, and the hundreds of billions of dollars that could have been saved. The point is that, had our governing silos functioned in ways that allowed for multiple agencies to work in concert, or had the individuals within our government worked more creatively at allowing innovation to take place, they could have changed the functioning of our civil society. They deferred to others and to the rules of the institutions. This shows you why the discussion about creating and recreating institutions is so important.

The FCC's institutional mindset was this: If you wanted to offer service in education, then you needed to talk to the federal institution that deals with education: the Department of Education. If you wanted to help improve commerce and the productivity of a future educated workforce then talk to the institution that deals with commerce: Department of Commerce. And if you were dedicated to the security of our economy and therefore the security of our nation, then maybe you might want to talk to the Department of Defense, or maybe someone else, somewhere else. Do you see the folly in all this? It is easier to defer to another institution instead of actually trying to solve a problem that could benefit society. Were these bad people? NO! They were bureaucrats who were not motivated to go beyond the confines of their own institution because the institution didn't provide for novel solutions to current challenges. This type of behavior is called *institutional incompetence*: behaviors that we as humans have created and perpetuated, disallowing solutions to problems.

Our ability to sustain ourselves as a complex species in the modern world is linked to our ability to change institutional behaviors critical for our survival. But first we must recognize a need to change.

This example points out how a private institution (a business in this case) was able to conceive how to develop new institutions that could address today's issues. But it came up against an existing government institution vested in doing things the same way for decades. An institution refusing to change, while rationalizing and justifying its detrimental behavior. This level of institutional incompetence affects our nation's ability to sustain itself. And this example is too common. It's one of the major reasons I want us to discuss creating new institutions and altering existing institutions.

Now, let's try to further link this issue of institutional change to the issue of sustainability. It's the basic underlying concept which has stood as a part of human understanding and many societies' founding of institutions since we humans started our trek towards being civilized. This concept of sustainability is quite simple. At one time it was part of our traditional knowledge, part of our lore passed down from ancient times. It has even been written about in the Bible. But due to our lack of education on the subject, applying it has become complex and, at best, difficult.

Why has institutionalizing the concept of sustainability waned so dramatically? How can we re-institutionalize this concept in all that we do today? How can we infuse it into all of our existing institutions and behaviors?

Let's think about this concept for a minute in terms of … real chickens and real eggs. Before we industrialized and automated much of our agricultural production, we as individuals actually had our own chickens. So we had fresh eggs, or we bought our eggs fresh from someone that had chickens. When I was a youngster living in Miami, my family bought our eggs from our neighbor Roger Baker, the most industrious kid you had ever met.. Mom bought fresh eggs from Roger once a week. Not because we couldn't buy them at the store, but because my mom thought they were better, or more likely to be safer to eat. Why? Because she knew where they came from. My suspicion was that she wanted to buy them fresh from Roger because it reminded her of her own childhood. My Mom's dad, Henry Young, raised chickens and taught kids through FFA (Future Farmers of America) about 80+ years ago, how to maintain your chickens and how to increase your supply of healthy produce. He taught how to increase your egg supply, and how to develop a chicken and egg business and industry. This was quite novel 80 years ago, so much so that the town of Hugo, Oklahoma actually named a building after him. He and many others in that region helped develop the egg and poultry industry. Today, we have the likes of Tyson who started out raising chickens in Northwest Arkansas. The company has become one of the largest suppliers of poultry, pork, beef and fish in the world.

Is egg production on a local basis like what Roger Baker did considered sustainable activity? Sure it is, to an extent. Is what Tyson does considered as sustainable production? Yes. There are economies of scale which coincide with the scope of the nation and world's economy and population. Here's the point: In earlier days, we understood that to survive you ate what you produced, and you didn't eat your means of production. If you eat all the chickens, then you don't have any more eggs or any more chickens to eat.

Oh yeah, I nearly forgot … the Bible story on sustainability. I'm sure many of you remember the story that you don't just feed fish to those who are hungry; you teach them to fish so that they can sustain themselves. In modern times we have developed a more complex sustainable economic system of production and distribution of goods. Our industrial mindset has individuals functioning within their own silos; concerned about eating and not concerned about the source of what they eat. They care about their individual lives and how Big Brother can take care of them in the event something goes wrong. That is not sustainable. And we have institutions concerned about their own function, not the functioning of society.

The issue of sustainability can, in fact, permeate all that we do. In the last 50 years, the sustainability concept has been institutionalized in organizations like Heifer International. This global nonprofit gives cows and chickens and other animals to poor nomadic and archaic agricultural communities around the world. It also teaches these populations how to farm and live sustainably. Heifer doesn't give them cows to eat, but for milk and to reproduce.

This concept of sustainability is not only applicable for poor nomadic and archaic agricultural-based first-wave economies. It also serves second-wave industrial economies. And as noted earlier with the direct broadcast satellite example, those third-wave ICE age economies as well. Connecting this concept to other facets in our modern life and economy can help us sustain ourselves. Infusing the issue of sustainability into existing industrial-based and post-industrial-based institutions would allow for functional changes within these institutions. This could facilitate the type of initiatives which would help us create functional sustainable communities, as well as a society able to sustain itself.

6

Connecting Dots

Six degrees of Kevin Bacon is getting ready to go into hyper-drive. The game that was developed by three friends from Albright College has a variation based on assuming almost anyone in the world can be linked to anyone else by six or seven degrees. The game holds true for the subjects surrounding sustainability as well. All that we do in life is connected.

Everything we do can directly connect to the development of our communities as being either sustainable or non-sustainable. We noted this in the last chapter with our example of the multiple connections made by Congressman Mills and Advanced Communications Corporation. Loads of subjects need to be discussed as we proceed in laying the foundation for developing sustainable communities. This constant connecting of one subject to every other subject is, in today's popular culture, more affectionately called "connecting dots." It's about getting away from decision making in a vacuum, or in those infamous silos; one of the reasons given for the happenings of 9/11.

This process of connecting dots or subjects can be laborious, but once institutionalized can allow for decision making to be more comprehensive. It can counter the silo effects discussed in the previous chapter. Connecting dots, or having discussions of subjects relative to other issues and subjects, helps those involved in their individual communities understand that to create a sustainable community is not about just one thing. The process allows us to consider a whole host of issues and subjects.

I can't tell you how many times I have sat in large and small community meetings with well meaning, bright individuals: from truck drivers to college presidents, to attorneys, to bank presidents and realtors to community activists and factory workers. Each brings to the table a passion for a particular issue and from a particular perspective. Each is convinced that, if we did just the one thing that they are concerned about, the world would be better off. They may be right. Most likely though, they are only partially right.

I actually get a kick out of hearing the various opinions of different people. When developers pose a solution, it seems there is always a real estate component. When an individual who lives in a poor, crime-infested area poses an ultimate solution, it normally involves a strong component of community policing or getting rid of drug dealers or prostitutes. It's a lot like getting advice about your ailing gall bladder from a surgeon versus a faith healer or a general practitioner or a chiropractor. The advice may range from pray more, to take more cod liver oil, to taking medication for pain, to having surgery to remove it. Each is going to bring to the table his or her own bias. I must admit that I prefer the advice based on science, but that's just me. I learned from a young age that some individuals in our communities base their opinions on emotions and feelings and not on logic. This is where I give advice again … Don't discount these individuals. Sometimes their opinions hold great foresight.

Anyway, each individual brings a view to the table as a solution to per-ceived problems. Some are convinced that fixing sidewalks makes their community a better place, some want trees, and others want the pot-holes filled in their neighborhood because it's ruining their cars' tires and shocks. Others believe that if we educate our kids better we will attract industry, which will increase our tax revenues, which will allow us to fill the potholes. All are important, and it is equally important to help our

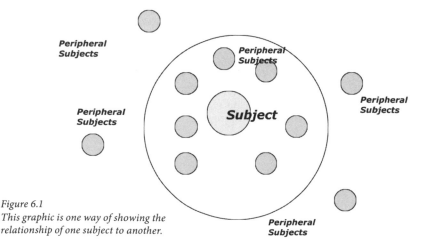

Figure 6.1
This graphic is one way of showing the
relationship of one subject to another.

communities to understand the connections among them all. Do we as communities discuss the connections of these things? Normally not.

Two points need to be made as we look at how we connect dots. The first is how we view the issues, and the second is the process of connecting the issues.

About 20 years ago many of the neighborhood organizations in my home community came together to form a larger organization. That coalescence of groups grew to a substantial size in the early years. At one time it encompassed 22 neighborhoods and had more people represented than in a typical congressional district, and more than the districts represented by a typical city board member. Due to the range and complexity of issues confronted at each month's meetings, we began to notice a pattern of big-picture issues that had to be addressed: an arena for our city as a part of an economic development initiative, as well as individual issues, like a series of break-ins in a particular area of town. The same thing that City Hall had to deal with on a daily basis, but we weren't encumbered with the city government's institutional restrictions. There were times when the small items would overwhelm the group to the exclusion of the big picture items, and vice versa. So as to keep our focus, we learned to address both big and small in context to the other. We termed that "potholes and promises." This big-to-small and small-to-big view is important in creating initiatives which can spawn the development of a sustainable community. We will see more of this concept's philosophical underpinnings when we talk about Frank Lloyd Wright and E. Fay Jones' philosophy in Section III.

A marvelous illustrative example of basic dot-connecting was explained to me many years ago by a wonderful fellow named John Matthews. We need to think of our overall, comprehensive view of the world as a house with windows on all sides, John said. If different people look in each window, they each will see something different. When we combine their descriptions from their particular perspectives, we can piece together a view of what the house actually looks like inside. Combining the views of the many to get a view of the whole: this is what we are conceptually trying to accomplish. I hasten to remind us that this gives a comprehensive view of the present, not a vision of the future. Again, we will see more of this concept in Section III when we focus on the Wright/Jones philosophy.

Asking the right questions will help us to think across multiple subjects. Knowing that everything can be "Baconized" entitles us to link various subjects together in our questioning. For example, we could ask questions similar to the following:

What is the connection between an extra three quarters of a trillion dollars spent on petroleum, and what does that have to do with our lack of an energy policy and to our lack of understanding the issue of creating sustainable communities?

What does the oil embargo of the early '70's, and the attempt to make the places we live and work and the vehicles we drive more efficient, have to do with the inefficient development of the built environment which has kept us from creating sustainable communities?

What do lower energy prices and new technology have to do with the inefficiency of the built environment?

How do our educational system and our media connect to us electing politicians incapable of recognizing a problem unless it is critical?

What do women's liberation, and Bill Gates have to do with U.S. consumer prices and economic productivity and the functioning of and interdependence of telecom economies all over the world? How did these events affect the inefficient development of the built environment and lack of necessary changes which could have led our society in creating sustainable communities?

What does ancient dogma have to do with an enlightened electorate, and can that affect our ability to sustain the human race?

What does an enlightened and educated electorate have to do with the sustainability of a democracy? And what does that form of governance have to do with the long-term ability of civilization to sustain itself?

What does worker productivity have to do with drug use and authoritarianism of drug cartels, and how do they relate to the functioning of capitalistic systems and the development of sustainable communities?

What do changes in our educational system have to do with creating competent students, and what does that have to do with electing competent people to represent us? How can that affect the development of sustainable communities?

How are all of these things connected to each other?

I am trying to be a little coy by asking questions which imply certain answers, but I hope to highlight the exercise of asking questions and trying to connect different subjects. Asking critical questions is an important component in discovering solutions. The more questions we ask which cross between or transcend the existing institutional silos we have created, the greater our chance to discover successful solutions. Greater is our chance as well to see deficiencies of existing institutions and what new institutions might be possible.

Creating sustainable communities involves lots of community meetings, which involve discussions about every issue imaginable. It is important for us to put each subject into context of the big picture, thus Baconizing to the subject of sustainability.

Another rule ... Connect those dots!

7

The "New World Order"
in your own back yard

Gerald R. Ford once noted, "A government big enough to give you everything you want, is a government big enough to take everything you have." As correct as Ford may have been, the fact of the matter is, that the more authoritarian a form of governance is, the stronger and potentially bigger and more powerful it can become. Understanding government structure and the anamorphosis of governing power, especially for the new economy, has huge implications for local governments and neighborhoods that want to create sustainable economies and communities. Creating a governing structure that can facilitate the development of a new ICE Age economy is what Toffler implied in his book *The Third Wave* when he talked about democratizing our institutions, including our democracies. The democratization of various governing and non-governing institutions will eventually take place as an outgrowth of necessary institutional and behavioral changes to sustain the new economy. Such is the nature of derivative change. We can help the process along as we have in the past through various forms of economic interventionism and free-market reforms, or fight it through various social or authoritarian forms of control.

Considering the nature of this anamorphosis of governing power, I think it is important to note this: The State having outright authority over an individual's property rights is antithetical to the notion of a sustainable third-wave economy. The use and nature of real property is inexorably altered in an era where the physical need for real property is minimized in developing product and creating wealth. A government which tries

to retain its right to control the owners of property, whether real property or intellectual property, is by definition more social or fascist than
democratic. Likewise, without radical changes for protecting intellectual
properties, we may begin to slide down the slippery slope of government
controlling creative thoughts which create wealth, something we currently
see happening in more authoritarian countries around the world. Having
said that, we can begin to see a degree of control over intellectual properties
here in the United States. I'm speaking of control through the agglomeration of media, causing a self-imposition or self-censorship over intellectual
properties, and at times a control over others' intellectual prowess through
legal institutions which help sustain the media's corporate institutions.
As we discussed earlier, these machinations are part of our history and
our origins. It is part of how we have created institutions to support and
sustain life as we understood it at that point in time.

Humans are, by nature, social. As social animals we have learned, for
survival purposes, to be kind, merciful, magnanimous, charitable, benevolent, philanthropic, and loving. We also at times can be anti-social. We
can be self-serving, envious, narcissistic, selfish, mean, chinchy, miserly,
and egotistical. All play a part in our survival and all are a part of developing our institutions. Understanding human nature is quite helpful when it
comes to understanding our institutions' origins and functions, especially
those institutions which function as some form of hierarchical governance. Institutions which include nearly every social and governing body
on earth, from the family to the chamber of commerce to the Knights of
Columbus and the local summer swimming association. This governance
component has come about through human behavioral and institutional
evolution. An evolution that is ongoing and never ending.

If we project into this evolutionary cycle's future, it's pretty easy to see
much greater emphasis on gender components based in real functional
division within our species. Most of our early institutions were based on
physical dominance of men over women—an institutional derivation from
the early division of traits and need for humans to survive. Our modern
economy requires different organizations and institutions which allow for
equity of men and women. This means that the functioning of our institutions will change and we will create new institutions for this new economy
expressing more female traits. That doesn't mean women will be in charge,
nor does it mean that men will be in charge. It merely means that evolving
institutions will reflect traits allowing us to survive into the future based
on further democratization. This allows for greater equity among all who
participate in the democracy, meaning both men and women.

Follow me for a minute. Over the millennia, human hierarchical forms have evolved into institutionalized forms of governance. The earliest forms were inevitably authoritarian, based on a pecking order that developed for survival purposes: clans, tribes, gangs and the like. They have been around since the beginning of time and exist in various incarnations all over the world today. These authoritarian forms of governance tend to be a little further down on the evolutionary government scale than democratic forms. Today's authoritarian forms are rooted in medieval and pre-medieval male-dominated institutions: The likes of Mullahs, the mafia, pirates in Somalia, Crypts in Los Angeles, drug lords in Mexico, the Saudi Royal Family, and most major religions on earth. Authoritarian forms tend to be archaic and, if not marginally enlightened, they can be brutal. If not kept in check, these forms of governance are able to grow and prosper, not just because of the forced submission of their constituents, but because they go beyond mere taxing to get their power. They can end up controlling an economy and they can actually be the economy. Too much power in the hands of authoritarian institutions tends to subjugate their constituents ... Tell me how that squares with the modern definition of sustainability, whose underpinnings are social and economic equity.

It's interesting to note why smaller authoritarian governing bodies don't tend to create sustainable systems or mandate sustainable initiatives. That's not what they do. Their decisions are based purely on short-term social and economic survival and enrichment of a certain few. If you've ever noticed, that type of governing behavior doesn't inspire confidence for economic development and capital investments. It's one of the major reasons why the bulk of at-risk capital tends to be invested in countries with communities and institutions that have democratic forms of governance. Even the authoritarian governments invest their money in capitalistic democracies. Here's the point: The fault of much of the world careening towards un-sustainability is, in large part, due to the various forms of governance that exist on earth. It's not because of big bad capitalists ... even though there is some fault that can be assigned there as well.

Remember what we discussed in earlier chapters? By their nature, capitalists are authoritarian. Their decision -making is narrow and focused. Only the large multinational corporations have, as a part of their global objectives, broad goals. So the next time you want to bash some democratic country with a capitalistic system in place for not allowing some poor archaic authoritarian countries to become sustainable, I might suggest that you call me and we can think this through in greater depth.

Picking up again on the discussions about modernity and sustainability in a modern democracy, we have to ask: Have there been glitches in the modern world? Have there been aberrations in modernity and in this enlightened age we live in? You betchya. Hitler, Stalin, the Ayatollahs, Sun Yong Il, Pol Pot, Saddam Hussein, to name just a few of the easy ones. On a more regional and local basis, we can all think of some real idiots who have bastardized the rationale for a functioning democracy so completely that we wonder how we ever elected some of them. The jails are full of them, or at least ought to be full of them.

Now, let's ask the more difficult questions that appear more directly linked to our daily lives: Have there been glitches to democratic reforms locally which impede our ability to question our programs, policies and expenditures? Have these caused us to become less efficient and to pollute our environment, and has this threatened the ability of our progeny to survive? I like that one! I think that is a good question.

Remember that sustainability is to a large degree about social and economic equity. Not equality … equity, fairness. Ordinarily, that can't occur under repressive and autocratic forms of governance. There fairness is normally not part of the governing composition, much less part of the discourse.

The global side of the democratization process has been going on for quite some time. The United States has played a pivotal role in this continued evolution over the last 100 years. World War II was a somewhat brutal way of allowing individuals to seek freedom and truth, yet the result was democratic reform in Western Europe. Kennedy at the wall in Berlin was a definitive statement, not for east versus west, but for the line being drawn in the sand: We were either for continuing those freedoms envisioned by Bacon, Descartes, and Locke, or we were to fear those principles. Then authoritarianism and oppression of the past would creep back to become the norm. Nixon's foreign policy expanded the influence of our … influence. The democratic propaganda machine entrenched and extended during that period. Carter's foreign policy's emphasis on human rights was one of the more brilliant periods; or more correctly stated, the timing was wonderful. It was the moral stance necessary to light the fire of desire for liberation. Ronald Reagan's push for democratic reform, or principles of modernity, globally was known as the Reagan Doctrine. His push for democratic reform domestically, the catalyst for the re-enlightenment or the re-invention of how we govern, was known as Reaganomics.

Under the Reagan Doctrine the orchestration of free markets' relationship with free people began to take hold. Under Reaganomics domestically,

Ronald Reagan went on record as saying that, if we got government out of the lives of individuals, even those who were less fortunate, then the system would work better. He then proceeded to take as much money away from state and local governments as he could to allow them to fend for themselves. The net effect:Everybody in the cities hated Reagan and set about to show that they could make it even without money from the federal government. From this grew the neighborhood movement both locally and nationally, where individual rights were further enhanced ... A democratization process with proven results in changing local and national elections and affecting various trends ... from Newt Gingrich to ACORN and now the TEA Party movement. This re-invention of government was underway with a fervor that hadn't been seen for 200 years. The resultwas the re-inventing of government. A record of this re-invention was documented in David Osborne's book *Re-inventing Government*. We had Mr. Osborne come and talk to us at one point about what had taken place in the 12 years prior to the Clinton Administration, and how we as a civilization have re-acquainted ourselves with the process of doing for ourselves, and how the grassroots movements of problem identification and problem solving actually work: **A movement which is the foundation for the development of sustainable communities.** That was the legacy of Ronald Reagan, and quite possibly will be for Barack Obama if he gets to do what he said he wants to do in certain areas of our society.

After Reagan came George H. W. Bush, who masterfully drew the correlation of individual freedom and democracy with economic freedom in his foreign policy as it related to authoritarian rule and oppressive power in the Persian Gulf. We'll hopefully see the effects of this in the next 20 to 30 years, where the suppression of authoritarian rule will unleash the brilliance of an entire section of the world possessing an extremely rich history of innovation. A geography where the creation of truly sustainable communities can occur faster than most places on earth.

George H.W. Bush also made a big push, what began under Reagan, redirecting the energies of the CIA to focus on economic modeling of foreign countries and **large multi-national conglomerates**: *The areas of our next democratic warfare, and I might add, one of the greatest opportunities and possibly greatest impediments to global democratic reform we may ever see.* This "new world order" had emerged globally with the free and massive flow of capital along with the concerns for the rights of individuals ... what was called "democratic capitalism" under the first Bush's administration.

For the next 16 years, multi-national business escalated under the Clinton administration and further entrenched under the latest Bush Administration. Their foreign commerce policy appeared to be schizophrenic, a result of a somewhat laissez-faire perspective and quite focused in that respect. For those not schooled in economics, "laissez nous faire" means "leave us alone" or "keep your hands off us." We had a period of global economic expansion at that time in which the expansion of production utilizing low-wage jobs grew all over the world—one of the great opportunities for democratic capitalism to expand, which it did with mixed results. Because of that period and the de-emphasis on the "democratic" portion of the democratic-capitalism, many around the world thought the new world order was about how capitalism, meaning America, could screw anybody they wanted to, and get away with it. Had this free-people, free-markets world order—which emanated from the virtue of the "greatest generation"—been allowed to continue more robustly and build more vigorously, the opportunity for equity, economic development, and eventually sustainability would have moved forward much faster. This opportunity stopped partly through our own doing as noted above, and partly by the clash of medieval religious-based cultural fanatics and authoritarian regimes seeking their own enrichment.

Sorry to do this to you, but I have to get this off my chest. Here's my bias: I believe the past 16 years are the result of a baby-boom generation being in charge: A self-absorbed, gimme-gimme, feel-good generation that the rest of the world has been learning to hate. The greatest generation spoiled us and we expected that by brandishing an olive branch, a peace symbol, and universal love we could express any form of freedom we wanted with no regard to others' cultural identities and with no backlash, while we took as much as we could from everybody on the planet. Warning to the next American generation: be wary of the baby boomers. That group has a history of being self absorbed and wanting everything for themselves, and believing all that they do is right and good. It's a group that has taught its offspring how to be as narcissistic as they were, and it's a generation that will take everything you've got including your future. Oh … sorry, I think that's already happened. The good news is that the actions of the baby boomers will compel the next generations to deal head-on with the issue of sustainability, much more rapidly than they otherwise would have, if they and their offspring are to survive.

So, off the soap box … back to the grassroots movement of re-inventing our forms of governance in this country and the great potential for creating sustainable communities. As I had noted earlier, the re-invention of government has been underway for many years with a fervor unseen for 200 years. The democratic movements in this country are expressions of this trend: women's suffrage, the civil rights movement, the women's movement of today, and even the men's movement. But here's the most exciting movement for rediscovering our own American Revolution: The grass roots movement within urban environments and the spill over to the rural environments. Individuals want control of their lives, their neighborhoods, their homes and with the help of the likes of Al Gore and others, their environs. They really want our leaders to start acting smart and in our collective self interests. This democratic movement—the foundation for the development of sustainable communities—requires people to actually *do* things. It's not just about telling people whom we elect what to do. Remember, politicians don't actually do anything. They just vote on getting our money from us to spend money to hire others to spend money to hire others to actually do things. The movement of *doing for self* means just that. The supposition that government needs to be involved or in the middle or in control of what you want done is an incorrect supposition. And it is counter-productive. This movement has been pushed into hyperdrive with this latest generation and the communications technologies that they employ and the mainstream media is now beginning to employ.

This neighborhood movement—democratization—isn't just in America. It is all over the world. It's only in democracies where movements like this tend to be tolerated and actually enhanced. This democratization movement of our local economies, coupled with the democratization and femininization of our institutions, bodes well for the possibilities of developing really sustainable communities. This process decentralizes decision making so individuals as consumers or constituents can actually impact their surroundings; an impact that used to take generations to see. These new institutions allow for power to move from the top down to more intimate governing levels, and pushes decision making and solutions from the bottom up. An additional part of this institutional evolution is having local communities and neighborhoods usurp power not voluntarily given up. Which reminds me of some wonderful meetings I had a number of years ago when I was at a national convention of neighborhoods.

Due to my semi-active participation in my own community's neighborhood movement along with my participation in a few conventions with Neighborhoods USA (NUSA), an active organization that is part of the national neighborhood movement. I was asked, along with others from around the nation, to engage in some in-depth discussions about the future of democratic governance in our local communities. These discussions, sponsored by a Los Angeles county commissioner and facilitated by a brilliant LA county commission staffer, went on for a number of evenings over a couple of yearly conferences, and lasted for hours at a time. They were great fun. The discussions focused on where we thought the future would take us, and what forms of governance we could utilize to facilitate that future. We talked about the flourishing of gangs, authoritarian forms of governance that fill governing voids and empower young people. We talked about how to counter that form by institutionalizing viable alternatives of empowerment through the democratic neighborhood movement. The results from these and other numerous discussions were staggering. Los Angeles voluntarily gave some of the power they had acquired over the decades back to the community through empowering structured neighborhood institutions: Individuals living in a community, whether registered voters or not, could have a say in their community's development, and where money could or should be spent. This is the democratization of our democracy that Toffler talked about 30 years prior, and the democratic activity that is taking place in the "New World Order" of democratic-capitalism.

How does this trend relate to each of us locally? For us to create the sustainable investments required for a community to sustain itself in a post-industrial age, alterations must occur in the male-dominated institutions which will allow for social and economic equity to take place. Not creating these necessary democratic-capitalistic institutions guarantees that anti-democratic forms of empowerment and governance will dominate us. Forms that will chase away investments, not attract investments. Look around and see where investments take place in our communities. You would have to be blind not to notice that, where vitriolic brutality and authoritarianism exist, disinvestment occurs.

The "new world order" is not some UN-led, left-wing or right-wing conspiracy to control the lives of everybody on earth, designed to take away the constitutional rights of freedom-loving Americans; or some multi-national business group intent on removing the unalienable rights of people from around the globe. It is merely the continued evolution of our political and economic systems. The new world order has emerged globally with the free and massive flow of capital *along with* the concerns for the rights of individuals. Simple as that. Democratic capitalism: the two systems require each other for their mutual existence.

Section II

Past

Chapters 8 thru 11

As a precursor to understanding this book, we just finished a section that dealt with a few broad issues underlying the issue of sustainability. This Section II is a continuation of those issues: those basic understandings of some of our Eggs' working mechanisms, but with a particular focus on the past. We will continue to talk about the foundations we developed in the first section: how some of the basic components in forming our institutions had developed out of our past, influencing our way of functioning and thinking. Looking at certain issues from the past's perspective, coupled with our understanding of these basic components, gives us insight into how we caused some of the problems which confront us today.

We can talk about problems which might rise in the future due to our past and present actions and trends. That type of talk tends to dominate our political discussions in our media and political institutions, and within the proliferation of nonprofit and private foundations which surround us. It is important to distinguish between future problems which might exist versus those which will exist. I don't know about you, but I find it a little difficult to identify future problems, not being there. However, the subtleties between the two should be noted. Knowing and projecting future problems are two very different activities, and many times cause us to not engage in reevaluating many of our institutions.

Many wonderful individuals have advised that understanding our past keeps us from making the same mistakes in the future. I am one who adheres to that tenet, although I'm not sure that is always the case. Much evidence suggests that we as humans will still make the same mistakes over and over regardless how well-educated we are about the past. Fay Jones used to teach us that we needed to connect our past to our future. He eloquently spoke to that issue when awarded his Gold Medal from the American Institute of Architects. He noted that for us to know where we are to go into the future, it is necessary for us to know our past ... One of those whole-is-to-part as part-is-to-whole things.

Designing our communities based on understanding the past, our nature as humans, along with the basic elements discussed in the previous section—this will allow us to delineate better the complex components involved in decision making. It will also provide greater consideration of important issues which may be peripheral, yet crucial for us to account. A greater understanding of our past world allows us to design communities which can potentially solve more problems rather than create more problems.

In this section we will talk about our problems and how we identify them. We will discuss the nature of bureaucracies and the role these institutions play in creating our problems and solutions. And we will see how institutionalizing the industrial model of specialization and division of labor may develop some severe long-term potential problems for us as a civil society. We will briefly discuss the concept of lineal versus spherical thinking, and how institutionalizing of "scapegoats" is important in the lineal world.

8

Problems, Problems, Problems

"The problem is!"

I thank my mother for a lot of things … including how that one particular phrase has affected my life. Finding origins of various problems and their solutions has been a lifelong endeavor. My brothers and I sometimes laugh about how some people can start every statement with: "the problem is." Over the years we have recognized that it isn't always due to a negative outlook on life; you know, the incessant belief that the glass is half empty. Rather, it's an overwhelming desire to figure out why the world works the way it does. It is, for some individuals, a way to empower one's self by making statements to affect others … stating one's opinion whether based in fact or not.

My mother, like most people on earth, can see when "things aren't quite right." The older she gets, the greater her ability to start many of her sentences with the statement … "The problem is." Actually, there are a lot of moms out there. If it weren't for moms and dads and kids and adults that are able to see that problems exist, and if there weren't people out there trying to fix the perceived problems, the world could become really scary.

One man's garbage is another man's treasure, or in our case one person's problem may be another person's solution. Many of the problems that exist are a function of perspective and perceived need. As discussed earlier, we as humans define our problems. Problems exist due to our existence. We can differentiate between our problems' causes, classifying them as systems conflicts and institutional conflicts. Try to keep in mind that these conflicts at times cause us to live in unsustainable ways. At other times, the conflicts are essential components in our ability to sustain ourselves.

The systems conflicts are fairly simple to understand. They involve our earthly existence propagating and spreading out all over creation, engaged in the daily behaviors of surviving. Things like eating and pooping. The more people there are, the greater the chance someone is going to poop upstream. With that, we just created a problem of our own doing; a problem that most civilizations have figured out how to remedy. Loads of these types of problems come along in our daily lives and endeavors.

The institutional conflicts, although brought on by human endeavor just as the systems conflicts are, tend to be a direct result of humans trying to solve problems. We've discussed some of these, and will continue to explore their ramifications.

This may sound odd to some of you, but we as a species create the problems, then we try to solve them. Kind of like what Congress does. Why do we have deficits when it seems like everyone in Congress is against them? Crazy, isn't it? This phenomenon is either an interesting anthropological development of the nature of humans so we always have something to do with our daily lives, or a kind-of cruel trick played on us by God. More and more, our existence is defined not by how simple we as humans can live on earth, but by an existence which attempts to create greater complexity and greater technical problems for us to solve. In any event, we constantly define our existence by our ability or inability to problem solve; problem solving in both a negative and positive way.

Finding commonality or consensus is one of our keys in solving problems within democratic institutions, as well as within authoritarian institutions which are becoming democratized. That's not easy when you have a countless number of institutions, along with corresponding institutionalized behaviors that run counter to that notion. Can that be fixed? Sure it can. Will it? Probably not, but we can sure sit around and talk about what needs to be done and do nothing about it. We as humans are real good at that. The myriad issues in which individuals see problems cause a great deal of frustration for some, especially if they can't fix the problem or don't know how. Here's the typical response to problems surrounding us: Blame someone because it is part of our hierarchical, top-down, authoritarian past (and present); and it seems logical that problems had to be brought about by somebody, and in some cases it is the fact. This perception has been institutionalized over generations. It has become an institutionalized form of creating scapegoats. Ergo, a person must be the reason for the problem. The fact of the matter is that many of our problems result from the definition and functioning of many of our institutions. Don't get me wrong. Plenty of people create problems, but for the most part, it is not a single individual that creates our communal problems unless that individual possesses an inordinate amount of personal or institutional power. For example, even with the power possessed by the CEO of British Petroleum, he didn't create the horrors inflicted by the oil gushing from the ravaged oil rig's base in the Gulf of Mexico, nor did President Obama. Yet with the institutionalized scapegoat mentality, we need to blame an individual, when in fact it is an institutional failure: a failure which we can fix through altering the systemic institutional incompetence in both private and public institutions. Having said this, I should note that vestiges of institutionalized individual personal responsibility still exist in modern society, where decisions cannot be protected by a corporate veil or body of law designed to shield the individual—professions like architecture, engineering, and medicine, in which the individual is culpable for his decisions and actions or inactions.

Differentiating between negative problem solving and positive problem solving is a matter of perspective which helps us to prioritize. For example, solving the problem of how to go to the moon is considered a positive problem. Communally it has a much different mind-set than solving problems of acid rain or chronic homelessness, considered as negative problems. I mention the matter of perspective because we have seen over the decades how we seek solutions by utilizing positive goals for some of our negative problems. Recently we have seen how President Obama helped define solutions to our latest energy crisis by proposing leadership development in science and technology. This would be our way to dominate the developing green energy market, providing a positive impact on our economy. It was similar to the positive-problem discourse used in putting a man on the moon. Has it been oversold? Maybe, but here's the point: Problem solving starts first with bitching about problems, then defining the problems, then defining a course of action to possibly solve the problem, then creating a plan to solve the problem, and then actually doing something to solve the problem … or taking actual concrete steps to implement the plan to solve the problems. It does help to have a positive spin on problem solving.

In my profession, the architectural profession, we talk about a process of dreaming before you conceive, conceiving before you plan, planning before you design, and designing before you construct. That simple process to which most of us, if not all of us, would probably subscribe can get terribly screwed up due to any number of reasons. I can't tell you how many times we get that basic problem-solving process wrong. For the most part, the majority of people only get to the point of bitching about problems, and sometimes actually talking about what to do to solve them. Rarely do they ever do anything about the positive or negative problems which they define. My gut tells me it's about 90% of the time nothing ever gets done. When you consider the amount of time that the media talks about problems, coupled with our politicians' and we the constituents' talk, that percentage may actually be closer to 99%.

The next group of people we should observe don't want to talk about problems ... they just want to do something. They want to make things happen. They want action. These folks are the ones who rarely engage in a problem-solving process. They tend to be the boisterous, type A, high-testosterone male, or female trying to emulate the male-dominated institutionalized pecking order. These are the people we hear talking on TV all the time about what "we" should be doing. They already know the solutions and they want their solutions applied without ... planning before we design and designing before we construct. It's important to note that these individuals may not be wrong; but the point is, if we are to solve complex problems in a complex world, it might be wise to consider multiple opinions. This is called consensus building. Now don't confuse consensus building with leadership or fact finding. All are different, and all are important.

We will see in Section V a real example of how a neighborhood engaged in the problem-solving process, how they identified a series of complex problems and got to the point of actually taking action.

As for the physical environment, problem solving becomes a critical characteristic because it's hard to un-build something after you've already built it ... even if you've built it wrong. It's essential that we focus on developing the built environment to assure our ability to sustain ourselves. Many of our problems today in the built and natural environment were created out of conflicts in human interaction or differing functions. They stem from what we think of as land use and zoning issues developed in the past. In most urbanized and partially urbanized areas around the world, there are expectations for conflict between land uses or zoning categories which differ. That is the nature of human activity in the built environment. We attempt to segregate land uses and create zoning categories to minimize those potential conflicts which will naturally arise from normal human activity. Throughout the past five or six decades, there have been continuous attempts to further diminish these conflicts with institutional and historical behaviors which allow for communities to spread further apart. This minimizing of potential conflicts has been reinforced so consistently in many areas around the United States and the world, it may now be considered an expectation or a cultural or community norm. Such expectations are continuously validated and institutionalized every time—for example—a community annexes more property for expansion. in direct opposition to the fact that enough available real property already exists within their communities to allow projected growth for years to come. The reinforcement of this type of institutional behavior causes us to become less efficient and less able to sustain ourselves over the long run. This is an example of a problem that exists in which we as communities implemented solutions ... we constructed before we designed and programmed. That comes from our institutionalizing behaviors which tell us what to think rather than how to think. Something we will discuss in more detail later on.

"The problem is" ... defining the problem. Again, the identification of problems is a matter of perspective. The planning and designing of solutions should be based on defining the problem along with a bunch of other things. If you can't define the problem properly ... or if you define it with such severe limitations due to the institutional mind-set ... or imposed limitations of surrounding institutions ... or limited focus of the individuals in control ... you will guarantee limited results which tend to create a whole other set of problems. Many times we tend to define problems with a limited scope, rather than in a comprehensive manner. We will see examples of that in following chapters.

From my experience, I have noted over the years that many of us wonder why and how we got to the point of needing to legislate all the little things involving common sense or acceptable or normal behavior. To a great degree, we've caused it by inculcating specialized processes within ourselves over many generations. We humans, in some cultures, have evolved into such specialized beings that our ingrained behaviors have caused us to not consider the ramifications of our behaviors in the aggregate. This fragmentation of functions has caused us to become less responsible, sometimes shortsighted, and at other times mindless and careless. Our communal response to our institutions creating people like that is to make laws to counteract irresponsibility. Extending this idea of systems and institutional conflict into our daily lives within our communities, we can see how our various daily functions, once considered in the aggregate, are subjected to laws and ordinances today in hopes that we act as responsible humans. For the most part, the laws are an attempt—in the aggregate—to remind us of the behaviors which we thought were givens. We created the problems, and we try to solve them. We've made lots of laws like that.

9

The Black-Hole Nature of Bureaucracies

Let's think for a moment about some of the things we discussed in the chapter about sustainability in a modern democracy. Keep in mind the relationship and the constant push and pull between institutionalized democratic organizations and those organizations' corresponding bureaucracies. I don't think we need to go into a great deal of detail about the tug of war that exists between these forces, but I have to assume that we understand an inherent incompatibility exists in some of the functioning relationships within various democratic institutions and their resulting bureaucracies: from federal government structures down to corporate structures and on to neighborhood organizations … Especially when various forms of "isms" come into play: capitalism, socialism, fascism, and communism. In more democratic systems, bureaucracies tend to be the philosophical antithesis. They are the reality necessary to implement the theoretical. In some less democratic governing structures, the managing class's understanding of functional reality dictates the structure and underlying philosophy. This antithetical structure to democratic governing forms is efficient, but tends to distort the individual's rights. Or maybe I should say it tends to alienate those unalienable rights that we have. It's one reason why we try to limit the responsibilities of our governing structures. These forms create a philosophical and functional dichotomy, the result of a bureaucracy managing an institution and trying to both sustain itself and perpetuate itself. I mention this because we must understand that bureaucratically laden institutions, or those less democratically structured, have an underlying focus and culture different from those in our underlying definition of sustainability, which is social and economic equity. Such a focus comes from enlightenment, not authoritarianism.

Various democratic movements have sprung up around the globe focusing on social and economic equity—part of the underlying definition of sustainability. Numerous ancillary or peripheral organizations have developed as a result of these movements. Each has developed its own corresponding bureaucratic institutions. Over a period of time, this tends to cloud the purposes of the original movement.

Bureaucratic organizations exist at all levels of human endeavor, in both functional and dysfunctional forms because we design them to be that way. I didn't say we want the bad ones to function the way they do, we just design them to function that way. I don't believe it is out of any malevolence toward others that the institutions are designed poorly and their bureaucracies function poorly. It's because over a period of time some institutions become bastardized and the entrenched bureaucrats become complacent. In most cases they are just unaware because their jobs are defined for them. Nothing wrong with that.

Dysfunction within certain institutions is often due to both internal and external conditions changing. Changing demands on an institution with an intransigent bureaucracy is a recipe for a great deal of frustration at best. If institutions refuse to change, they run the risk of becoming dysfunctional and possibly irrelevant. In our quest to develop sustainable communities, we must recognize the existence of both functional and dysfunctional bureaucracies, understanding that both can drain productive energy from achieving very important accomplishments. My advice: Stay shy of bureaucratically laden institutions. They can suck the heart and soul from anything that gets close. They, at times, can become the black holes of reason and success.

As for how this connects to our daily lives, all of us can probably relate to the frustration of dealing with a defective, malfunctioning bureaucracy.

Can you imagine being stuck in a dysfunctional organization knowing that you don't have the power to alter it. How many of us really have the frustrating experience of being a bureaucrat in a dysfunctional organization? I suspect that the number of stymied bureaucrats is large and growing. It's not the purpose of this book to discuss the frustrations of bureaucrats, but I am of the opinion that the larger that number becomes within the total workforce, the less sustainable our economy becomes. We won't be addressing how to fix these particular problems, but we will hopefully show how to recognize and work around them.

It's important to remember this: If you let bureaucrats and bureaucracies participate in what you are trying to accomplish, your outcomes may mirror theirs. That, at best, would be considered redundant. Moreso it would be a waste of time, energy, and money. If you are trying to create a sustainable community, why would you consider asking for help from those organizations that have historically not helped, and may have for many years been part of the problem? Asking established bureaucracies to change their ways so they can work with you to create innovative new initiatives is not terribly validating for those bureaucrats within existing institutions. If you want them to do something that they believe they are already doing, then you are telling them they aren't doing their jobs properly. That's not terribly validating either. If you can get them to do what they normally do *as a component necessary to fulfill your sustainable initiative*, now they become a partner. That can be wonderfully validating. Remember, bureaucrats know what they are doing. If somebody from outside is telling them they are not doing what needs to be done, it can be an affront. Getting them to change what they are doing should come from within by enlightened leadership. That's their job, not yours.

Here's a quick example of dealing with bureaucrats: My colleague Dave Barlow and I decided to focus our attention on just one of the numerous objectives that I developed many years ago to create a sustainable community. This particular initiative dealt with the educational reforms necessary to create a post-industrial work force, with all its quirks and manifestations. About 30 years ago, he and I and a number of other business people and educators started a career-education organization, working with similar organizations in other states around the country. We figured that being ahead of the curve was always better than being behind it. Being less seasoned then, we decided to work with some of the existing institutions in our home state. That was the kiss of death. After a couple of years, the existing bureaucracies gradually dismantled all that we had done. They did so under the guise of the State knows best, and hastened to keep the existing institutional structures in the same forms as at their inception. Twenty years later the State developed a career component within an existing department. This was an example of bureaucrats not being validated in what they do by the introduction of new ideas, yet coming to the conclusion that they needed to change two decades later, but under the same structure that allows them to validate themselves. Notice that such mindset and action becomes a function of preserving the institution, not of accomplishing a goal.

Not to be deterred, about seven or eight years ago Dave and I set out to do something a little different: To structure a university of the future by combining and expanding several progressive approaches: the EAST Initiative, the development of various third-wave institutions, some Adler, ideas from the origins of the University of Chicago, and other philosophical concepts. We again wanted to address the workforce demands of the future. A bright wonderful banker in Northwest Arkansas decided that this was exactly what the University of Arkansas needed to do, so he had me meet with deans of various departments. This time I approached it much differently. I didn't ask for them to get involved. I merely had the discussion about creating new institutions within the system's existing structure. After some wonderful talks about educational philosophy, institutional structure, and the new educational model, each of the deans and professors came to the same conclusion: this needs to be done, but don't include them because, if their bureaucracies got involved, it would end up looking just like their institution. What did I learn? I learned that bright, honest people do in fact inhabit our earth. Bureaucrats do, in fact, know what's going on and, if your initiative is couched properly, they can be helpful. The implementation of various sustainable initiatives came to life for us, as a result of bright, motivated individuals within our local established planning bureaucracy, as you will see in Section V. The world can work.

An institution may have laudable goals, and the bureaucrat's stated function may be to accomplish those goals. But the real function of the individual within an institution involves doing a specific job, looking out after self, and perpetuating the organization. That singular focus of trying to sustain an institution determines the actions of both management and labor. It is the focus of both governing bureaucracies and corporate bureaucracies. Their intent is not to seek truth. It is to manage a process or to do a job. At times, the individual may seek enrichment at the expense of others, or in lieu of money they may seek self-aggrandizement. That form of organizational governance has become systemic globally over the millennia. In some circumstances, it is in direct conflict with the collective need to sustain the human race. Twenty-five years ago, Alvin Toffler discussed the trend and need to democratize our institutions, which means the actual functioning and organizational structure of our bureaucracies. Couple that with the nature of hierarchical structures that are authoritarian by either design or by their nature, and you begin to see why and how various institutions tend to fall short of their original visions. You also see why you must evaluate long and hard before you get existing institutions involved in helping you create your own sustainable community. This problem isn't new. It has existed forever.

I've got another half dozen examples that deal with the nature of bureaucracies and the quandary that surrounds them, but I need to spare you because I want you to keep reading. Here's what I believe is of issue: Your heightened vigilance is required, or possibly some sort of an organizational re-evaluation may be necessary, for you to maintain the focus of your own movement of creating a sustainable community.

10

What to Think vs. How to Think

Skipping back to Chapter 8 for a moment, I would really like for us to think about the institutional mind-set which has developed over the past couple of hundred years or so, and how that mind-set relates to the multitude of problems we have created. I would proffer this: our past expansion of this mind-set and continued magnification of this institutionalized way of thinking and behaving has been, and could continue to be, detrimental in our quest to become sustainable.

Behaving in specialized ways is a natural outgrowth of human endeavor, and is, in fact, good at times. However, fortifying the industrialized institutions has us behaving in specialized ways. Many years ago we began to defer our thinking processes to these. For some reason, at times we seem to have accepted that specialization and limitations of individual thought are one in the same, and in the best interests of us, the masses. It is suggested in some circles in this country, and in other industrial, pre-industrial and emerging industrialized countries around the globe, that industrialized societies work more efficiently if we, the worker bees, do our jobs and don't worry our pretty little heads over complicated things that should be left to "experts." This is not what Adam Smith envisioned when he wrote *The Wealth of Nations*. That type of patronizing belief has its foundations in pre-modern institutions—Restrictive institutions, the likes of sexism, racism, anti-Semitism and other regulating beliefs. These patronizing beliefs, sometimes based on certain rational philosophies and sometimes on limiting rational thought, are why we've accepted the unacceptable: like pollution, poverty, homelessness, invasion of privacy, and any variety of other ills to which we don't feel compelled to concern ourselves. We rationalize that experts out there "specialize," and so know better. These types of restrictive beliefs are foundational to some institutions, including some of the major world religions. They have been fortified by a bastardized version of the industrialized processes. These processes can become anti-democratic, and as noted earlier, terribly problematic if we are to create sustainable communities.

Many industrialized modeled institutions have developed in the past which concern themselves with limiting individual thinking. They are insidious by their nature. They are unwittingly involved in decimating our rights which we consider unalienable: those rights allowing us to think, the philosophical underpinning of all our human rights. Remember Rene Descartes from earlier … as humans we exist and we think. This is why we are entitled to our rights. Our rights are not endowed to us by any institution: governing, religious, business, or other. Any restrictive institution—if declared necessary for efficient societal functioning while not enhancing but restricting our collective education and ability to think—degrades our rights. Restrictive institutional thinking shackles our freedoms and our ability to find truth. Subject to such restrictions, we cannot create sustainable communities under our definition.

One last thing before we move on to some examples: the press and media. Thank god they exist. According to the philosophical definition of a free society, their thought processes are not restrictive. In practice, their functions maybe restricted by the nature of their business in this communications age, but their thoughts in the aggregate are not. They aid us in our collective quest for the truth. It's the reason our forefathers affirmed the necessity of a free press. By actual function and practice they can at times be specialized in their attempts to simplify for today's consumption standards … for sound-bite consumption. They, in fact, can be and at times are restrictive. However, when taken in the aggregate, the media actually considers more not less. They are involved in all subjects, at least all subjects that are deemed of interest. The media is in the awkward position of either not covering enough or covering too much. They're damned if they do and damned if they don't. The reason I bring this up: Their situation is much like what you will experience if you involve yourself in the redevelopment of your community. If you talk "big picture," some critics will say you have your head in the clouds. If you focus on the small details, others will argue you are not dealing with the real problems. It is always too much or too little. Don't be dissuaded. Always keep in the back of your mind Frank Lloyd Wright's adage: The whole is to the part as the part is to the whole. The point is that, if you see each of the small issues like the media does with a story, in the long view, in the aggregate, and with all of the complexity, you are more likely to see the whole picture. Then you will engage in the lofty yet necessary endeavor of creating sustainable communities and possibly saving our species.

I've always been amazed when an individual is introduced with near reverence as a Renaissance Woman or Renaissance Man because he or she does more than one thing. In some circles such traits are venerated, in others not. I believe that is because most of us have been taught from a young age that you have to select one thing to do in life, and you need to do that one thing well. Nothing wrong with that unless it is taken to the extreme. That division of labor started from the beginning of time and has been institutionalized. Being taught to do one thing is much different than being taught to think and act in limited and specialized ways rather than in holistic terms.

We may have evolved as specialists in some respects out of the necessity to survive and sustain ourselves, and out of institutional behavioral reinforcement. But prior to the institutions developing around the Industrial Age, we humans were more generalists. Part of our survival and daily activity was sustainable. We thought sustainably and we acted sustainably. There still exist around us various remnants of those holistic thought processes. Look at how small farms and family farms function today. The same exists within some of the archaic and authoritarian societies around the world. Industrialized nations' and societies' specialized institutional behavior is one reason why some cultures have difficulty understanding some of our actions and can be a source of conflict.

Two of the most brilliant individuals that I have known in my life were considered as being "all over the place." They could connect dots better than most and find seamless solutions to problems. Today, we would dose them with Ritalin because others might believe that they need to focus on one thing at a time. Described as holistic thinkers or renaissance people, these individuals were said to lack focus. In our specialized world, some believe that those doing more than one thing or thinking in complex ways, like most people actually do, lack focus. The group you are with will determine whether holistic thinking will be valued or dismissed. Remember, being dismissive is a way to limit debate or discussion. Knowing what to think in this social scenario is of greater value than knowing how to think. Those that tend to dismiss may see the broad thinker as a threat, and may fear a loss of their own power.

This discussion of what to think versus how to think reminds me of a wonderful story about something that happened to me when I was a young architect just a year or two out of architecture school. I had won a competition for the bell tower design on a university campus. I won't mention the university, but as a result of my minor accomplishment, I was asked by the university's president to work on the area's master plan. Here's where it gets good. Some of my bosses wanted to tell me what to design. This was contrary to what the university guy wanted. Even though the nature of specialized hierarchical business structures had been gradually changing during this period—30 years ago—my bosses had not internalized this cultural change. They had supposedly embraced it, but that was merely lip service, and all of us young architects knew it. The old guys wanted desperately to be in control. This particular firm's specialty areas were controlled by the top echelon; a top down approach. But in this particular case they couldn't tell me what to do and what to design … and how to think. It was actually comical watching them constantly come by my cubicle to see what I was doing. Some of the other young architects and I had wagered a case of beer on which boss would freak-out first. I probably should have been a little more sensitive and accommodating to them, but I didn't want to lose a case of beer.

Needless to say, I bled this situation for all it was worth. When I was finished with the design we had a meeting with the university president. He loved what I had done. When I rolled out the plans in front of him, he actually said, "It looks like something Frank Lloyd Wright did." That was likely due to the drawing technique I used, and not because it was a good design. The funny part: Even though the project was well thought out and the rationale was well articulated, my bosses couldn't bring themselves to say anything good or constructive. The university president was perplexed by their conduct. You've never seen grown men squirm so much. Their fear of a young architect who they couldn't control taking over their perceived specialized tasks wasn't very palatable, and from their perspective couldn't be allowed. The specialized, structured way of thinking and doing, with which most were comfortable at that time, could be at risk. After everybody had a chance to critique the design, the client turned to me and asked what I thought. My reaction was simple. I wouldn't have designed it as I did if I thought it was bad. That was good enough for him.

Later that day the big boss called me into his office to talk about the project, but he really wanted to discuss how I needed to be more compliant. After some friendly discussion, he finally got around to telling me what my problem was: "You think too much." I couldn't believe what I heard. Are you kidding? Something like that just didn't seem to be a problem to me. What better compliment could be paid to someone who took pride in independent thought and creativity; the best compliment that could be paid to an architect. My reaction was simple. "Thank you." I could tell that my reaction really pissed him off, but I was truly sincere.

The younger folks that read this will probably be dumbfounded, but this is how the old-school worked and, assure yourself, it still works that way in many circles. What is important: Always be aware of this hierarchical approach to design, in which someone tells you what to think. It is antithetical to the approach necessary in designing sustainable communities today. Always embrace the thoughts and talents of those around you and those in the community, and never demonize a person's talents. The trick is to extract others' talents and help them express their thoughts. This overwhelming desire, that many of us in the industrialized societies have developed, to specialize and control all aspects of human endeavor may not serve us well when we undertake developing sustainable communities. Lou Kahn used the term "thoughtful creation" in describing the built environment. Thinking is the crux of sustaining the economy and the environment, and how to think is much more important than what to think.

The specialized thought processes we have been discussing have been reinforced for numerous generations. It has occurred through our educational processes typified in the industrial model most of our educational institutions employ today, including our universities.

The earliest forms of these institutions date back to around 2257 BC from China, around the 7th Century BC in Pakistan, and the Greeks around 387 BC. Depending upon your definition, the modern versions or foundations we know today emanated from a medieval model from either Turkey in 849, Italy in 1088, or France in 1100. These medieval forms were to a great degree about educating the children of aristocrats in the ways of land management, and how to protect their properties against incursions or over-indulgence. Same as we do today. We enlighten the individual about managing the economy's basic sectors and peripheral service sectors. You can say what you want, but that is about all there is to it. It's just broken down into a bunch of specialty areas. The point: In a post-industrial economy the type of basic-sector managerial skills required are in some ways a different animal.

As a quick aside, a wonderful educational organization, the EAST Initiative, has spread into maybe a dozen U.S. states It is one of those newly established institutions that helps a student learn how to think, not merely what to think. Critical problem solving from a young age—through which we learn that all things have relevance, is vital to our problem-solving tools. Which brings me to my bone of contention: Today, at universities around the world we are still teaching students what to think in the specialty area of planning.

For the most part, young planning students are taught what to think and not how to think. I'm sure a collective gasp will rise from educators who teach the subject all over the world. But the fact of the matter is the world wouldn't look the way it does, that is to say the bulk of the United States wouldn't function so inefficiently within its built environment, had young students been taught how to critically think about the world in which we live. I can't just blame planning students for that, although they are supposed to be the advisors to all of us on all things pertaining to our communities' physical development. It is a general failure of the educational system to teach the critical skills necessary to evaluate comprehensive problems in a specialized world. Before you jump to any conclusions, I am not blaming educators for that failure. This is just another systemic failure due to our hierarchical industrial model based on ancient and medieval life and institutions. Back to the planners for a moment. It would help if they at least had a basic understanding of economics, but that's not an educational requisite for being involved in developing the environs in which nearly all commerce takes place. It's hard for me to fathom such inadequacy in preparing those who represent such a vital link in the development of our communities, sustainable or not.

During the early phases of working on the project I describe in Chapter 32, a young planner kept trying to pigeon-hole our effort into one of the methodologies that she had learned in planning school. She was terribly competent at regurgitating that learned information, but was not able to see what the community was doing. That wasn't what was taught to her. She was terribly infatuated with the knowledge she had acquired in college, relying heavily on it as she argued how the community should proceed in its endeavor. She was, however, terribly frustrated that the methodology the community employed couldn't be called something specific. She was likewise frustrated that the community was unwilling to change its process to fit nicely into her world: the world that she had heard about or learned about in school.

The gross inefficiencies we experience in today's built environment result from this specialty division of labor that should require more general knowledge rather than less. Our need to create curriculum to support a planning profession based on an industrial model has led us to this: We have created an entire language specific to the profession which excludes those who don't have the same educational background. We have relent-lessly worked at making the profession's minutiae, and for that matter other professions' as well, more involved and more complex while narrowing the profession's scope into specialty areas. *We have created a specialized, sim-plistic profession in an ever more complex world.* Do you see the beginnings of a problem developing here? This has been going on for so long that most in the profession would probably wonder what the fuss is all about. They are taught s what specifically to think about any number of situations. No options available.

Most of the public discourse we see today, just like most of our edu-cational instruction and collective knowledge passed from one generation to another, involves others telling you what to think and not how to think. This book is about understanding these institutional conflicts, how to identify them, and possible actions to take in finding solutions to the conflicts. The management and eventual solving of the problems are a function of how we think about them and the thought processes we use to connect dots in a complex world.

11

Once Upon a Time

Once upon a time some wonderful people knew, if they could educate future generations of designers and planners, they would transform their built environment into a more efficient and beautiful place that could sustain itself. IT DIDN'T HAPPEN. The 1973 Oil Embargo was the impetus for the U.S. becoming energy independent and hopefully sustainable. In early February 1974 Henry Kissinger unveiled a federal-government initiative called "Project Independence" to free us from foreign sources of petroleum. THAT DIDN'T WORK. Even though the embargo was really about punishing the U.S. for helping Israel, it actually turned into an issue purely about money and greed, wrapped up in the cloak of religion, fueled by hate. The proof is clear when you see the graph of oil prices adjusted for inflation from 1861 to the present. The prices rocked along as a stable commodity for over 100 years until a consortium of oil producers figured out they could squeeze more out of the world's industrialized nations. They could collude to get higher prices and a greater piece of the action.

What the oil producers did then and are doing today is not that much different from what we do with welfare and foreign aid. It's a transfer of wealth from certain productive sectors of the economy to less productive sectors. The difference: This transfer of wealth occurred for a commodity which has greater value; and it occurred not through competition within the private sector, but through collusion, something we as a democratic country used to disallow in our businesses practices, and somewhat in our labor practices. The free market tends to create stable and lower prices, where collusion tends to increase prices and can create great wealth for the few in control ... That doesn't quite square with our definition of sustainability.

From 1973 to today the prices for oil have continually increased, even adjusted for inflation. Is it because of the future available supplies of oil that the price has escalated? Yes, partially, but not really. Prior to '73, oil companies within the private sector competed, which kept prices stable, even considering the pre- and post-divestiture of Standard Oil. Since collusion took place on this global scale, the prices have been escalating. What the oil producing business/nations want is simple: what they consider their fair cut of the wealth which we and others produce. The oil producers are brilliant at testing the market to see how much they can squeeze before the U.S. and the rest of the world start to go into a recession. What I mean by "squeeze" is to affect the supply so that they get the highest returns. That is to say, they maximize their profits. That's what businesses do, and that's what authoritarian countries that are actually businesses do as well. The difference is that they can actually affect the availability of supplies by different methods that we as a democratic nation tend to disallow. How do they affect supply? Depends on who you are, how powerful you are, and how you can affect and take advantage of business and political affairs around the world. It depends on if you are part of the power structure of a Middle Eastern country or Russia or Exxon. But be aware, they can affect prices whenever they want.

Here's the bad part of all of this increase in energy costs: The price of all that is produced becomes higher, and in some cases wages stagnate. The good part: This situation may force us, if we are smart little chickens, to become more efficient, and will hopefully cause us to become more sustainable. European nations tend to tax the heck out of the consumption of oil to affect ... consumption. They would like to see us do the same. It would make them more competitive with us, or you could say it makes us less competitive. That is to the advantage of nations all over the world that want to create greater wealth for themselves. Problem for some nations that produce things is that it will also affect their overall propensity for consumption.

So, the oil embargo started out to be a catalyst for planning and design schools as well as communities throughout America to focus on ways to decrease dependence on the possible depletion of fossil fuels. But somewhere along the way we all forgot about the big picture, as noted in previous chapters. I have mentioned in this book that the *green* chicken came first. This is the notion that we are in control, or should be in control of the things around us. This chapter is a mere recognition that we humans have evolved within an ecosystem. Through trial and error, we developed local, indigenous systems, buildings, and institutions which sustained us. Today we still exist within this same human ecosystem, but we seem to not recognize that. In the not-so-distant past, (once upon a time) we were, as an organism in the Petri world, more "green." The time before the industrial revolution, and even through the early days of the industrial revolution, we functioned more in sustainable ways. The proliferation of inexpensive energy which helped us as humans to do "work" (defined by Junior High science class) allowed us to discover ways to do so many things differently than we had for so many millennia before. All this was seen as good, until we began to understand the implications and ramifications of all we had done. Please understand I am not advocating that we go back to a point in the past. As I had noted in an earlier chapter, that's really not doable. I am advocating that we understand better those attitudes and actions for generations before that had made us the green chickens, and begin to reintegrate those things back into our daily lives. Fay Jones had always taught that to know where we want to go into the future, you have to have some idea as to your past, because from that past exists a historical knowledge as to who we are and how we function. From that we can then acknowledge those things which are infinitely important for our survival. That means we need to educate our kids in certain ways, as we had done in earlier times, showing how it relates to us sustaining ourselves and our communities.

The aggregate functioning of the organism we call a community is the biggest user of energy, and for the most part forgotten when it comes to saving energy. We as a society have reevaluated some components of what helps a community to become energy efficient, but not all. In the early '70s, after the oil embargo, many of the existing community, business, and governmental structures appeared ill-equipped for increasing the efficiency of our environs while focusing on the "livability" of our communities. The common belief was that the two issues were mutually exclusive. Turns out, that's not true. As a result of the perceived inadequate action by established institutions, a handful of individuals began to analyze the systems necessary to alter our processes and institutions, hopefully allowing us to compete more efficiently as a nation and as communities.. During this period, the most interesting transformation took place. The knowledge base which existed within government, coupled with those who were developing sustainable initiatives along with some really brilliant engineers, surfaced to help create laws requiring more efficient buildings and transportation systems. The federal government created various policies to lessen our overall dependence on depleatable resources. It mandated efficiency within buildings through more stringent codes, and a little bit on autos through standards for increased vehicle gas mileage. Something President Obama has addressed again. Many states and local governments have followed the lead of the federal government in adopting building codes and energy codes which help to make our buildings more energy efficient. Where we continue to be lacking is in our attempts to deal with land-use policies as they relate to the functioning and efficiency of our built environment and of our economy, which directly impacts our ability to sustain ourselves. Has all the work that we have done over the past 40 years helped in the big scheme of things? Sure it has. And community planners will tell you about all the wonderful and difficult things they are doing, and the efficiencies created within the various systems which affect the efficiency of our communities. But the fact is that, since the oil embargo, our communities have become even more grossly inefficient than in the previous 40 years. The design schools and planning schools have created specialists who can't see the forest for the trees. If they could, our environment wouldn't be getting more inefficient, and our communities wouldn't be getting uglier.

Although not part of the main-stream discourse at the time, the need to decrease dependence on petroleum products on a more massive scale manifested discussions, academic exercises and eventually implementation of strategies. They revolved around the development of post-industrial sectors of the economy. It was surmised that the coming post industrial "ICE" Age could more rapidly usher in the development of efficient urban environments and more sustainable economies, the types more capable of sustaining fluctuations in the oil markets and any number of other markets by relying on sound basic economic principles. Recognizing that the communications age was well under way, those of us involved in this movement set out to evaluate and develop new institutions and methodologies. They would facilitate creating more efficient and livable environments and sustainable communities required to sustain their populations in a more competitive global economy.

At the heart of the discussion, it became apparent that the existing methods of planning and the corresponding planning institutions would have to be significantly altered. Only through substantive change could our communities become more efficient and more competitive without causing local environments, economies and communities to degrade. We've developed third-wave technologies and resulting industries and institutions. This has allowed for more rapid development of new levels of governing institutions. These are necessary to re-evaluate our planning methodologies, and have further increased pressures on existing governing and planning institutions to alter their perceptions of how we develop our economies and built environments, and how we manage our environment and our resources.

What does all this have to do with creating sustainable communities? EVERYTHING!!

I hate to get into monopolistic and oligopolistic competition and the function of price leaders and price followers in the market place, but just understand this: Any business will act the way OPEC did during the oil embargo, and would act just as the more recent consortium of oil-producing countries and oil futures traders. The point: If you don't change how your community deals with the overall efficiency of the built environment and our ability to compete and produce in the face of these pressing issues, then you're an idiot; of course I mean a Jay Leno-defined type of idiot.

Section III

Present

Chapters 12 thru 15

Most of us think of our pasts, live in the present, and dream of the future. The development of many of our institutions is based on these human attributes, institutions that deal with the past, the present, and the future.

If you haven't noticed by now, I do love to talk about the past. The past is what has created me and you and everyone else around us. The importance of the past (our history) is to help understand why and how we got to where we are today (our present) and how our institutions developed to operate in the fashion they do (their present function).

The key, I've learned, is to work with people willing to honor our history, face present realities, and plan for a sustainable future. Those folks aren't always easy to find, so I've had to learn to be flexible.

Many years ago, my friend Jim Lynch was in my office discussing one of the many issues confronting the neighborhoods in our community. Typical me, I was expressing my frustration with those who couldn't see into the future and figure out what we needed to accomplish. Jim sat me down to help me become less frustrated with those around me. He explained the various types of people that exist on earth, how we can treasure the talents of others and utilize those talents for the betterment of society. I've found the people who really care about that have the courage to do their research and publicly state their views on what society needs to become better. They see the potholes and the promise.

A small town mayor that represents the International Council for Local Environmental Initiatives, now called the Local Governments for

Sustainability, has noted: "Cities make up two to three percent of the geographic mass of the globe, but we generate 75 percent of the greenhouse emissions." That's where we are right now. That is the present. That is the big pothole that needs to be fixed.

The construction techniques and energy efficiency of individual buildings is not the focus of this book, but I think it is important to note that the composite of individual buildings is partly what makes up a community. It's important to know where we are at present as it relates to the efficiency of buildings in America. A great summary was presented to the U.S. House Select Committee on Energy Independence and Global Warming in 2008 by Michelle Moore of the U.S. Green Building Council. She noted that buildings are an essential part of the solution to the energy, resource, and climate issues our country is facing. She went on to say that buildings in America typically have a lifespan of 50-100 years, throughout which they continually consume energy, water, and natural resources. (Actually buildings don't consume those things, people do, but we know what she means.) She also said that buildings are responsible for 39 percent of U.S. CO_2 emissions per year. If the U.S. built half of its new commercial buildings to use 50 percent less energy, it would save more than six million metric tons of CO_2 annually for the entire life of the buildings—the equivalent of taking more than one million cars off the road every year. (Now you're talking some savings on money and health.)

In her presentation she also noted that buildings annually account for 39 percent of U.S. primary energy use, use a little over 12 percent of all potable water (or 15 trillion gallons of water per year), and consume 40 percent of raw materials globally. That equates to approximately three billion tons annually. She continued with some other statistics which I find goes to the heart of our throwaway culture. She noted that the Environmental Protection Agency estimates that 136 million tons of building-related construction and demolition debris are generated in the U.S. in a single year, and that we create around 210 million tons of municipal solid waste per year ... I've got a great slide somewhere in the office from my original slide presentation that I used to give over 30 years ago. It shows a wonderful piece of architecture built from construction scraps and throw-away items.

The most staggering statistic to me—remembering that I grew up in a Miami, Florida home with no air conditioning and with solar hot water and windows oriented to channel the breezes, and screened-in porches where it seemed like my brothers and I nearly lived outside—is that Americans spend over 90 percent of their time indoors. It amazes me that today almost all buildings are sealed up and air-conditioned, which removes us from the direct effects of weather on our long-term decision making. (There is a hidden discussion here.) Ms. Moore finished by saying that "buildings have a profound, if little understood, impact on our health and well-being as individuals."

It is obvious that, if we were to seriously address the design, construction, operation, and deconstruction of buildings, we could reduce greenhouse gas emissions. It is my hope that we pull back from the individual buildings and see a bigger picture, our communities. If we address these same concerns in the broader built environment as we do with individual buildings, we could significantly reduce greenhouse gases, create greater efficiency, compete more effectively in a more competitive global economy, and be healthier doing it. So let's address these concerns.

12

Is T. Boone Pickens Right?

Before I answer that question, I just want to say ... **DON'T SELL YOUR SUV.**

Now, on to Mr. Pickens ... For those of you that don't watch TV, T. Boone Pickens is a very wealthy oilman that had been paying for his own television commercials in hopes of getting each of us, and the government, to understand that there are real solutions to our latest energy crisis. He's trying to get us, the consumers, to be aware of other forms of energy and to demand these alternate forms. He is trying to get us to put pressure on the elected lumps in Congress to get off their collective derrieres and help the private sector supply alternative forms of energy to us the consumer. That way the markets for these alternatives will develop more rapidly. He is also trying to nicely browbeat the transportation industry into accelerating the implementation of their R&D and technology into the marketplace. His plan is to end America's dependence on imported oil. Not unlike what President Obama is trying to do as he announced on June 29, 2009 ... just in different ways.

Let's back up for a minute. The terminology of energy crisis may or may not be technically correct. It's more of a fossil-fuel price-escalation crisis which affects the consumer and the economy. Mr. Pickens is trying to tell everyone that there are plenty of "energy" resources available that don't include petroleum from overseas. He's saying the crisis is of our own making due to our shortsightedness—us the consumers/electorate and the people whom we elect to public office.

Sorry for calling our elected officials lumps. They're not actually lumps, they just act like it. They either don't know what to do, or they're stuck in a system that doesn't allow them to do anything but spend our money in hopes that solutions will befall us. I don't want to berate all of Washington. In reality, for the past 30 years exceptional resources and exceptional people—including the Department of Energy as well as organizations like the Alliance to Save Energy, and individuals like the brilliant Carl Stein in New York City, and even Malcolm Verdict at the University of Texas in T. Boone's own back yard—have had the answers. They've been sitting on "go" for years just waiting for the day to implement real energy-savings solutions. Actually, some have been extremely successful at implementing solutions, but I contend not at the scale necessary. Otherwise we wouldn't continue to have the energy problems that we have.

What Mr. Pickens is doing is wonderful. His focus is on the supply of energy. In his lectures he points out that foreign oil makes up about 70 percent of U.S. daily use, and when oil hit $140 a barrel we would spend $700 billion a year: a situation that has affected our national security. As he says, "the largest transfer of wealth in human history." What he is saying with his commercials—to us the masses—is don't blame Congress, Washington, Bill Clinton or George W., and don't blame the car companies. We the consumers are not driving the market where it needs to go, and he wants us to alter the demands we have on Congress and those folks who supply energy to each of us. He is pointing out that we have put our own nation at risk, and we need to understand that the free markets work just fine when people actually act in both their best interests and in our collective best interests. Both however, just like in a democracy, work as long as there is an educated populace. Mr. Pickens is trying to educate us.

Mr. Pickens is using the media … doing a series of commercials to persuade us to alter our collective behaviors, just as every company in America is trying to do, relating to their "green products." It's all pretty much the same. It's all good. The most current commercials for every green product from happy cows to recycled carpet will have you believe that, if you buy their green products—and every company will eventually have one—you will save the world. Some of that is true. It will help for each of us to do our part. Mr. Pickens, however, wants us to focus on products that will make us less dependent on other countries and more dependent upon ourselves. **THIS IS ONE OF THE KEY COMPONENTS OF CREATING SUSTAINABLE COMMUNITIES,** and the reason why I have a chapter about Mr. Pickens. He is trying to show that utilizing replenished, local, easily accessible resources is advantageous to our collective futures. Alleviating the reliance on depletable resources shipped in from all over the world is very good … most of the time.

Mr. Pickens would like for us to create demand for different forms of energy produced here in the U.S. That's good. What I would like to point out is this: Increased supply of conventional and alternate forms of energy is important; but decreasing demand on a per capita basis is as important. And it's not as hard as it seems, and can have a much more dramatic effect in a shorter period of time.

Mr. Pickens has noted that the unbridled purchasing of oil from foreign countries can affect our national security. Knowing that the Department of Defense was involved in national security, and being somewhat less seasoned 28 years ago than I am today—a nice way of saying I was naive—I figured that all I needed to do was call up the DOD and explain the importance of decreasing our dependence on foreign oil. I'd note how to go about it through the alteration of land-use policies, and other things like that. I figured from that first step, these wonderful folks would help push this discussion where it needed to go. You know, because the Defense Department would be concerned about national security. Boy, was I ever wrong. Looking back, I can now laugh, knowing how institutions actually work, or should I say how they don't work. I'm sure the people that talked to me were wondering why I was calling them, even though I told them why. Point is, 28 years later the net effect is that the Department of Defense, Congress, Department of Energy, Department of Commerce and others have talked about the relationship between our purchasing of oil from foreign countries and our national security. But not much has been done. They will say that a lot has been done. They'll explain all the things that have been done. But the fact is that we are more dependent on foreign oil and less secure as a result. Facts don't lie.

I can assure you, if the results which have come out of government were mimicked in Mr. Pickens' own companies, he would have fired the individuals that act like our Congress for gross incompetence, or he would have been out of business. What do we do as the supposed informed electorate? We keep electing these folks and they keep acting like idiots and not leaders. As I said in earlier chapters, they really aren't idiots; they're just caught in a system that ought to be overhauled so that our outcomes aren't so consistently idiotic.

As I noted earlier, government institutions are not established to create profits, and capitalists invest where they are not encumbered by outside institutions or individuals who are not concerned about profits. The reason why T. Boone does commercials is to get consumers to drive the energy markets, rather than allow Washington to drive the markets, so that risk capital will find its way into the market more rapidly, creating sustainable investments and profits for the private sector. Rest assured, what he is doing is significant. It may have a more beneficial long-term impact on the development of the energy markets than what Washington has done in the past 30 years. Thank you, Mr. Pickens.

To finish this chapter where I started ... Keep your SUV and buy a small car as an extra. The worst thing we can do is dump a whole bunch of gas-guzzling monster trucks on the used-car market, flooding it and bringing down the price of used SUVs so every person that wasn't able to purchase gas at $5.00 a gallon will be tempted to buy one of these vehicles.

Did the "cash for clunkers" program worked? In the short run, absolutely. Will it have a positive effect? Yes. Will it help the auto manufacturers in the long run? Maybe yes, maybe no. It depends on whether the program is a real catalyst for changing consumer behavior over the long run. Just looking around, my informal poll, I have noticed more electric and hybrid autos on the road, but I am also seeing more new Sport Utility Vehicles.

Years ago, I thought I wanted a SUV. I was telling all my hunting buddies that I thought I should get one of those vehicles because they had trucks for work and for farming and hunting. Dan Hooks looked at me and said, "Yeah you need one of those ... you and every other woman in Little Rock." He proceeded to tell me if I ever needed a vehicle to haul stuff around in, I could borrow one of his. His concern was for all of us being economical so the price of petroleum wouldn't go up. That's how farmers and other businesses survive, by producing products as economically as possible so they can compete and not go out of business. This is why decreasing demand for energy is so important for all of our businesses. Increasing the supply of various alternative forms of expensive energy possesses a degree of folly.

The story of Dan chiding my desire to get an SUV reminds me about a woman in Little Rock and her SUV which was parked across the street from my office. A little over two years ago I walked out to get into my car, which was stupid, because I live only two blocks away from where I work. I noticed a young lady with a box of liquor that she was getting ready to put into the back of her SUV. She was probably five foot three or five foot four inches tall and was driving one of the biggest SUVs that exist on the road. She was dwarfed by the vehicle. I was mesmerized by what I knew I was getting ready to witness. After she got the tailgate down, which was not easy for her, she picked up the box and strained to get it up and onto the tailgate which stood at near shoulder height. She was not big or strong enough to push the box in past the tailgate, and she couldn't hop up on it because it was too tall for her. So she proceeded to climb up on to it so she could push the box in far enough to shut the drop-down door. It was marginally fun to watch, partly because she was an attractive gal, but it was by far one of the silliest sights I've seen in a long time. This was a young person that bought one of these vehicles because everyone else had one, or because she wanted to feel safe, or—one of the big reasons—because it's convenient to cart stuff around in it. What I saw was not convenient, so it must have been for one of the other reasons. She could have driven a Mini Cooper and fit all the groceries she would have needed for a month in it, and she wouldn't have had to look so stupid.

As an Architect, if I were to design a home for an individual that was as inconvenient and awkward to use as this young lady's vehicle, I would be fired or sued. So why do individuals make these type of poor decisions? That's a discussion for another book. Anyway, this type of insane decision making on the part of consumers is what we need to be addressing. It may result from crafty advertising over a period of years by the car companies, or from peer pressure that caused her to tool around town in a small house. All I know is that this is not wise for us as a civilization: to spend untold amounts of our productive capacity on energy and our treasury to secure oil resources on the other side of the globe so we can drive around in vehicles we use to boost our self-worth. If we spent the same amount on exploration within our own borders as we have on the wars in the Persian Gulf arena, we would have had a very different foreign policy today. Personally, I blame myself and people like that young lady for the wars that we have fought.

If you want to do something for the economy, keep your monster vehicle and use it only when you need to transport a half dozen kids or lots of building products for renovating your house or food to feed a football team. These large vehicles are useful and marginally efficient if you are transporting lots of things or lots of people. If you are one of those hot dogs that want people to believe you have money, or if you actually do have a sizable quantity of disposable income, and if you want to help the economy and yourself, keep the SUV. Then go out and buy a Fiat 500 or something that transports two people if you're just driving yourself around or commuting to work by yourself. Neil Cavuto said that Fiat doesn't make a car big enough for Americans to fit in. He's wrong. They do make cars big enough for Americans; and until recently, they have tended to be more efficient. As I've noted in other chapters, the transporting of humans and goods is about using the least amount of mass as possible for the job at hand. The issue for us: Start using the high-school education that we've received; flex our brains to limit our individual consumption of energy.

Be conservative—conserve. Don't you find this dichotomy interesting: how the liberals are the conservatives on this subject.

Always remember ... when the car companies see truck sales climb, which means SUV's, what do you expect them to do but supply the demand? When you see gas prices go down and we consumers go right back to our old ways of (as the "Saturday Night Live" Coneheads used to say) consuming mass quantities of gas, what do you expect the car companies to do but give us more of what we have been buying?

When I grew up, if we left unused lights on in the house, my dad would yell out, "This house looks like a Christmas tree." That was our signal to start turning out the lights and cut waste.

Mr. Pickens' focus is on other forms of energy to keep this terribly inefficient system humming along so the economy's fluctuations are not so drastic. His focus is on supply. I'm talking about making the system more efficient with a focus on demand. We need to consider both.

If you want to do something for our economy and our security, buy a little car and turn out some lights. This country looks like a Christmas tree.

13

It's Not an Information Age!
the new ICE Age

If you are rich and exist within an agricultural- or industrial-based economy, you can be a benefactor of the arts. If you are upper-middle-class, if you aren't quite as rich, you can be a patron of the arts, and if you are lower-middle-class or just downright poor, you can be a helper. Or you can, through public policy, vote for taxing those with money to supply you with your demand for the arts. The fulfillment of the individual and societal expectations for the arts has been accomplished through private expenditures and through public programs, policies, and expenditures. That's how we can have public art and symphonies and the like. This is the conventional model which caused artists to suck up to the wealthy. This hierarchical social and economic model has been with us from time in memoriam. The artists are the fools who are required to entertain, who are given a pittance out of the goodness of those in the social stratum above or through the public sector. I give you money … you entertain me. Be the monkey on a leash.

Today, if you're rich in a post-industrial or third-wave economy, you make money off your creative efforts and the creative efforts of others, and you want your production costs to be minimized so you can be globally competitive. If you are upper-middle-class, again not quite as rich, you make money off your creative efforts and the creative efforts of others. You want your production costs to be minimized so you can be globally competitive. And if you are lower-middle-class or poor, you make money off your creative efforts and you want your production costs to be minimized so you keep your job and your job isn't sent to India. Each knows that the function of the "creatives" is not to be a monkey for others, but to create wealth by using our creative talents to send 1's and 0's all over the world in creative "products" that people want to buy.

The differences: In one model the creative individuals suck up to the wealthy, whereas in the other scenario the "creatives" are the wealthy and everyone has to suck up to them. The paradigm shift has taken place. Creative talents create wealth. The artist—under a new and expanded definition—is the new industrialist. If there is any question about this, look around and see who makes the biggest salaries and creates the greatest wealth in terms of our balance of payments.

Regardless what Al Gore and others call it, it's not an Information Age … it's a Communications Age. We communicate, or distribute informational product and entertainment product in digital format all over the world. Just as rice and soybeans are products we distribute in the agricultural sectors of the economy, and just as widgets are the products we distribute in the industrial sectors of the economy, we distribute information and entertainment in the communications sectors of the economy. It's the "New ICE Age:" Information, Communication, Entertainment. But be aware, the same economic forces that control production and distribution of first- and second-wave product still exist, with possibly one exception. There are times where the chain of events of making things, storing and retrieving and distributing things, is altered in a third-wave economy. There are times when distribution occurs simultaneously to production.

The implications have far-reaching impact as to how to create our communities … that is, the communities based on this new ICE Age economy.

Art is not a luxury, it is a human necessity. It wouldn't have existed in the forms that it has over the millennia otherwise. Understanding the scope of that human necessity and the creative needs in a global third-wave economy which consumes ICE Industry product, is at the core of understanding corporations' and communities' future needs for altering existing programs, policies, expenditures, institutions, and current methodologies.

The agricultural sector produces, let's say, rice that creates wealth for our nation. A single grain of rice or maybe an entire handful of rice doesn't have much value coming out of the fields. But, if you put millions of grains together or produce tons of rice and package it nicely, and distribute it to consumers efficiently and effectively, you can create lots of wealth. Same thing in the digital world. Digital 1's and 0's have no value in and of themselves, but if you take bunches of 1's and 0's and put them together in *creative* ways, you have information which can be of value to others, or you have entertaining products that people want to see and hear: movies, music, art, sports, "American Idol," and on and on.

As the Tofflers talked about nearly 30 years ago, this is a new Basic Sector of the economy where wealth is created and things are created that people want to buy: products that can be distributed all over the world in the blink of an eye. Snap, and you've sent your products to every market in the world. Now you're talking the potential for some real money. The economics are pretty simple. The basic sectors of the economy are where wealth is created. No matter what product you are talking about, you either create it, you store and retrieve it, or you distribute it. That's all.

What some had called the post-industrial age, others called the information age. What Alvin and Heidi Toffler called the third wave, and what I termed about 20 years ago as the "New ICE Age," has been with us for over 100 years. When Edison developed the light bulb and the Kinetoscope, the ride began. Motion pictures, radio, television, computers ... we are merely seeing the inevitable maturation of a basic sector of the economy that has been around a while, continually enhanced by technology, just as the agricultural and industrial sectors have been continually enhanced by technology.

Back in November 1986 I was quoted as saying, "Creativity is the foundation of a post-industrial economy." I wish our educators and business community would have paid attention. The nature of the new ICE Age is such that to have a viable economy in the world of the future, the last thing you cut from a school district budget when times get tough are the arts. Educators need to stress that, if you want to sustain your educational system over a long period of time, you fund those areas which will generate returns in the future. Sorry, but hair salons don't create wealth and don't generate the returns necessary to sustain your economy. Sports programs do if you are in or near a major metropolitan area that has a professional sports franchise. That's the topic for another book. In the meantime, keep in mind that corporations' and communities' changing impetus on the arts and entertainment will yield higher expectations for arts education and creativity as an underlying foundation for a viable third wave, ICE Age, economy. Such expectations will drive public policy for those communities that get it, and will be the genesis for institutional change.

There are some major institutional issues we must address for the ICE Age sectors of the economy to develop fully, and for us to create efficiencies in the built environment which will sustain this economic sector. These will be addressed in more detail in some of the following chapters. For now, let's begin to think and ask questions about them: First, the bodies of law which have developed around our concepts of toil of the back and of the mind: the foundation for lien laws and the protection of those who work with their hands and their minds. Second, the nature and impact of intellectual property rights which has its foundation in the toil of the mind, and has huge implications on the development of the built environment.

Be aware that, in this new ICE Age, for the first time human civilization has no physical constraints to developing product and creating wealth. The implications of this for the built environment are staggering. For developing sustainable communities, they are critical for those communities wanting to diversify their economies and participate in creating wealth and opportunity in the New ICE Age.

14

Land of Oz

I feel like I am stuck on the wrong side of the rainbow. Worst part is that I'm not sure at times which side is the right side. Have you been to Kansas lately? What would Dorothy think of it if she were to leave Oz and go back to western Kansas today to Auntie Em's farm? Would she be able to survive? Maybe yes, maybe no. In that part of the country the chance of farm survival is no longer dependent upon having a storm cellar to get away from the tornados, but upon whether you have water resources: the essential component for sustaining life.

One of the major tributaries on the North American continent is the Arkansas River. I mean it is a really big river where it empties into the Mississippi. At that spot, it is near equivalent to that of the Ohio or Missouri rivers. It's one of those rivers that starts at the continental divide in the Rocky Mountains and flows through Colorado, Kansas, Oklahoma, and Arkansas, spilling into the Mississippi River in Southeast Arkansas. Technically, it doesn't actually flow through Colorado. They dam it up and use all of the water that comes from the mountains. It picks up a lot of water from various tributaries along the way outside of Colorado. It's good that it does, because if you were to go to western Kansas, you could stand in the middle of the Arkansas River in a dry river-bed. I mean no water. It's surreal. Seeing the actual bed of a river—cause for settlements and eventually the development of a railroad—with no water in it is eerie. All the trees on the old river bank look like skeletons. Colorado uses every bit of the water from the Arkansas River so that no water makes it to Kansas. You ask: How can that be? The answer is a lot of mumbo jumbo and legal issues surrounding riparian rights. But the real answer is because humans need water for survival: survival for one group of people within one jurisdiction over another group's survival in another jurisdiction. This can put people and jurisdictions into direct conflict with each other. Is this type of conflict over water a forecaster of things to come? For now it's a legal conflict, but as global population increases, the type of conflict over water will change, just as the conflicts over oil have changed through the past hundred years. Fighting over water is just beginning. This is a critical issue that will only get worse as we continue to populate our Petri world. You think fighting over oil is bad, wait till the fighting over water really heats up, and heat up it will.

Lucky for the farmers in western Kansas and other parts of the world, and lucky for you consumers that need groceries that allow you to eat and survive, there are other sources of water. In that part of the country, the chance of farm survival is dependent upon whether you have water resources from one of the aquifers. For those of you who are not familiar with aquifers, they are bodies of water below the surface of the earth. Some are stationary like a lake and some are moving like a river. The food that we have on our tables has become more and more dependent upon these bodies of water from under the ground, just like we have become dependent on the oil that comes from under the ground.

Farmers have been using aquifers since humans figured out how to pump water from them. The problem that some farmers are beginning to face, which you the person who eats food will face, is the depletion of water from some of the aquifers. That means the water supply from subterranean sources is drying up. As a result of this man-made phenomena, some areas in the United States have begun using more sustainable methods of recycling water for certain types of crops. This is good, smart, and must be done because the demand for surface water has increased for other human needs as the aquifers are being depleted. What all of this means, if not properly addressed, is that the price of water will go up. Which means the price of food will go up. Which means the price of survival will go up. That means that those who create wealth will be able to survive longer and sustain themselves. Remember Chapter 4? Sustainability is about the stupid economy.

When developing sustainable communities, meaning communities able to sustain themselves, the demand for water resources needs to be considered very seriously. The list of uses for water include drinking and bathing, watering our lawns, sliding down a slip & slide, cleaning our cars and clothes, transporting goods up and down tributaries, assuming the tributaries don't go dry from upstream folks using all the water, and growing crops for us to eat. As the decades pass and the population grows and the demand for water increases, here's the question that will arise: Which on our list for water use is most important? Is there a hierarchy of need? We have seen this rating of water uses for decades. Every time there is a drought we curtail the consumption of some things and allow water for certain other things. In the deserts of New Mexico and Arizona the folks live with this list of hierarchical needs all the time. Where it gets more complex is in large population centers with high demand for water so lots of people can survive. Should that be given precedence over the need to water the produce in the fields so that we have food to survive? We are beginning to make those types of decisions.

An even more complex question is the need for water levels in our navigable waterways. Massive amounts of water are required to float the boats that bring goods cheaply to and from markets. The same water that one day may need to be used for sustaining our food supplies, and possibly the same water being diverted for consumption in an upstream jurisdiction. Will we see the time come when we are more concerned about getting the things we want than growing the food sources required for us to sustain ourselves and survive? We are confronting these issues today in some parts of the country. If you, the chicken, don't take note and address this issue in the development of your own community, the existing businesses and political institutions will make the decisions for you. Then in 50 years your kids will wake up and ask: What the hell were they thinking? Were our parents idiots? Of course, I mean the Jay Leno type of idiot.

Should we use water for distribution of products or for the creation of products? If we are not able to develop agricultural products to create wealth to buy things, then why do we need to transport things? It is a given that we can and do buy products from all over the world, including farm products. We can create wealth in other sectors of the economy and then use that wealth to buy our food from other parts of the world. That is somewhat counter to the notion of sustainability, but doable. Here's another reason why we buy more of our food from other parts of the world: The decommissioning of farm land for housing our growing population, or what we call urban sprawl. We have lost billions of dollars of wealth-creating revenues into the U.S. economy due to this phenomenon.

We, and others around the globe, are finally making the link between the over- dependence on foreign oil and national security, as well as the link between water needs and farm production to national security. Basic sustainability for humans does imply a safe supply of water for survival. It is imperative that you consider such a supply along with all of the other issues when developing public policy as your community tries to become more sustainable. Many years ago, the dilemma between adequate supplies of safe drinking water for millions of people in south Florida came head to head with the state's food production and wealth creation. The issue was not about how we can sustain ourselves over the long run, with the implication of controlling population growth, but how do we sustain an ever-growing population. The answers are normally a function of the questions asked, and this was no different.

Back in the middle of the last century, cattle ranching in Florida was a huge industry. Florida at that time was the largest cattle producing state in the nation, or maybe it was the second largest, but you get my drift. All through Central Florida were wonderful ranches. My home away from home during the '60s was one of those areas … Yee Haw Junction. It was actually called Jackass Junction but the powers that be decided that, when the Florida Turnpike was to be built through the area, the name should be changed. We hunted these areas as kids, but we had to be real careful while walking from one side of the ranch to the other not to get too much cow dung on our boots … you know, cow chips, i.e. cow patties, a.k.a. cow poop, crapola, and every other word that young boys could think of to describe the dung minefields. The quantity of cow crap through which my brothers and I would have to navigate was multiplied by the tens of thousands throughout the state. That's a lot of poop, and it's important to remember that the runoff from storms runs downhill. That means that when there's a storm and the water mixes with the tons of cow poop littering the Central Florida countryside, then the cow poop would go down hill, and in Florida it meant landing in the water supply.

One of the first things humans learned thousands of years ago was to not pee upstream. Under the leadership of former Florida Governor Reubin Askew, after he was out of office, the amount of effluence allowed to run from the cattle ranches down into the water supply was decreased radically. It decimated the cattle industry but it saved the ecology of Lake Okeechobee and the Everglades, which is the filtration system for south Florida's water supply. This type of forward thinking has saved the water supply for millions of people, and has preserved a magnificent environment. But we still haven't addressed the real issues pertaining to sustainability.

Kudos to the State of Florida for acknowledging that you shouldn't pee upstream, and then doing something about it. And kudos to us for having the foresight to understand that it is not healthy to dump a lot of particulates into the air that we breathe. The federal Clean Air Act was an attempt to address this problem. Here's a novel idea: If we view air and water like they are part of our human ecosystem, which means we can use them wisely to produce things necessary to sustain ourselves and also produce wealth, then maybe we can start making better, more rational decisions about the growth and development of our communities.

The sustainability issues from the Kansas and Florida examples aren't about whether one state has the rights to water over another, or should we choose water for people over production of food for people. It is whether our land-use policies which cause shifts in economic production and population are wise.

There are answers to these types of problems, and we chickens have them. But for us to make these types of really difficult decisions, it will take, as the cowardly lion in the *Wizard of Oz* says ... "Courage."

15

Frank Lloyd had it (W)right

Some think that Frank Lloyd Wright created architectural master-pieces that were organic … "Organic Architecture." Architecture derived from the characteristics of nature and living organisms. Well, yes and no. That's not quite it. It actually depends on how you define nature. But Mr. Wright's definition of organic had more to do with the origins of, the nature of, or the essence of an idea, whether from nature or not. As Fay Jones described it, it is a concept distilled down into its essence, where the elements of the whole are harmoniously related through one control-ling component. There it is:"The whole is to the part as the part is to the whole." That's the adage made famous by Frank Lloyd Wright, and a key component in developing the processes necessary to create truly sustain-able communities. It's a controlling component that runs throughout all decisions made, from big to small at the same time. That's organic.

When I say Frank Lloyd Wright, most of the time I am also talking about E. Fay Jones, unarguably the most successful disciple of Mr. Wright, and the harbinger and broadcaster of his philosophy. My relationship to Mr. Wright was nonexistent. However, my connection to him and his philosophy is a direct link through Mr. Jones, one of my architectural professors, and one of my mentors, and as the years progressed, eventu-ally one of my friends. My philosophical understanding of Wright results from both Fay Jones and my other architectural mentor and friend, Ernie Jacks, a onetime brilliant designer at Edward Durrell Stone's office in New York. My exposure to Wright's philosophy through Fay was considerable, as were the tenets espoused by Ed Stone through Ernie. Even more impor-tant for me is that my philosophical understanding of Fay is because of Fay, and my philosophical understanding of Ernie is because of Ernie, which resulted in my own underlying philosophy riddled throughout this book.

In the early '60s Mr. Wright came to visit Fay at the University of Arkansas. It was not just a special occasion for those in the profession, but for those in the larger community as well. Having Frank Lloyd Wright come to your town of 15,000 people, and in essence anoint you as one of the chosen-ones, was big for a young architect. Some years later, during my first year of architecture school, I went to an event at the arts center on the University of Arkansas campus to honor Edward Durrell Stone, one of the early pioneers of architecture's modern movement. The building where the meeting took place had been designed by Mr. Stone and the team of architects in his office. He and his team had also designed the New Deli Embassy and the Kennedy Center for the Performing Arts, and many other buildings all over the world. One of the most influential architects of the 20th Century, he had, at one time, one of the largest architectural firms in the United States. He had returned to his hometown of Fayetteville,

Arkansas to donate his papers and architectural models to the University of Arkansas' School of Architecture. It was a wonderful occasion for many because of Mr. Stone's importance to the profession.

As an aside, I took a photo of Ed Stone and Fay Jones at that event. Fay kept it on his desk for many years. (Photo to the left, Stone seated, Jones standing.) About the time Fay received his Gold Medal from the American Institute of Architects, he sent me an autographed copy of the photo. I have kept it on my desk for the past 20 years; a great memory for me. To top that, a few years after I took the photo, I was helping Ernie Jacks close his office after he had decided to concentrate his efforts and talents on teaching at the University. As we packed up all of his final gear, he handed me four or five T-squares that he had used over his career, with one that had his name etched into it. I have them hanging up in my office for others to see. I tell stories about those being among the tools used for designing the North Carolina State Capitol Complex and the New Deli Embassy and others. Ernie never has told me if I was pushing that story too far or not, so the lore continues.

Mr. Stone was one of the originators of what was then termed as the International Style. Both Wright and Stone decided to buck the modernist trends of the time. Some believed it was because they wanted to distinguish themselves from the crowd; but they had real philosophical problems with the established school of modernists. I believe that Tom Wolfe has described better than most what was happening at that time in the world of architecture, and where many in the profession fit in the big scheme of things. Wright and Stone were brilliant individuals who had big egos, but they were thinking about how and why the world worked the way it did, and they tried to make it a better place in which to live. They did that through the expression of their own philosophical beliefs and art form … architecture.

I would like to discuss a number of issues making Mr. Wright's and Mr. Jones' philosophy applicable to the development of sustainable communities. First, the origins of the modern movement of architecture and the eventual bastardization of those origins: A cause for much of the inefficiencies in the built environment today. That issue is the foundation for understanding the divergence of Frank Lloyd Wright and Edward Durrell Stone and others from the mainstream Architectural Modernists of their time. Through this discussion, I would like to assert what I believe should be the real meaning of modernism in the architectural world, and the effects this can have on the built environment. That then leads me to the subject of this chapter: how and why the true modernist underpinnings of the Wright/Jones/Stone/Jacks beliefs are applicable today in developing sustainable communities.

Modernism in the architectural sense emanated from modernity, which we discussed in Chapter 2. The essence of modernity rises from the two foundational institutions in civilization's quest for truth: science and democracy. These grew out of the demise of medieval institutions. The earliest originators and developers of architectural modernism worked under the medieval institutional system, and the remnants of the medieval mindset as they began to define modernism. They attempted to throw off the old institutions and wanted to define architectural modernism in a new way and with new terms; but they defined it, not in terms of true modernity, but in terms of anti-establishment. They were constantly defining in terms counter to the remains of medieval thought.

Their thoughts, expressed in new definitions, were these: If the world had been controlled and designed for such a long period of time by the bourgeoisie, then the new modernists defined the new world as anti-bourgeoisie. If the world had been grand and imposing in scale, then they defined the new world as demure. And if the bourgeoisie's architectural world had been rife with detail and color, then for the masses it would be defined as colorless. Here was a terribly fun and exciting time for the artisans and creatives of the day. They were looking to redefine the foundational origins of all that would be created in our physical world, describing its essence as austere and non-indulgent. They ended up *wrongly* equating modernity with their new anti-bourgeoisie political philosophy, a philosophy which co-opted the modern architectural movement. Wright and others continued to explore the *true* meaning of modernity, and explored such in their works, including Wright's city of the future, Broadacre City, an exploration in form of modernity's democratic principles.

This original movement from its inception was brilliant. But it rapidly became bastardized. It was hijacked by intellectual lightweights who decided for those around them what to think versus how to think. (See chapter 10) They became the thought police. They were educators and professionals that had a vested economic interest in others believing what they espoused as the only correct or viable way to think. Some of the art and architectural creations coming out of this movement were magnificent. The resulting built environment became the craze and envy of the world for a period of time, but it was unsustainable. The equation of industrialized forms and the resultant physical environment as an offshoot of modernity is now being questioned around the world. Because of this misconnection, modernity is now something to be despised in parts of the world. Let's correct that misconception. Our built environment is not a result of modernity, but rises from a bastardized version which was incorrectly termed as modern.

This architectural movement turned into an extremely poor expression of the human spirit, the human experience, the complexity of human life, and the new freedoms being experienced by people all over the globe: liberty and democracy … the essence of modernity. They knew that they were embarking on a new journey into uncharted territory. The movement went wrong when it became defined by a few individuals whose definitions became institutionalized in the same way that the authoritarian leaders of the medieval period defined their own institutions. They became intransigent and undemocratic in short order, and disallowed experimentation and the quest for innovation and truth. The movement became anti-democratic and by definition opposed to the principles of modernity.

The modern architectural movement rapidly became the antithesis to modernity. The movement was hijacked by itself until the so-called "postmodernists" came along. The truth be told, in the big scheme of things, the post-modernists are merely a narrow experimentation in resurrecting the original modern movement. Post-modernism implies that modernity is dead. Nothing could be farther from the truth. Architectural post-modernism was breaking the shackles of the misdirected modern movement to express modernity as it should be expressed. Architectural "post-modernism" is actually a wonderful expression of modernity and a part of the modern movement.

Not only is modernity alive and well, it is continuing to spread all over the globe: the dominate philosophical movement. Point is … there is no such thing as after (post) modernism. Abraham Lincoln told a dog story when trying to make this point. If a dog has four legs and a tail, and you count the tail as a leg, how many legs does the dog have? Four. Just because you call the tail a leg doesn't make it so, and just because you call a movement "post modern" doesn't make it so. Architectural post modernism fits squarely within the confines of modernity and the origins of the modern movement.

The bastardization of architecture's modern movement and the infatuation with a counter movement caused us as planners and architects to take our collective eye off the ball. We were not embracing the democratization of our institutions and the design process as an expression of modernity; we were designing for the technologies of the day. We began designing buildings independent from our collective past, with little or no consideration for human context or in the larger context of community or the environment. Some great pieces of architectural art were created, but most modernists' adage that "form follows function" was from a minimalist perspective. In today's world, it rings hollow. Forms were following function, but the functions being considered didn't have context to much. In the bigger context, we were designing for the automobile and not the human. As the automobile became dominate in the landscape, the design trends and underlying philosophy of the day were following the advances in technology, and not any objectives based on a civil or sustainable future. We built our environment to be extremely inefficient during this period. We didn't know it because we didn't think about it, because knowing how to think wasn't part of our functionality. It wasn't part of the functional requirements we imposed on ourselves. We forgot that we could use our brains, and that we humans can in fact be in charge. We again allowed for the eggs to dictate.

We built inefficient housing forms, which we still do, and inefficient communities, which we still do, because energy was readily available and cheap, and because it was easy and inexpensive to build that way.

In reality, not a lot of thought was required—a prerequisite for the proliferation of the emerging real-estate development industry. And that
profession became the kiss of death to the development of thoughtful and
sustainable communities. Here's all that was required: Build as cheap as
possible and return borrowed monies back to the bank. This is the legacy
of the modern architectural movement. It is not the legacy of modernity,
nor of modernism.

I mainly want to write about Mr. Wright and Mr. Stone, and their
divergence from the mainstream modernists, because they didn't act like
eggs. They didn't do what the institutions of the architectural world told
them needed to be done. They are the origins of my own philosophical
underpinnings and much of why I do what I do. Understanding this might
help you get into my mind, and help you figure out where I am coming
from as we discuss the development of sustainable communities.

The divergence of Wright's and Stone's philosophy, as well as
Buckminster Fuller's and the like, from the modernists of the time, was
held in contempt by those who espoused the pure perverted version of the
Bauhaus modernists movement. This was a movement which was typified
and driven by a lack of abundant rational thought. Don't get me wrong,
modern architecture is an art form which at its highest echelon is beautiful
and magnificent. It's rife with justification for what the artists wanted to
do, but not truly indicative or expressive of the day and time in which the
world's democratization and greater complexity of life were taking shape.
The forms emanating from the so-called modernists were terribly anti-
democratic. Contrast that with what Stone was doing and what Wright was
doing. The philosophical counter to the modernists were the likes of Ed
Stone and Morris Lapidus, who began to usher in the age of the so-called
"post-modernists." Again, a real misnomer.

Frank Lloyd Wright was, in his time and to a great degree today, the
preeminent philosophical expression of real modernity in the architectural
profession. A comprehensive nascentistic philosophical expression which
is being built upon today by brilliant architects from around the world ...
philosophical trends typified by greater introspection, greater freedom,
greater emphasis on allowing local conditions to dictate both function and
form, and a real intellectual approach to asking real pertinent questions:
A real quest for the truth. This is a philosophical trend which accounts for
more and greater complexity rather than less, and forms which express
this complexity. The newer generations of architects are not burdened with
the same institutional shackles with which the old ones were, and are free
to express the tenants of modernity more fully today. From my perspective,

the future of the architectural and planning professions looks really bright. The big question is whether clients will pay for brilliant planning and brilliant architecture. The influences from the real-estate development community and the consumer of architectural services have been in the opposite direction.

The philosophy of E. Fay Jones and Frank Lloyd Wright has great promise because it allows for a comprehensive approach to decision making. It is not limited unless there are functional needs for limitations. The whole is to the part as the part is to the whole. This philosophy implies greater knowledge and a holistic vision: A process which facilitates Baconized dot connecting, and a matrix of decision making. Let me explain.

Some folks deal better with the big stuff and some better with the minutiae. As noted in earlier chapters, this type of specialization and division of labor has been institutionalized for good reason, and many times to our collective detriment. The conundrum that we've discussed about the tug-of-war between big-picture issues to small-picture issues, i.e. potholes and promises, is for the most part solved by utilizing this comprehensive nascentistic process. The issue of where to focus one's attention becomes moot because the process creates opportunity to consider all. This comprehensive trend, typified by Mr. Jones' and Mr. Wright's philosophy, extracts the essence of all that exists around us, and expresses it in the built environment. It is a process which considers the essence and origins of all that exists, and decision making in the whole. It should be easy to see that decisions made in context to all that goes on in life have extreme applicability to the development of sustainable communities.

Fay Jones' work has involved many principles used in creating sustainable and green buildings, and to a great degree, so has Wright's work. Fay taught that these same principles can be utilized, not just in the creation of individual buildings, but in the creation of the bigger picture—our communities and the world. This philosophical bent has one foot in the origins of modernity and the other in the origins of human endeavor dating back to man's enlightenment. I believe it has a greater chance to affect our ability to sustain ourselves, our communities, and our civil societies than does any other proposition.

These underlying principles were at the heart of my conceiving the first third-wave sustainable city of the future, and implementing these principles in redeveloping the existing community we will see in practice in this book's last section.

Frank Lloyd had it (W)right. E. Fay had it (W)right, and there are wonderful architects and planners all over the globe that have it (W)right as it relates to the sustainable development of our communities. This comprehensive organic process considers the implications of all that goes on around us as we make decisions. Not in isolation, as we normally do, or as a perversion to the ideals of modernity. This is a process which considers the big picture, the "whole" picture as it relates to individual decisions ... the "parts."

Section IV

Future
Chapters 16 thru 21

We're going to cursorily address some important issues which impact our ability to sustain ourselves. Issues like education, health care, global warming and transportation. Seeing what these issues may look like in the future is important, but what they *should* look like if we are to sustain ourselves, in my opinion, is equally if not more important. We should note some interesting trends and whether these trends can or should be factors in our decision-making processes.

Let's stay aware of the difference between projecting the future and creating the future. In the first case, we assume that certain things will happen. In the second case, things will happen the way we want them to if we make them happen that way. In simple terms, the former looks at the past and considers along with various trends, innovations and advances in technology, where we are going. These are typically projections that communities, governing agencies, and most of us use to determine any variety of future needs: from transportation planning, to revenue projections for the IRS, to what I am going to buy at the grocery store, and on and on. The latter involves establishing numerous viable future scenarios based on various trends, along with the human decisions made with regards to those trends. It then assumes the selection of one of these scenarios as a goal, based on needs, dreams, and desires. Then, resultant to the selected goal, programs, policies and expenditures are developed to accomplish that goal.

My focus is on the latter because I'm a Chicken and the future to me is an Egg. I may want to know what the future holds, but I really want to help determine the future that can be to our collective liking. Don't get me wrong, lineal projections from the past into the future are helpful, and can be great tools in determining various futures.

This subject can get quite complex. Loads of books on the subject are fun to read, if you think fun is bamboo shoots under the fingernails. As an aside, I have focused on this way of thinking over the years because it has made sense to me to do so. Also, I am a student of Fay Jones who unveiled this process to me many years ago. I have decided over the years to confine myself to the philosophical parameters we have discussed in earlier chapters. Otherwise, I'll get bogged down into the philosophical discussion that my friend Dave Barlow believes is basic to the determination of futures: the dispute between actualism and possibilism. Sorry, I'm not going there. That's for another book. Dave needs to write that one.

When I work with others to determine the various futures that might exist, from which a community can select, I like to describe how trends and cycles affect decisions and outcomes. This will be described in further detail in Section V. When decisions are made about the future—or I should say, when decisions are made about taking advantage of what the future holds—it is vitally important to distinguish between the trends and cycles.

Sometimes it is hard to distinguish between the two, especially when a cycle takes so much time to unfold that it seems like a trend. Some fun facts are floating around the Internet that have lots of people trying to figure out what they mean to our collective futures. Some of these look like trends and some are actually cycles, and some are just trivia with no great implication as to determining our future. Things like:

- One in eight married in the U.S. in 2008 met online.
- In 1984 there were 1,000 Internet devices. By 1992 there were one million, and by 2008 there were a billion.
- The top ten in-demand jobs in 2010 did not exist in 2004.
- We are currently preparing students for jobs that do not yet exist using technologies that haven't been invented.
- There are 200 million registered users of My Space. If it was a country it would be the fifth largest in the world between Indonesia and Brazil.
- By 2049 a $1,000 computer will exceed the computational capabilities of the entire human species.

A bit of advice: Don't be bamboozled by the glitz of statistics that you haven't been aware of prior to this time. It's all predictable, and it's not as amazing as you think, if you just sit down and contemplate it.

Think about the implication of this to your future:

- During the 19th and 20th Centuries, there was great movement of people throughout the world. At the close of the 20th Century, and in these early days of the 21st Century we are moving or communicating information and entertainment product.

- In 1880, agriculture, manufacturing, commerce, and industry employed 86 percent of the U.S. work force. By 1975, that proportion dropped to 33 percent, and it is projected to drop to less than 25 percent within the next five to 10 years.

- In 1991, for the first time ever, companies spent more money on computing and communications gear than the combined monies spent on industrial, mining, farm and construction equipment.

This pattern offers hard proof that we have entered a new era: the Industrial Age has given way to the Communications Age... the "New ICE Age." What does that mean to the composition of your economy, your educational system, your transportation system, your land use, your laws, and your political system?

There's a behavioral pattern that most communities in the U.S. embrace which governs how they enter the future. It's a pattern which many times is counter-productive in dealing with the critical issue of creating a sustainable community. It typically starts with the business leaders wanting to expand the economy as defined in their mind, ergo advertised to the masses as growth and progress. Again: It is done this way because the business institutions are set up to function this way, and because media doesn't know any better. Also, educational institutions support and reinforce this human and institutional behavior.

So ... the question for our communities, which encompasses individuals, community organizations, as well as the governing and business institutions, is: How do we take advantage of the various cycles and trends by prioritizing policies for the communities' economic prosperity, and for the sake of the economic well-being of present and future generations? Also, can we be aggressive enough to compete globally in a sustainable way? Asking the questions about the future allows for greater participation. The easy way to say it: you are asking rather than telling. Asking questions about the future implies that the community is going to be involved in creating the future, rather than just predicting the future and trying to get in front of it.

Many times a disconnect occurs between the questions which address long-term issues for the community as a whole versus the long-term issues for the business community, which many times look like short-term issues. The long-term issue for a community might be having a more sustainable environment, and a more beautiful place to live; the focus is on creation of wealth and developing higher incomes versus the business community that may want to attract jobs through various incentives. These are two different models. As discussed earlier, one is a focus on expanding the economy through sustainable investments, and the other requires a continued influx of people so the entire system can continue to function. More people? Is that the sustainable approach?

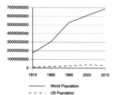

To the left is a chart that was compiled by Johnathan Lumpton showing the population trends for the U.S. and the world. What does it show? It shows that there are a lot of people in the world, and there are going to be more in the future. From this trend, we can project future population.

When we take the dashed line from the chart above, which shows the U.S. population trend, and we show it by itself, it looks a little different. These charts show us that, over the past 100 years, population has grown quite a bit and that the U.S. share of the world population has gone down from 5.3% in 1910 to 4.5% by 2010. Does any of this help us as community groups, or city boards, or states or as nations to determine policies as they may relate to the development of sustainable communities? Yes and no! Here's what is important: more information, not less, is brought to the table and discussed as to its relevance.

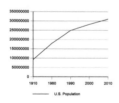

Lumpton's next chart shows U.S. employment trends: Total employment shown with the solid line, private sector employment with the dashed line, and public sector employment with the dotted line.

What's important to note within this chart: The public sector share of the total employment has risen from 2.6% in 1910 to a projected 16.9% by this year (2010), with a 1% fall during the decade of the '90s. Could this tell us something if we were to connect these dots to a bunch of other dots dealing with productivity, capital investments, and let's say income levels, tax revenues and foreign industrial production. YES! It's not for me to tell you what it means, it is for you and your community to make that determination for yourself, with help from people like me. But do it with more information and data, not less.

Here's what is most important: These types of charts and the statistics within the charts can help us as communities make decisions about our future; a future that used to be relegated to some government bureaucrat. We can now empower ourselves to make decisions about our future rather than being a subservient citizen with no control over anything. This is what's so important about the communications technology trend. It is as liberating today as what was experienced when Columbus and Copernicus upset the applecart of their day. We will see how the shift in this trend has allowed for greater citizen input and control in Chapter 24, and I'll mention again: this is what Toffler described as the trend in the democratization of our institutions that would follow our inculcating new communications technologies throughout our society.

Lots of people have noted how important it is to know your past, and to link that past to your future when you are planning and designing your future. There is a wonderful story, let's call it the Ancient Horse's Ass Link—that some folks like to use to drive that point home. It goes something like this:

> *The US standard railroad gauge (distance between the rails) is 4 feet, 8.5 inches. That's an exceedingly odd number. Why was that gauge used? Because that's the way they built them in England, and English expatriates designed the US railroads. Why did the English build them like that? Because the first rail lines were built by the same people who built the pre-railroad tramways, and that's the gauge they used. Why did 'they' use that gauge then? Because the people who built the tramways used the same jigs and tools that they had used for building wagons, which used that wheel spacing. Why did the wagons have that particular odd wheel spacing? Well, if they tried to use any other spacing, the wagon wheels would break on some of the old, long distance roads in England, because that's the spacing of the wheel ruts. So who built those old rutted roads? Imperial Rome built the first long-distance roads in Europe (including England) for their legions. Those roads have been used ever since. And the ruts in the roads? Roman war chariots formed the initial ruts, which everyone else had to match for fear of destroying their wagon wheels. Since the chariots were*

made for Imperial Rome, they were all alike in the matter of wheel spacing. Therefore the United States standard railroad gauge of 4 feet, 8.5 inches is derived from the original specifications for an Imperial Roman war chariot. Bureaucracies live forever.

So the next time you are handed a specification/procedure/process and wonder, 'What horse's ass came up with this?', you may be exactly right. Imperial Roman army chariots were made just wide enough to accommodate the rear ends of two war horses. (Two horses' asses.)

Now, the twist to the story:

When you see a Space Shuttle sitting on its launch pad, there are two big booster rockets attached to the sides of the main fuel tank. These are solid rocket boosters, or SRBs. The SRBs are made by Thiokol at their factory in Utah. The engineers who designed the SRBs would have preferred to make them a bit fatter, but the SRBs had to be shipped by train from the factory to the launch site. The railroad line from the factory happens to run through a tunnel in the mountains, and the SRBs had to fit through that tunnel. The tunnel is slightly wider than the railroad track, and the railroad track, as you now know, is about as wide as two horses' behinds. So, a major Space Shuttle design feature of what is arguably the world's most advanced transportation system was determined over 2,000 years ago by the width of a horse's ass.

And you thought being a horse's ass wasn't important? Ancient horse's asses control almost everything...and current horse asses are controlling everything else.

You get the point. It may be obvious that in making plans for our future, we need to consider so much from our past. Do we always defer to that past? No! Just be aware and use what is applicable.

Let me explain this another way. A number of years ago the state I live in wanted to know what type of jobs they should pursue. "Pursue" in this case means buying or stealing from other parts of the country. Local Chambers of Commerce and State Economic Development organizations define success this way. How do you attract companies from outside, and what do you have to give them to convince them to move to your location? This particular time, the state decided to hire a company from New Jersey to look into their crystal ball and tell what jobs of the future the state should pursue. The company looked at the existing infrastructure, composition of existing jobs along with the educational standards and proficiency. They determined that the state should go after low-end and moderate-income service sector jobs for the post-industrial economy. Things like telephone answering centers ... You know, so we could compete head-to-head with India.

Some of us took exception to the report. Not because of what was suggested from the data compiled, but because it made a lineal projection into the future. It basically said, this is where you have been, this is where you are now, therefore based on the direction you are heading, this is where you need to go into the future. The state swallowed it hook, line, and sinker. Our position was simple. Throw that report in the nearest trash can, or in keeping with the fishing analogy, in the nearest river.

My state, like most states, has never created a long-term plan—futures plan—for the development of a post-industrial, third-wave, communications-based economy. The only plan that I know of in my state? The one I created nearly 25 years ago that I have been gradually implementing. There is also the strategic plan developed by the community which we will highlight in Section V, but that is not a comprehensive futures plan for the development of a third-wave economy. It's a plan for developing a sustainable third-wave community, and in my opinion quite impressive.

We suggested the state not just look at who we are to determine our future, but who we want to be. Such an approach has a much different result than the approach initiated by the New Jersey company and bought by my state.

As we noted in our chapter about the Stupid Economy Stupid, wealth is created by being net exporters of product rather than net importers of product. This holds true with creatively based communications products as well as with every other type of product. We pointed out to the state economic development organization that *millions* of ICE Age jobs had been created over the last couple of decades. The questions we needed to answer: Can we develop the jobs from within, and can we be aggressive enough to compete globally? I knew the answers before I went in, but I thought I should ask them anyway.

As you discuss the future with any of your governing institutions, the public-policy questions should have a focus on those trends shaping the future and the future outcomes you desire. Issues based on trends like jobs in Higher Education, Entertainment Tourism, Eco Tourism and Cultural Tourism. Also the relation these have to product creation and distribution, and issues based on trends like jobs in first- and second-wave industries becoming less plentiful as a percentage of population; and the trend that shows that the route to a prosperous future lay in the development of a sound "creativity based" communications-related economy to augment the existing economy.

From those types of projections one could begin to build public policy around the augmentation of an existing economy. Policy developed around ICE industries and technology-based companies as a foundation for a community's' future economy: an economy able to sustain itself and its built and natural environment far into the next century.

If there is nothing else that you take away from this book, I hope you always remember this: A HUGE difference exists between projecting the future versus *creating* the future. We're Chickens. We can cross the road to get to the other side. We can create the future.

16
Dear Barack

Dear President Obama,

When you and Congress spend our money on infrastructure under the various stimulus packages *(which by the way, for those who don't know, much of our infrastructure is part of our nation's wealth)* please don't spend it on the same forms of infrastructure that has (1) made us so inefficient as a society and (2) caused us to become more and more dependent upon depleatable forms of energy. A continuation of expenditures for infrastructure using the same model for our society's physical development will do nothing but guarantee that we will continue the trend of the past 60 years: We have created a physical environment that mandates we spend an inordinate amount of our wealth on all forms of energy. This has caused us to become less competitive. The money we spend for these energy resources, in the aggregate, actually goes into the price of everything we produce as a nation. In part, along with globally uncompetitive wage rates, it's the reason why jobs go to other parts of the world.

We must change our programs, policies, and expenditures as they relate to developing our infrastructure. Not doing so will guarantee that we continue to be less efficient and less competitive. It doesn't make sense to continue the trend that has made us nearly twice as inefficient in our use of petroleum for individual transit since the 1974 oil embargo. To date, we have not had a rigorous approach to refocusing our public infrastructure. For our nation, such a continuation of the sameness over the long-run will continue to reduce our competitiveness, and make our society unsustainable.

It is our hope as a nation that we create greater efficiency in the built environment so that we can become more competitive in this global economy. We can do better.

Bill Asti

17

Educational Reform
with advanced technology

To sustain ourselves and our economy in a democracy, the purpose of education must be much more than preparing a workforce for the available jobs. An enlightened electorate is necessary. Watch Jay Leno's "Jaywalking" sometime, then tell me how you think we're doing in that respect.

In the real world, education is about knowledge, competence, morality, and the resultant condition: enlightenment. In the public institutional world of education we've created here in the United States, education is sort of about those things, but not really anymore. It is basically about knowledge, and in some communities around our nation that's even iffy.

Throughout this book we have discussed five components fundamental in creating a sustainable community. Of paramount importance is economic sustainability and the economic reforms which coincide with that. In our modern democratic society this can only occur with a focus on educational reforms. In today's world of heightened competition, with a need for fiscal constraint, reforms mean utilizing advanced technologies. We have shown how advanced technologies can have a dramatic effect on telecommuting and the eventual structure and efficiency of the built environment. Likewise, advanced technologies can have as dramatic an effect on educational outcomes, meaning the civility and competence of the individual, at a competitive cost.

I tend to repeat this strong belief: "Creativity is the foundation of a post-industrial economy." I have also noted in lectures and writings over the past 25 years that trust, as an adjunct to morality, is a necessity. This is true when doing business around the world in a post-industrial or third-wave economy. Our educators and business communities must pay closer attention to these simple concepts and begin to re-infuse them into our educational systems. Actually, some of this is being done, but probably not where you think.

As the public K-12 (kindergarten thru twelfth grade) educational marketplace has evolved, education has become a conduit for imparting certain knowledge and marginally enlightening the individual.. This narrow focus results from workforce needs within certain basic and service sectors of the economy as well as the effect of litigation within the educational marketplace: litigation which has driven curriculum and costs. We actually see the same thing in the construction industry, the manufacturing sectors, the medical marketplace, as well as every other sector of the economy. I'm not saying this is all bad. I am just merely pointing out that this is the nature of the beast in our social system and economy.

The demands of the consumer within the K-12 educational marketplace, i.e. parents and businesses, have not decreased over the last 50 years. The demands have actually increased on the educational marketplace. But the public educational services supplied have been constricted in some areas while the responsibility, liability, and paperwork demands on individual teachers and administrators has increased dramatically. Let me explain.

Public educational institutions have been and will continue to be outgrowths of the demands of individuals and families and various other institutions. Only in recent decades have demands for educational services emanated, not from actual market demands, but from the benevolent hand of government. As the numbers of individuals requiring services has increased, and the institutions have justifiably become more complex, the focus on supplying the demands of the marketplace were replaced by the social interests of fewer and fewer individuals, exacerbated by our legal system. As the structure of our economy and the composition of the workforce have changed, the demands on educators have begun to grow more and more. The consumer of educational services, along with the labor markets, required the educational systems to fill the voids created by a constricted educational market and a waning home and church environment. These components were part of the educational experiences of the individual up until that time. These phenomena, along with the infusion of more females into the labor market—exacerbated by the intransigence of traditional religious institutions which refused to change with the times—widened this void in the overall educational marketplace. That is to say, the consumer's demand was for our public educational institutions to become mothers, fathers, preachers and teachers training students for jobs of the past, jobs of the present and jobs of the future. At the same time, we began taking away the ability of the educators to perform any function but to impart knowledge, and we wanted them to control their costs. We sent mixed messages to the educators. Then we expected them to do more and be more, and then we chastised them if they did what the market demanded. Then to beat all, we didn't want to pay them commensurate to the pivotal position they held in the transition of our economy and competitiveness of our workforce. We wanted them to impart knowledge without any moral underpinning, in settings which disallow discipline, authority, and physical control and safety.

This institutional gulf between the demand for and supply of services began to grow wider and wider. Some 25 years ago, when I used to lecture to educational groups all the time, I would foretell the coming of private education's proliferation. It was not easy for the existing institutionalized educational systems to see this because they somehow suspended within their minds the economic laws of supply and demand. From my part it was easy to see. That's all that private education is about: supplying the demand. Today we are seeing some public educational institutions dealing with the issue of supplying what the market wants as a knee-jerk reaction to falling enrollment and falling revenues. They are beginning to compete with private education. This is merely a reaction to the demands of the market, demands which have been there all along. These demands emanate from the nature of who we are and what we want for our offspring. They have been ignored by the nature of the institutions initially established to fulfill those demands.

Have I made the point? Let's go on to what teachers actually do, why we make it hard for them to do it, the use of technology in the educational market, and the effect on the evolution of existing institutions and creation of new educational institutions.

Congressman Wilbur Mills used to say that a teacher's purpose was to nurture, or something to that effect. He talked about the need for the teacher to be given the time to be the mothers, fathers and preachers, and the tools to be great teachers. For those of you freaking out right about now, the reference to preachers doesn't mean religion in the classroom. This was the underlying basis upon which he established his educational tax-exempt foundation, The Foundation for Educational Advancement Today (FEAT). I mentioned a little bit about this in Chapter 5 when talking about institutional change. This educational organization was to deliver educational product utilizing advanced technology.

For those of you unfamiliar with Mr. Mills, he was at one time the most powerful elected federal government official in U.S. history. He was the longest-serving chairman of the House Committee on Ways and Means, back when the seniority system in Congress allowed him to select the chairs of nearly every other committee. He nearly controlled the budget of the United States.

Mr. Mills' premise was this: If we want to alter educational outcomes, it is not going to happen by making teachers more accountable. It won't happen by testing the hell out of students to make sure that the teachers are feeding them all the right information on standardized tests. It will occur by decreasing the loads and pressures heaped upon teachers so that they can spend time doing that which has proven results: teachers supporting, encouraging, and nurturing their students. This doesn't mean that the teacher doesn't impart the requisite knowledge. It just means that technology can give the educators the tools to do their jobs without overburdening them. Mr. Mills' proposed utilizing telecom technology to distribute to teachers all the components needed to fulfill their individual lesson plans. This included the required components mandated by various governing authorities, whether funded or not. Filling out a lesson plan would be similar to filling out an automated tax form at H&R Block. As you answer the prompts, the requirements would be brought forward along with selections of engaging lessons. These lessons would compete for the media-age student's attention along with the necessary visual aids, documentaries and more. The educational interface would also automatically grade specific knowledge-based tests. It would automatically graph each individual student's achievement, putting it in context to the rest of the class. These results could also be linked to the district, the region, the nation, and the world. Then the individual teacher and administrators could see any deficiencies in achievement, then responding with lessons to close any gaps. The net effect: to off load individual teachers so they have more time for focused individualized instruction … whether in school or at home. Individuals and groups have been working on this type of hardware and software interfaces for quite some time.

This initiative was well underway, but was killed by the Clinton Administration. It wasn't done to be malevolent to teachers and students; it was due to institutional incompetence and greed. We go about our daily lives believing that governing institutions and the people we elect are bright, competent and enlightened. They are not. They are just like all of us. Most of them really don't know what to do without institutional rules and regulations. The only difference is that we allow them to have power over our lives, where we don't allow the guy living across the street to treat us that poorly. And you wonder why groups like ACORN and the TEA Party exist?

Mills' goal was to allow teachers to do what they do best, and to bring down the per capita costs for educating our kids. He understood that educating students is a part of our tax burden. It determines the costs of all we produce as a nation, and also impacts our basic competitiveness.

A knowledgeable, competent, trustworthy, and enlightened workforce operating at a fair price: This will allow us to compete effectively globally, and will sustain our economy and our communities in the long run.

18

Global Warming in the "New ICE Age"

On a global scale, we can begin to see a distinction between those communities, states, and nations which allow for free and open distribution of information, and those that don't. The former tends to be more democratic. These more democratic governing institutions tend to allow the populace to be informed and educated, and even more important, enlightened. These free societies relish certain principles of sustainability, among the most essential being a functional social and economic equivalence amongst its members: real parity. This is one of the great legacies of the new ICE Age, the fervid immediacy created in leveling the playing field within many of our social institutions, which were originally a result of democratic institutions emanating from the foundations of modernity. In this new age, we can now see how behavioral mores can be rapidly adopted around the globe, contrasted to the old way through local institutional change and conflict, legislation in some cases, and in a worst case, war. The proliferation of informed, educated, and enlightened people around the globe brought on by this new age is a paradigm shift. It is distressing to some, but holds out great hope for many others. It's a legacy of the institutionalization of mores considered to be of great value and life-sustaining.

What does this have to do with global warming? First and foremost, we can now openly debate the validity of the global-warming theory in open societies, where others can't. Hundreds of millions of people on earth don't know about the issues of global warming or the sustainability of people on earth resulting from the way we pollute our environment. Openness that comes from democratic institutions can more rapidly help shape behaviors which effect outcomes. Not knowing what may or may not be happening relative to the pollution of our global environment doesn't tend to alter any behaviors, and the likelihood is that outcomes won't be altered. Openness and free flow of information can alter behavior and outcomes, which means it can alter consumer purchasing.

It matters not what type of economic system you live in. The masses who consume goods and services drive the markets. Sometimes there is greater government control over the markets and in some cases less. Unless you've been asleep for the past 25 years, you can probably figure out which economic and social systems deliver these fundamental precepts better than others. The bottom line: The populace is the consumer. By definition those modern societies with open, free markets and free people with social and economic parity either are or will be more sustainable in the long run. As an aside, social and economic parity doesn't come from dictates in a democratic society; it comes from the rule of law. That means attorneys doing what they do.

The younger echo-boom generation and those that surround them are infused with information from more sources than any other group in history. We can lament all we want about how we think the Internet and other forms of communication are ruining the world, but the fact is this group of consumers has greater possibility of becoming enlightened. As they mature, as has every other generation before them, they will, through their behavior, alter not just their consumption habits, but the consumption habits of their parents and their offspring. This is already happening. Part of this phenomena's proof is the proliferation of the enumerable green items being produced just in the past few years. This is consumer-driven, not manufacturer driven and not government driven. Supply follows demand. This alteration in consumption habits, and the corresponding proliferation of green, will rapidly become the norm in those open societies. It will eventually trickle down to those less-open societies that produce the green things for us.

Many wonderful governing institutions all over the globe have tried for the past number of generations to push this market. Those that have educated and enlightened their constituents have had a much more dramatic effect on the consumption decisions and behaviors than those that have tried to legislate. Fact is, the real expansion of the "green" market didn't happen until demand began to increase. The market has grown because of the enlightenment through the proliferation of information, and due to the investments made by the public sector, followed by the more massive investments by the private sector that brought us the communications revolution. It is laudable that governments want to help, and they can; but many of the institutions which evolve from that desire to help can become part of the problem.

As for global warming, will it continue? Personally, I don't even know if it's happening, nor does Al Gore. Through scientific discovery and through observation of human behaviors, i.e. the underlying derivation of the study of economics, we do know this: that most if not all organisms on earth, including humans, will propagate; and if left to their own devices, will consume all that they don't destroy. There is a limitation to our environment. The globe in this context is a closed system, and communities are the operating components within that system, the place we humans live and in which we sustain life. The human behaviors best able to sustain our communities are those in which the supportive institutions affirm and assure enlightenment, as well as institutional and individual freedoms and individual parity.

We must understand and enlighten humans about the nature and function of communities in the new ICE Age. It is a precursor to the physical requirements which can lead to altering human behaviors. This in turn can lead to our ability to sustain ourselves; not through authoritarian dictates, but through the enlightenment of consumers brought on by the new ICE Age.

19

Creating Efficiency in the Real World

Former AT&T Chairman Randall Tobias once noted that computer power had become 8,000 times less expensive than 30 years prior. He went on to say, if we had similar progress in automotive technology, you could buy a Lexus for about $2, it would travel at the speed of sound, and would travel about 600 miles on a thimble of gas. His reflection should give some insight as to why our economy had continued to do so well over the past 20 years. The workforce's productivity has been affected greatly by the advances in technology and the continual decrease in its price.

As we relate his statement to physically transporting people and the things that people want and need, two things are implied. First, the physical transporting has limitations due to the sheer physics involved, i.e.the amount of energy required to move a mass from one point to another. Secondly, even if we have new technologies in the automotive industry, the physical layout of our communities will not appreciably decrease the quantity of energy it takes to move the same mass from point to point. That is, unless we alter how we move around in the physical environment, or unless we move more efficiently, as hybrid vehicles help us to do. Understanding this is key in altering the land use patterns necessary to develop sustainable communities.

If we extend the thoughts expressed by Mr. Tobias, we might see some trends to explore. Beyond the discussion of costs in computing and how that correlates to the auto industry, let's first extend the discussion to agriculture, manufacturing, commerce, and industry. Those sectors in 1880 employed around 86 percent of the work force. By 1975, that proportion dropped to around 33 percent, and by 2000 I believe it was around 24 percent. This shows that, as technology is employed throughout our economy, the efficiency of each sector increases, and the level of skill and knowledge required increases as well.

As I noted earlier, around 1991, companies spent more money on computing and communications gear than on industrial, mining, farm and construction equipment combined. This spending pattern proved that the Industrial Age had given way to the Communications Age. Keep in mind that the forms (the physical layouts) of our communities result from the type of economy that each has. For the most part, our land-use policies and the way we physically develop our communities have not kept up with the changes or composition of our various local economies. This is important. Had our existing institutions changed to keep up with the economic changes, and the advances in technology, we wouldn't have had to go through this latest energy crisis. It, in turn, was part to blame for the current recession, as noted on Capitol Hill by Daniel Yergin of IHS Cambridge Energy Research Associates in May 2009. He emphasized that the car companies didn't get hurt by the Lehman Brothers debacle, but by high energy prices. Economics professor James D. Hamilton from the University of California, San Diego testified at the same House and Senate joint committee meeting that the higher prices at the pump ate away about $280 billion of consumer spending. From my estimation, that's a lot of money. Money that didn't need to be spent on energy had we altered the efficiency of our built environment after the '70s oil embargo. Bottom line: We wouldn't have been spending trillions of extra dollars over the past 30 years to travel from point A to point B. That money could have been saved or spent in our own economy. Point here: If we don't take the opportunity to create greater efficiency, as we should have 35 years ago, we will be talking about this again in another 20 or 30 years.

Looking forward, here's one question for us: How do we as a society connect the dots to create the technologies that could transport us more efficiently, and bring down the cost of energy as it did with Mr. Tobias's example with computers? The congressional response a number of years ago was to not appropriate funds for a supercollider and the attendant science. Is there a direct connection? Yes. This type of simple dot connecting is important for developing solutions, and hopefully creating a sustainable world sooner rather than later. However, we the electorate continue to refuse to make the connections between high-school physics and the basic functioning of the world around us. To compound the problem further, we vote for people that don't see the urgency in developing the science and technology necessary to sustain our civilization far into the future. Developing a project that could help us unlock the physical world's mysteries would be invaluable, including being especially cost effective. I find the irony here inescapable. Science helps us to unlock the secrets of the universe, the TRUTH. But our government, that is supposed to be in a quest of the truth, doesn't see the need to engage in that quest. If you didn't sleep through basic physical science class in high school, you should be able to understand the basic physics of mass and energy. The hope is that we will all do a better job at connecting high-school science to voting on issues which can secure our future.

Back to Mr. Tobias for a minute: He was correct in noting that technology can, in certain circumstances, bring about the types of solutions we need to become more efficient. In one scenario, if certain technologies are developed, the price of energy could become cheap enough that we can continue to live unconstrained within our physical environment as we have for the past 50 or 60 years. The point that the environmentalists, and greenies, and sustainabilitiests are trying to make is this: It is not wise to bet on a future that is not guaranteed. If technology saves the day, GREAT. But in the meantime, let's at least plan for a future in which we use our resources more wisely. Let's use them in ways that will allow us to compete more effectively in the long run, and that will maintain and sustain our economy and our wonderful society for future generations.

From Mr. Tobias's words, we can see the correlation between technological advances in computer power and the phenomenal decrease in costs, all quite wonderful and true. Where he went on to correlate that scenario to the world of automotive engineering, and what that world would look like if the same advances in technology were to take place, was cute, but not particularly insightful or helpful. This was just another example of an industrial institutional mind-set playing coy with us. –The truth is, the real world has already experienced a paradigm shift in technology. The resultant changes in the economy—that this same technological revolution has brought about increased productivity—has done the same for our commuting. At the time Mr. Tobias made that statement, technology had already allowed us to surpass the two dollar Lexus traveling at the speed of sound on a thimble of gas. As I had noted earlier, our ability to telecommute has been here for decades. The problem: The recalcitrance of existing institutions to recognize, to push for, and to utilize the technologies that are already in front of us.

When Mr. Tobias made that statement about moving at the speed of sound, we could already move at the speed of light. The federal Department of Transportation could have advised Congress 25 years ago or even 15 years ago (as I had suggested to the head of the Department of Transportation) how to develop legislation for transportation and road funds to be utilized for telecommunications infrastructure and software development. This would have facilitated telecommuting, and we wouldn't be pissing away the fortunes of this nation today. For some reason, Mr. Tobias seemed compelled to include the auto industry in his analogy for no reason. He merely stated a problem. He didn't create a solution or solve a problem; he merely stated the obvious, like most of us do most of the time. We like to hear ourselves talk by constantly stating the same problems over and over in a million different ways. Quit that!

Will there be problems in advancing the use of telecommuting into the realm of the Jetsons? Yes and no. I would surmise that the most problematic area will be that of the real-estate development community, along with the investment community and banks that invest and make loans for those businesses. They will have to get past the land-use regulations and building codes which address the separation of various classifications of uses. It will befuddle them for a while, but it's not that difficult. It will be a paradigm shift in that industry. It will be difficult for some to understand and not very easy for others to implement. Those who could rapidly help drive the market are the employers who could implement transportation policies for their employees. For those who have to physically be in a certain location, allow for sliding levels of incentives or disincentives in income, based on proximity or whether a person walks, rides a bike, drives an energy-efficient car, and so forth. For the rest, which could be a sizable portion of the commuting workforce, develop a type of subsidy for degrees of technology utilized in telecommuting. If started tomorrow, most companies could begin implementation within four to six months. The effects would be dramatic and rapid.

In America, for communities not totally based on agriculture, a prosperous future and a sustainable future lies in creating a sound communications-related economic base to augment the existing economy. These ICE related industries and technology-based companies, coupled with altered land-use patterns, can be the foundation for greater efficiency—a foundation for a community's future economy able to sustain itself and its built and natural environment far into the next century. These efficient, visionary, sustainable communities will become the competitive City/States of this millennium.

The letter to the President in Chapter 16 is really intended for every elected official in America and every leader around the world. Redeveloping

our communities and our infrastructure around a model of greater efficiency will allow for our communities to thrive and prosper, and become
sustainable. The question for global communities is this: How do we take
advantage of the trends by prioritizing policies for the communities' economic prosperity, and for the sake of the economic well-being of present
and future generations?

With the realignment of the real estate market currently taking place
as a result of the global recession, now would be the best time to begin
implementing this model ... I think I hear a muffled scream ... must be
from the folks in the real-estate industry. Their concerns are legitimate and
justified, but if they were bright enough and bold enough, they could lead
us to becoming a sustainable nation in the blink of an eye. Considering
what we have been seeing coming out of Congress recently, as it relates to
the reforms in the financial industry and lack of connection to the real-
estate market, it probably won't happen. Unless YOU decide to MAKE it
happen.

20

Transporting Goods and Humans

The current need for various forms of transit has gone far beyond what is necessary due to the structure of our built environment. That transit demand can change as we develop efficient sustainable communities.

The Chief Executive of Segway, Inc., Jim Norrod, was quoted in an Associated Press article by Bree Fowler and Dan Strumpf as saying, "We're excited about doing more with less." *(Figure 20.1)* We've gotta love this guy. His statement stands at the heart of the definition of sustainability.

How is it that the tree-hugging liberals are able to embrace the essence of sustainability, which is the bedrock of conservatism? You know, conserving, conservation, conservatism. And how and why have the conservatives in this country and other countries not embraced this … and why aren't both groups working with each other? That is beyond me. Actually, it isn't beyond me, it's just again proof that lunacy comes in all forms, shapes, sizes, and political persuasions. It's again the institutional incompetence which drives the process and allows for idiots to control the world in which we live. (You know that I am referring to the Jay Leno type of idiots.)

Have our leaders been unaware for the past 35 years of our dependency on foreign oil? I recall how Jimmy Carter tried to term the whole energy issue as the moral equivalence of war? What have they been doing other than allowing for greater inefficiency to abound in our transportation systems, and then acting shocked when more jobs go overseas? Now, along comes Mr. Norrod and he continues to say, "Less emissions, less dependency on foreign oil, and less space," and for one-third the cost. Here is someone that makes sense, outside the existing institutional framework.

How novel! Do we want to implement initiatives which will have a positive effect on the economy and can lay a foundation for developing sustainable communities and sustainable economies? Then we should do some pretty simple things. This initiative of Mr. Norrod's being one. Others include dealing with the land-use issues surrounding the efficient movement of people and the things we buy. And then there are numerous individual initiatives which can alter the behaviors that cause such great inefficiencies in our transportation systems.

Figure 20.1
GM/Segway two wheel electric
vehicle for urban transportation.

Remember: It's not the use of energy that is at the core of sustainability; it's the per capita use of energy that drives the issue. It's the per-unit of energy attributed to all production and distribution that drives the issue. This chapter's focus is on the distribution component, not the production one. It is vitally important to remember that all work is done with the utilization of energy. All wealth is created with the efficient use of energy. **Using energy is good.**

Using energy in ways that will sustain our economy in the long run— that's what we have to come to terms with. Believe it or not, the reason why we are able to create wealth in this country is due to the use of energy. And guess what else? The reason why we are losing jobs and will continue to lose jobs is because we aren't as efficient on a per capita basis in our ability to create wealth as are others. And that includes the use of energy, especially in the transporting of the things we need to survive, and in transporting of us,the humans. If we transport ourselves much less expensively, and if we utilize the technologies for keeping so many humans from needing to be transported, then we take one of those essential components in determining the costs of goods off the table as an unrestrained variable, and we increase our abilities to create wealth.

Without getting into converting different forms of fuel into British Thermal Units and the like, remember that it is the "doing of more with less" as Mr. Norrod said. This allows us to sustain ourselves and to sustain our economy. It goes to the heart of being efficient and competitive in a global economy. Using the least amount of energy for all that we do. A constant drive for increased efficiency and lessening costs in our transportation systems, as well as other systems, results in sustainable productivity, a sustainable economy, and jobs that last in a more competitive global economy. We compete more effectively.

We've talked about high-school physics. Remember junior-high science? The use of energy has a byproduct of what? HEAT. It matters not if you create the energy with nuclear power or fossil fuels or from wind stored and transported and then used. The use of energy to do work results in heat. Actually, there are some differences in the production of energy; some forms produce more heat and use more energy in the extraction than others. For the most part, however, without getting into carbon emissions, a unit of energy is a unit of energy, whether you are driving a gas or electric vehicle. It's all about how much you use on an individual basis to get a mass from point A to point B, or how much is used to get an item from supplier to market … Thank you Wal-Mart. As an aside, Wal-Mart is better at logistics, that is to say getting the things we need to market, than anyone in the world. There's a lot to be learned from them, and a lot that they have given to sustaining our economy and our environment. I'll get into the negative side of Wal-Mart in a minute. Anyway, less energy use, less heat byproduct.

So you can see, moving a mass, meaning people and the things we want, from point A to point B, is to a great degree what this book is all about. How to decrease the distance between point A and point B, *or* in some cases how to alleviate one of the points is important. How this is manifested in the built environment in the next 20 to 30 years will determine our ability to compete with the rest of the world, and our ability to sustain ourselves.

Okay, this is where we damn the Wal-Marts of the world, or more appropriately, damn the developers and planners and politicians who have guided our land-use policies over the past 50 years: policies and practices which have allowed Wal-Mart and others to take advantage of us the taxpayer.

We build roads and interstate systems at our own expense. This allows for people to travel to remote locations where there are cheap prices for land. This is where the Wal-Marts built cheap large structures and filled them up with all sorts of neat cheap stuff that could undercut the prices of the existing community's businesses. If we didn't build those transportation networks, then the Wal-Mart forms wouldn't exist as they do today. Had we built the transportation forms and regulated the land-use surrounding them, then the Wal-Mart forms wouldn't exist. Had transportation planners, urban planners and politicians known what they were doing, we wouldn't have created such great inefficiencies in the built environment. The developers and Wal-Marts of the world would not have taken advantage of the land-use policies and exacerbated the inefficiencies of the built environment had those who conceive the land usage as it is today looked into the future. Why do we blame Wal-Mart and developers for making limited and focused decisions? That's what they are supposed to do. We are the ones at fault for creating a system that allows for this terrible inefficiency to take place.

If we take into consideration all the money we spend transporting ourselves to the remote hubs to buy our goods from the Wal-Martss, and the amount that we spend on the roads to get to the remote hubs, we might find that we actually didn't save as much as we thought we did. If we take our transportation infrastructure costs and our transporting costs into account, what we see is that the Wal-Marts of the world have shifted those logistics costs to us. They are merely taking advantage of the business model that we the taxpayers have created.

Here's the first thing you learn in Economics: There ain't no such thing as a free lunch. The Wal-Marts have merely shifted some of the costs of distribution to us. We build the infrastructure and then we pay to go get the things we want, rather than those things coming to us so we can walk to get them. You'll pay one way or another. The difference is that the money goes to Wal-Mart and the petroleum producers rather than to the mom and pop stores, and into a different form of built environment which could be more efficient.

Remember the problem-solving math questions we had to learn in Junior High? You know: There are two trains traveling at different speeds in opposite directions. When do they get to Chattanooga, and how many time do they cross the RR tracks in Poughkeepsie? I hated those math problems. But today I find myself thanking my math teacher Mr. Vreedenburg for teaching them.

MATH QUESTION:

Martha is a New York engineer who needs to meet with a client in Los Angeles. Her boss has given her the option to fly or drive, but with this caveat: She must select the one transit form that uses the least amount of energy.

Her company car gets on the average 25 miles per gallon. (A typical car.) The 747 that she has preliminarily booked has 568

*seats; but when she checks the seat selections she notices that only
500 seats are occupied. Boeing's website notes that on longer flights
the 747 uses approximately five gallons of fuel per mile, and that
the distance from New York to Los Angeles is 2,144 miles.*

*Which form of transportation should she use if time and money
were not of concern but only energy use?*

ANSWER:

*The company car that transports Martha gets 25 miles per gallon,
or uses 85.76 gallons over the 2,144 miles between New York and
LA. The 747 is transporting 500 people one mile using five gallons
of fuel or 0.01 gallons per person per mile or 100 miles per gallon
per person. At 2,144 miles she uses 21.44 gallons of fuel.*

*The 747 is better than a car ... unless Martha decides that she
could sell four of her seats in the car and could stand packing five
people in the car in the same amount of space that the airlines give
you, then she might be comparable in the amount of energy used
per person.*

The **Real Answer** is, why didn't Martha tell her boss that she could
telecommute to the meeting and the energy use would be a fraction of a
fraction. For the price of a few airline tickets they could have some real
cool technology that could also allow for telecommuting to work which
would save a massive amount of energy. Multiply that by about 30 million
of the 130 million or so people that Alane Pisarsk notes commute everyday
to work, and we wouldn't have an energy crisis. Depending on the price of
gas and the average distance traveled in a commute, let's say the average
commuter would save $850 a year. Times 30 million commuters, that's
a mere $25 *billion* in savings. These types of savings can have massive
peripheral effects on all aspects of the economy, and on the built environment. Can you say "stimulus package?" It would have a dramatic effect
on our short-term and long-term competitiveness, and eventually on our
nation's balance of payments? Real usable technology of this sort has been
around for 20-plus years. It ought to be an integral part of our transportation planning and our public transportation expenditures. It would save us
hundreds of billions of dollars NOW!

As an example, Congress appropriated $155 billion in the 1991
Intermodal Surface Transportation Efficiency Act. Had we put 20% of that

into telecommuting, as I had suggested to the Transportation Secretary at a Neighborhoods USA conference, we would have seen $31 billion go into technology. That would not only have made our companies extremely efficient. It would have reshaped our communities so they could become more efficient. It also would have freed our agricultural-based and industrial-based economies from having to compete for scarce energy resources, which tends to drive up product costs. If you want a real farm policy, this is where Congress can begin ... connect that dot, Washington.

Update this type of 20% goal to the federal 2005 Safe, Accountable, Flexible, Efficient Transportation Equity Act's: A Legacy for Users' and the 2009 reauthorization of the same (SAFETEA-LU). Then you would have $50 billion plus which could be spent on the technology of telecommuting. This would decrease the need for the constant paving of every bit of land surface in the United States. It would decrease the amount of energy expended to build and use the roads. It would shift the expanding appetite for new roads to the maintenance of the existing system of roads. Fewer hard surfaces have an effect on the hydrology of our communities (flooding) and the absorption of the sun's energy: A part of the puzzle that causes "global warming." This suggestion will probably meet with more opposition than any other, and is a topic that should be discussed in a Chapter of its own, and must come in a later book.

All this talk about airplanes versus cars is easy when it comes to analyzing the per capita use of energy over the long haul. Add motorcycles and mopeds and Segways to the mix, along with ships and trucks and trains to move the things we buy. It gets to be fun ... but not difficult. It's simple.

Our transportation needs are at the heart of how we can collectively move towards a sustainable economy and environment considering how many people currently exist on earth, and considering how many will be on earth in the next 50 and 100 years. The less mass moved or the shorter the distance to move a mass means less energy used, less heat produced, less dependency on foreign fuel, less dependency on domestic fuel, less dependency on nuclear fuel, etc.

Some simple thoughts with a high DUH factor could shape our energy policy, as well as our transportation and economic policy. Some thoughts like: When more people transit, we use more energy than when fewer people transit. When we use larger vehicles to move people, vehicles with greater mass than what is necessary, we are using more energy than if we used vehicles with less mass. When people travel far, then they use more energy than when they travel shorter distances. When we move things longer distances, then we use more energy than if we move them shorter distances.

Figure 20.2
The Hummer. One of the largest vehicles used for personal transportation on the road today.

These statements should tell us something about how we should design our world and our built environment, and how we should establish our taxation and import/export policies. And it should tell us something about the functioning of our institutions. These statements should tell us all of that and more, if we are connecting the dots.

For example, the institutional function of the Department of Transportation and its leaders isn't to alter the future. Their goal is to manage a massive institution that ***does not*** have as its primary goal to recreate our communities and our technology, so that we and our transportation networks are more efficient and better able to compete in a global economy.

Much of our economic problems today stem directly from this institutional inability to make the changes that could bring about the type of future for which our populace is crying out. These changes would allow us to compete more effectively and sustain ourselves. Changes that are real expressions of the changing economy and changes in human behavior required to sustain the species.

The suggestion I made to the Secretary of the Department of Transportation and the regional Transportation Advisory Council (on which I have served for the past 15 years or more) was simple then, and it is simple now. Redefine transit so that billions of dollars can be redirected by communities into telecommuting at their discretion. And, to keep the road lobbies from going nuts, separate goods transporting and expenditures from consumer vehicle and technology expenditures. The amount of dollars would shift rapidly, and would be staggering; especially once the truck lobbies figure out that their profits would go up. The re-creation of our communities based on this paradigm shift would happen fast, and our dependence on foreign oil would lessen overnight.

Figure 20.3
The Fiat 500. One of the smallest vehicles used for personal transportation on the road today.

Had this been done 28 years ago when I called the Department of Defense to explain how land-use issues relate to the over-consumption of foreign oil and the security of our nation ... we wouldn't have the energy problem that we have today. I suspect we also wouldn't have the same foreign policy issues we have today, and there is a distinct possibility that we might not have had to fight the recent wars in the Persian Gulf region.

For many years, statistics showed that the faster the speed limits the more dangerous and the higher incidence of death. It was a stark reality check when the speed limits went down after the oil embargo, and the death rates on roads went down. When the government decided to raise the speed limits, they never said that we want more deaths on the highways, but the consumers knew it. Some believe that's the reason we have such large autos: parents want bigger cars for themselves and for their kids so they will be safe in a crash. The government made the conscious decision, setting an acceptable level of death and carnage, and actually pushed for additional safety requirements on automobiles. This sent the message, to those who could afford it, to buy bigger and safer cars if you don't want to be one of those death statistics which fall within that acceptable level. The bottom line result from the actions of the government: bigger vehicles became the norm. You gotta be safe, and if everybody has a big vehicle, then by god I'm not going to buy one of those tiny little tin cans. The system that the government created, and that we currently employ, has this odd proportional relationship between the speed that a vehicle is allowed to travel on the interstate system, by law, and the size of the vehicle which equates to safety to many.

Did Detroit, Japan, South Korea, Germany, and others sell cars that the consumer felt compelled to buy? Look around! The auto companies built bigger autos because that is what you as a rational consumer wanted to buy if you were concerned about the safety of your kids and yourself. That's what you do. Thanks to our own government.

The question now isn't how do we take over the car companies and redesign the autos so that in five to 10 years we will be back doing the same thing we are doing now. The question is how do we alter the transportation policies, and eventually the behavior and buying habits of the consumer, and eventually the composition of the auto market? How do we change the demand for private and public transportation so we develop greater efficiency in our transportation systems so that we can more effectively compete on the world stage?

In addition to the suggestion I made on how to develop telecommuting infrastructure, I've made numerous other suggestions which would

alter our transportation behaviors. One of my early suggestions was immediately following the 1974 oil embargo. Again, as a nation we decided to
lessen our dependence on foreign oil by lowering the speed limits on our
interstate highways. That was the easy way for Congress, which produced
some interesting consequences years later. My suggestion was to impose a
system of gradient speed limits based on mass. We have had that type of
differentiation for autos and trucks for a long time. The suggestion was to
develop the radar and computer technology for auto recognition. Then,
when a cop is checking the speed, the radar would allow those with less
vehicle mass to travel at higher rates of speed than the more massive vehicles. If you want to go fast, you drive a smaller car. Had this been developed,
maintained and enhanced over the past 35 years, you wouldn't have seen
the SUV phenomenon. Actually, that technology exists today from groups
like Vera Technology and others.

The more drastic the variation in speed to mass that would exist,
the faster the consumers would gravitate to the smaller vehicles. I do
understand that at times such is a function of the demographics, but none-
the-less over many years, it would have an effect. This change would be
market-driven and consumer-driven, not car-company driven.

Another suggestion that I had made on numerous occasions, which
could be implemented fairly rapidly, is having subsidized parking in urban
environments. Let me explain. If federal, state, or local governments
wanted to alter the amounts of energy used in commuting in and out of the
cities of America—130 million people daily—we should install visual recognition technology in every parking deck in America. The cars with less
mass would park free and there would be a gradual increase in parking fees
based on the mass of the vehicle. With free parking, you would see smaller
cars popping up all over the place. Again, technology like that is readily
available from groups like Vera Technology.

There are dozens more suggestions that could alter driver behavior
and the consumers' use of energy for transportation. The purpose of this
discussion is to help us all recognize that transportation remains one of
the keys in structuring the built environment, which is a key in creating
sustainable communities.

21

It's Called Health Care
not health I don't care

I get a kick out of T. Boone Pickens, Donald Trump and others that love to state the obvious. I've heard them say time and again that the latest energy crisis has created the biggest transfer of wealth in human history. It has. They're right. I've fallen into the same trap that they have many times. I made the same statement during the middle '70s and have continued to make it over the ensuing years. I know that I have said it hundreds of times over the past 35 years. But the difference here is that people actually listen to what they have to say because their financial stature gives them access to a media that, until recent years, was more concerned with the messenger than the message. Until recently, the traditional media could not have cared less what you and I had to say about the subject. That is what my friend Joe Glass used to call "municating." There wasn't any (co)mmunicating going on, just municating: A uni-directional dissemination of all information. Then technology created a really substantive change in the delivery methods of the message. Don't get me wrong, it is very important that those with mass media access and appeal say the types of things that The Donald and Mr. Pickens have been saying. I only wish that they would put this into perspective for all of us: the harsh reality that the biggest transfer of wealth in human history will happen in the health-care industry. The difference is, that instead of the transfer of dollars going to various foreign economies, they will transfer from consumers of health-care services here in the United States, which for the most part means the elderly before they die and taxpayers, to the health-care sectors of our economy.

Be forewarned, the transfer of dollars in the health-care sectors will dwarf what has happened and what will happen in the energy sectors of the U.S. economy. The good part here is that the transfer will be to different groups within our own economy. How many will try to get a piece of the action, and how many will try to touch the money as it goes by, is one of the questions that will affect the cost of health care and the potential inflation-ary effects of the health care market on the economy as a whole. The more who touch it, the greater the costs and the greater the inflationary potential within the industry.

Indulge me for a moment. If, let's say, 30 million people spent an extra $40 a month due to the increased petroleum prices from overseas, then we would be transferring an additional $14.4 billion more a year out of our economy to others. That's a lot of money that can buy a lot of things, including health care. We all know that making a visit to the doctor can cost a lot of money; but let's assume, for argument's sake, 30 million more people will see the doctor just one more time during the year at an average cost of $500. I don't know about you, but when I go to the doctor it seems like that's about what I spend. We aren't breaking out how much is insur-ance and how much is directly from your pocket in this scenario. We are merely trying to get a handle on the scope of the market. That's an extra $15 billion spent. So far, the best part is that the bulk of that money will spread out and trickle down within our own economy.

Now, if we consider the increase in visits from an aging baby-boom population, which will be a dramatic increase in doctor visits over the next 30 years added on to the insuring of those 30 million from above, with an increase in patient visits from the present to 30 years from now climbing to let's say 200 million additional visits, along with normal inflationary pressures, this could bring us to an *additional transfer* of dollars from the consumer to health-care providers on an annual basis of $150-200 billion. There would have to be a really large increase in petroleum prices to get to that point. The good part: most of the money will stay within the U.S. economy. The bad part: everybody wants to get a piece of the action, including the government. The more that touch it, the higher the costs will be and the higher the inflationary pressures become within the industry.

It is important to understand the significance of this issue as it relates to the functioning of certain sectors of our economy. Health care has a lot to do with our ability to sustain ourselves in an advanced, globally com-petitive, democratic capitalistic, post-industrial economy. Whew! That was a mouthful.

The cost of doing business in a competitive global economy for advanced civil societies includes a lot of components. For large-scale at-risk investment capital to find its way into the production chain, a number of things are considered. Remember what we have talked about in other chapters, that everything on which we spend our hard-earned cash, eventually finds its way into the things we produce ... into the price of the goods and services we produce. The more we spend on petroleum for transiting ourselves to and from the grocery store three times a day, the greater the pressures for higher wage rates which affects the price of what we produce. Higher wage rates mean higher prices for production, which at times drives jobs to another part of the world; and the same with health-care costs. The higher the hospital costs, the more we see doctors, the more litigation in the health-care industry—all this will eventually work its way into the price of everything we produce as a nation. If we don't cut costs somewhere or create greater efficiency, (as is part of the focus of this book: efficiency in the built environment) then someone, somewhere else in the world will produce what we want at a more-competitive price. This type of downward spiral means jobs go somewhere else, which causes us to have greater need for cheap prices. This causes us to purchase more from those economies which have cheap labor and don't spend on health care or clean production, which means more pollution and more jobs overseas. And this causes pressures on our own ability to sustain ourselves. That type of scenario doesn't jibe with any of the definitions of sustainability that I know.

This need for everyone from the investors to managers and executives and workers wanting more is the greed that fuels higher costs. But if managed properly in a competitive situation, that same greed can control costs and inflation, as it has for centuries in capitalistic economies. Problem for the health-care industry is that it is not, by its nature, a competitive industry.

What happens when a person is sick or in an auto accident? Everybody rushes to the hospital. No one calls around to see which hospital has the cheapest rates before a patient is transferred. (Hospitals aren't in the market to drive down prices like Wal-Mart is.) Then, when the doctor comes out to visit with the family, the family members in distress say, "Doc, please save my (blank)." (You fill in the blank.) With health insurance in hand, the mom concerned about her child turns to the doctor and says, "I don't care what it costs, please Doc, you gotta help my baby." That's what I mean by no competition. The hospitals know this and they can get away with charging four dollars for a Q-Tip or eight dollars for a pack of tissues that cost them seventy-nine cents.

As for family practitioners, meaning your family doctor, here is where some competition begins to take place. That's why more doctors, as a percentage of their population, have chosen to go into specialty areas within the medical profession. It's a cut-throat business and, for many doctors, not worth the risk considering patient attitudes and legal liability in today's world ... We wonder why there's a crisis.

Because of the nature of this beast, the need for health-care reform *should be* about caring for people as the title of the chapter suggests. Humans have known about the idiosyncrasies of the profession and this industry for eons; well, at least since the late Fifth Century or Fourth Century B.C. when Hippocrates or one of his students or one of Pythagoras' students wrote what today is referred to as the Hippocratic Oath. Why do you think the oath exists? It's because of the nature of what doctors do. The oath doesn't say, first find out if the patient has insurance; it says "first, do no harm." That's why in today's world you don't GO TO a doctor. You go to a clinic or a hospital where there is an intermediary that can ask you that question, where the doctor doesn't have to. This intermediary was established to help manage and to maximize profits. The problem now days is that there is an expansion of intermediaries. The more and more intermediaries that exist, that take a piece of the action, means the doctors are no longer in a position to "do no harm," or for that matter, maximize their own personal profits. Due to the development of the medical marketplace, the only way doctors can affect their incomes is by either selecting to practice in a specialty area in high demand or by limiting the aggregate number of doctors in the marketplace, meaning limiting the numbers that go to medical schools and eventually are licensed; limiting supply.

This expansion of the health-care market, along with the nature of the industry, has and will continue to cause a considerable inflationary trend in that sector as companies jockey for a piece of the action, and as more groups try to get a piece of the pie, and as demand for services outstrips the supply. If there was a greater ease of entry of companies and doctors into the marketplace, you would see a rush of companies and investment capital into the marketplace. This would create greater competition, which tends to lower prices; but the chances of that happening are not good.

Again, the good part of all this is that the monies spent in that market will go into the pockets of businesses and health care providers. Then it will either be spent in the economy or saved, which means into some type of financial services company, which means it will be invested. Let's just hope that those investments occur here in the U.S. economy; otherwise there will be a further erosion of the size and scope of the economy on a per capita basis. That means we would have less wealth as a nation on a per capita basis, not greater wealth.

In the doctor's Hippocratic Oath, the Latin phrase of primum non nocere translates to "first, do no harm," but after being altered over the centuries, the phrase from the original Greek text translated into English is "never do harm to anyone." It is interpreted by some to infer that, given an existing problem, it may be better to do nothing than to do something that risks doing more harm than good. Wow, that doesn't sound anything like the ads on TV that I see for any number of drugs; they rapidly spout off a litany of ills that can come from taking their drug as a supposed legal disclaimer. Maybe we could get an oath like that for members of Congress. Too bad it wasn't mandated before they considered any number of pieces of legislation, including the recent health-care legislation.

Let me deviate for a moment. As we talk about spending more money on health care, or saving money within the health-care system by trying to limit certain expenditures, we must take notice of those human behaviors which cause our workforce to be less healthy and potentially less competitive. Let's just take pollution and obesity as examples.

According to the World Health Organization, air pollution is a major environmental risk to health. It is estimated to cause approximately 2 million premature deaths worldwide every year. The number of premature deaths resulting from air pollution is now at levels comparable to deaths resulting from traffic accidents and second-hand smoke. In California alone the health impacts from air-pollution exposure, such as premature deaths and illnesses, costs $28 billion annually. From an economic standpoint, here's the bad news about all of these people dying early: They tend to have health problems which costs not only the health-care system, but it costs in terms of lost productivity. Again, as an example, just in California alone, estimates show an additional 4.7 million school absence days and 1.4 million work days decreased every year due to air pollution. The pollution seemed controllable in the earlier years of industrial expansion and of the automobile, but as noted earlier, it begins to become a real problem when we are competing for the same air to breathe that is being used to create billions of controlled fires in combustion engines, as well as industries that need massive amounts of energy to produce the things that we want.

If you don't smoke cigarettes at all, your lungs or heart can be damaged from second-hand smoke as well as exposure to ozone and particulate matter. Worse still, there are some long-term workforce implications with respect to the pollutants in the air. Breathing air with lots of particulate matter is a bigger problem for children (our workforce of the future and those who will pay for our retirement) partly because their lungs are still developing. With the exposure to a higher amount of air pollution, kids are five times more likely to have underdeveloped lungs by the age of eighteen.

Exercising outdoors during high levels of smog or other air pollution can lead to exacerbation of asthma, decreased lung function, and some suggest even DNA damage. Air pollution near freeways, high-traffic roads, seaports, and rail yards is generally higher. Research has shown that people who live, work or go to school near these transportation areas with higher concentrations of air pollution are at a greater risk for cancer and decreased lung function. They are at twice the risk of a heart attack, when compared to those who live farther from traffic-induced pollution. That fact alone should cause people to not want to live in auto-congested areas. Yet, if they all moved away from the congestion, it would cause even greater pollution based on the land-use and transportation models we currently employ.

As for the effects of obesity on the health-care system and on our economy; where do you start? According to the medical journal *Health Affairs* the proportion of spending on obese people relative to those with a weight that falls within a historical norm, accounts for 27 percent of the rise in inflation-adjusted per capita health-care spending between 1987 and 2001; and that obesity prevalence accounts for 12 percent of the growth in health spending. The authors of that report, Kenneth Thorpe, Curtis Florence, David Howard, and Peter Joski have an awful lot to say as to the effects and implications of obesity on the health-care system. They have done some great work.

Even more interesting to a guy like me was an estimate from the Institute of Medicine of the National Academies. After converting to 2004 dollars and adjusting for inflation, the U.S. health-care expenditures related to obesity and being over-weight range from around $98 billion to $129 billion dollars annually. That's a lot of money.

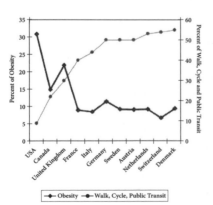

Obesity —●— Walk, Cycle, Public Transit

About a year ago a friend of mine that sits on a multi-county transportation advisory council with me, Kelly Coughlin, emailed me the graph to the left. Over the years she has been insistent that we try to better understand the various statistics and studies that pertain to public transportation and mass transportation. In this particular email she wanted me to become more aware of the positive health effects that decreasing pollutants can have, and how mass transportation can help to bring about these positive effects.

Most interesting in the email was the graph that shows levels of obesity in many of the industrialized countries relative to mass transit. If we go back up a couple of paragraphs we noted a hundred billion dollars or so spent annually to deal with the effects of obesity; money that if we thought about it could go into land-use and transit projects to decrease pollution and the effects that pollution has on our health-care costs. (Sorry for the digression, but I just wanted to connect a couple of these dots. Some food for thought.)

Money always creeps into the discussions of both the health-care issue and the sustainability equation. Keeping the relative non-competitive nature of the health-care industry in the back of your mind, let's try to figure out how this industry sector affects our ability to sustain ourselves.

Remember that the important factor in addressing appropriate health-care market reforms is a healthy stable workforce, which becomes a risk factor in determining the whys and wherefores in the investing of at-risk capital. If you thought that better health care is about giving you a cushier life for more years, think again. First and foremost, the primary issue in the world of sustainability as it pertains to health care is not about being warm and fuzzy and helping individuals in distress. It isn't about saving lives and helping people live longer so that they can do nothing for the remainder of their longer lives in good health. It is about either keeping them alive and healthy so that they work longer and can pay off greater debt over a longer period of time, or about keeping them alive and healthy for a longer period of time so that they spend everything they have before they die. Why do you think governments want to take the bulk of a person's estate after he or she dies? Their rationale is either you're going to spend it before you die, or they're going to spend it for you after you die. This notion is an affront to a system that creates wealth to sustain itself.

Let's try to figure out this enigma of better health care causing our population to get older, and how that relates to our ability to sustain ourselves. There is a direct link (dot connecting) between our health care and the age of our work force. If everybody hasn't figured it out by now, living longer may not only have some pretty detrimental effects on our Social Security system, but it has an awful lot to do with how we should approach our collective health care and the sustainability of our health-care system. Living longer also means more people will be needing care from the health-care system. This means an increase in the probability that we will go broke even faster than anticipated unless something a little more radical is done. The good news: If we can create a healthier workforce which can work longer, produce more, it may affect the actuaries which could allow for us to amortize our personal and governmental debt out over a longer period of time. The Chinese, who own a fair amount of our debt, would probably like that. The assessment of risk and amortization of debt has a direct correlation to the development of our communities; a key component in creating sustainable communities in a modern economy.

For the United States to sustain the financial health of our communal retirement system and our health care system, we can't retire at 65 or 67 or 68 anymore. And for those wanting to retire at 60 or 62 … thanks but no thanks. Eventually you will have to do it on your own dime. Fact is, you're not helping anybody, especially the next generation or the massive nonproductive sectors of the workforce.

I guess we can continue to retire at 65 or 67, but it entails that we either increase the birthrate, which will take too long to accomplish, or bring in more foreign workers to pay for the retirees. Remember, there's only one way for the system we have created to function properly: The current workforce must pay for the needs of the past workforce. Sounds vaguely familiar to me, kind-of like what Bernie Madoff was doing, but on a much larger scale. Social Security and the health care for elders … the ultimate Ponzi scheme.

In the world of the future, an efficient workforce must be competitive and comparatively inexpensive. It must produce for longer periods of time and for a longer span within a lifetime, and with fewer days off for being sick. All this affects the actuaries used in determining insurance and financial markets' income, as well as the ability of an individual to repay long-term debt. This has a huge influence on what we noted in an earlier chapter as sustainable investment strategies. Healthcare impact on the increase in longevity MUST be a part of the discussion as to the effect on an insurance company's portfolio as it relates to your community. Equally, with the increase in longevity it will mean individuals will HAVE TO work to an older age and pay into whatever form of retirement for a longer period of time, or increase their contribution to the system in some form. Again, here's the conundrum that we have created under the current model: Better health care allows us to live longer, which means more money going out of our communal retirement fund than going in. The result is to go broke or raise the amount that goes in. This means either increase taxes, or finance greater debt, which means straddling your kids and grandkids with the debt and greater taxes. The greater the debt and the greater the taxes will create more pressures on our ability to create wealth, which means more jobs will go to other parts of the world, which means sending jobs off-shore. If this scenario continues to play out over the next couple of generations, it means less per capita production, higher levels of unemployment, which means people will vote for more help for those that don't work. Or worse, people who do have work will get upset at those who don't, and vice versa, which is unhealthy, which is a euphemism for problems in paradise. You know, we're talking about the basis for fostering a revolt; similar to what we are beginning to see with some of the anti-tax and anti-government movements today. I could go on and on about various scenarios, but I hope you get the point.

If you don't take away anything else from this chapter, please note what I am getting ready to say. The issue of health care on the functioning of our economy is critically important. I have tried to correlate the energy sectors with the healthcare sectors of our economy for good reason. They both are very important factors in determining our ability to be productive, and in our ability to create wealth. Just as we need a stable supply of competitively priced energy for our economy to function and sustain itself, so too do we need a stable supply of health care for the productive members of the economy.

Let's step back for a moment and start from a different place and with a different perspective. A post-industrial, third-wave economy functions somewhat differently than that of a first-wave agricultural economy and a second-wave industrial economy. Even more significant, there are appreciable differences in the institutions which developed around each of these sectors, including health care. A few quick questions come to my mind as a result: Why is it that we try to make the different sectors and attending institutions function the same when they are so different? Is it because we are trying to be just or equitable or are we just dumb? As for third-wave sectors, remember that the nature of human capitol (labor) in this sector is somewhat different. It is not toil of the back, but toil of the mind. The nature of the institutions and the demands placed on institutions which grow up around this sector, including health care, may need to function differently. All of the implications associated with the functioning of institutions which surround the very different sectors of the economy is fodder for much in-depth analysis and commentary, and could be a wonderful discussion or maybe another book. For right now, it would be best for me to just say, give me a call and let's talk if you want to explore these implications.

Back to where we started this chapter. The types of statements that Mr. Pickens and Mr. Trump have made are intended to shake people up, and can act as a call to action. We should applaud them for using their celebrity in bringing the energy issue and the health-care issue to the forefront. Whether you do or don't like where Congress has taken the health-care debate, you have to give credit to the President and others for using their good offices in exacerbating the crisis so that the media will actually report on the goings-on. The majority of people in this country may not like where we are going, but at least there is a debate, and if we are chickens and not eggs, then we can define the health-care issue any way we want ... regardless what Congress has done.

What does all this mean? It means caring for our health is good for the bottom line, and will help to make our communities sustainable. It also means simply this: The economic argument for health-care reform has more to do with expectations for longevity and the impact such expectations have on actuaries than on the compassion for individual lives.

The purpose of health care is to minimize risks by minimizing work-force illness. This allows for getting more money out of the work-force over the long run. That means that the workers can pay greater long-term debt. If people in the U.S. are willing to work longer or to be more productive for a longer period of time, as they are in some parts of the world, then better health care in the United States means increasing the likelihood that investment capital will be attracted to our economy.

Solution: Better health care equals healthier work force. You work longer so you can pay more into the system, increase the ability to stretch debt out for longer periods of time, and make the banks and the investment community happier. Easy enough.

Section V
Developing a Model
Chapters 22 thru 34

Many of you have probably figured out by now that there are two components to this book. First, there's the "whys and wherefores," or the justification and rationale for us developing sustainable communities. This is the first four sections of this book. Then there is the implementation of the whys and wherefores, which is this last section.

The bottom line: This book was written for those who want to help push this world more rapidly towards becoming more sustainable. The intent is to help give a nudge or some basic guidance to the lay person, providing some motivation or help. I've additionally intended to create a common understanding and vocabulary for working with your communities' leadership and professionals. It allows you the tools to move forward rather than always just talking about what needs to be done. Most importantly, it can help to create a dialogue and a common understanding between all of the various participants within your community. It can help to demystify some of the community planning processes so that your community leadership and planners can develop a viable long-term partnership based on mutual respect and engagement with you, the constituents. If enough people in your community read this book, a collective understanding can develop as to what we all can do together. It can help generate a wonderful impetus within a community to move forward in creating an economically viable and sustainable future.

As for those communities large enough to have professional planners within their ranks, many planners will see a greater understanding by the consumer, you the constituent, as a welcomed political catalyst or a way to help get the ball rolling; a way that the pressure can come to bear on the decision makers and bosses.

This section of the book takes all that we have discussed in the first four sections, along with the models on which I have been working for the past 35+ years, as justification to describe how you can develop your own sustainable community. This means for those who are community leaders, or are in the business community, or are activists, or those who have decided that it's time to get involved in changing the world around you, you will want to read this section to see some of the technical things that we have done to implement this model. If the technical side doesn't appeal to you, then you might want to jump to the last chapter. If you decide to continue to read on through this section, I promise that I will try to make it as fun to read and as engaging as I know how.

Chapters 22 thru 30 and Chapter 33 are compilations of some of the work done by the neighborhood described in Chapter 32, and some of the work done by me over the past 35 or more years. Chapter 32 describes the neighborhood and shows some of their work product, but does not attempt to detail all that has occurred over the past 13 or 14 years. I have file cabinets full of the work that they have done.

As mentioned in previous chapters, a community physically grows as a response to the growth in population. It can develop new areas or redevelop old areas as a response to higher expectations, quality of life issues, or a need to retain population. As civilized societies, we are constantly building new communities and remodeling old ones. The new communities are pretty much like the ones we have built before, with one major exception: they are becoming more inefficient, even taking into consideration the wonderful strides made in the efficiency of our buildings and our transportation systems.

As you move forward through this section, keep in the back of your mind the discussion from Chapter 13, that "creativity is the foundation of a third-wave economy." Remember that the focus of this book is how the integration of this paradigm shift in the basic sector of the economy is manifested in the built environment and how that can create greater efficiency. This changing impetus on the arts and the expanded definition of the arts on the part of corporations and communities will yield higher expectations for arts education, as well as the creative labor forces as the underlying foundations for expanding the third-wave sectors of your economy. Such expectations can and in some cases will drive public policy. It can be the genesis for institutional change that will allow us as humans to solve one of the major hurdles that has confronted us: humanely dealing with the effects of global competition brought on by a communications revolution.

22

Creating New Communities
it happens every day

Every day, all over the world, we are constantly designing and building new cities and communities. A new neighborhood developed by a home builder here, a gated community by a developer there, and when there are enough roof tops to support some commercial activity, a shopping center developer comes in and builds some strip commercial developments. That's what's called in today's world, here in the United States, a growing community ... where the typical definition of growth is more people that need more stuff. We've had that discussion in earlier chapters about supply and demand and about lots of people in the world, and some of the implications of unfettered growth in the numbers of people on earth.

Let's back up for a minute and look at the history of the built environment. Throughout history, each time the underlying economy has changed, there were changes to how humans developed their built environment. These types of changes are what some call a paradigm shift. Alvin and Heidi Toffler helped us to understand some of these shifts or waves of change nearly 30 years ago.

When humans were nomadic we lived in caves and tents and wherever we had to. Let's call that community type 0 (zero). The shift to an agricultural-based economy caused us to put roots down, or what we as architects like to always refer to as foundations. The forms of our communal living began to become more complex. The land uses were segregated into a clump where we lived and everything else was where we farmed. As population grew, we added public spaces and began to add governing functions and other clumps of functions, what we call zones. Zones sound so much more sophisticated than clumps. What would it have been like had we developed clumping ordinances and clumping regulations instead of zoning ordinances and zoning regulations? It just doesn't have the same ring to it. I'm in my zone would instead be, I'm in my clump. Naw, that doesn't work. Anyway, we'll call the agricultural community type 1(one).

When we began to industrialize our economies, our communities took on new forms to facilitate the functions of the new economy. The forms followed the function, meaning the communities didn't change before the industrial revolution came about; they changed after the economy began to change. We'll call the industrial community type 2 (two). Changes to the agricultural communities occurred when the industrialization of certain parts of the world took place. The same thing is happening today with the change in the built environment to accommodate a communications-based economy. That's what my "City of the Future" was all about nearly 30 years ago: what shapes our communities would take on as a result of the changes in the economy.

During the various stages of economic development, technological innovations came about that revolutionized human movement. Early humans tended to stay near water resources to sustain themselves. Resultant to that they utilized boats for movement. Much of human commerce developed around water until innovation during the industrial era brought us trains. From that, our communities strayed away from where they were. Communities began to develop around watering stops for the trains and eventually began to develop where rail spurs could be connected. During the industrialization of our communities, and many of our institutions, some innovative technology came about that inexorably altered the form of the built environment ... the automobile. Every time I think about the development of the automobile it reminds me of Jerry Reed's song "Lord Mr. Ford." If you get a chance and you want a good laugh, download that one from i-Tunes.

The automobile along with all of the other transportation forms based on the steam engine, the internal combustion engine, and jet engine, along with humans pumping water to locations where it doesn't exist, has allowed for movement that has spread us out to nearly every nook and cranny of the earth, because it was now quick and easy ... and, based on that model, sustainable. The forms of our communities changed to facilitate the functioning of this type of altered economy. We'll call this type b as an adjunct to both community type 1 and 2. So we now have community types 1a, 1b, 2a, and 2b. This is significant because type 1a and type 2a were, in their infancy, borderline sustainable. I want to mention type 0 here because the modern transportation forms and flow of capital have made our society function in some ways like the nomadic forms ... like type zero. You know, mobile homes and travel busses and the like.

We saw constant movement and spreading out all over creation during the period of time that the United States was the productive engine for the world. As long as we were creating lots of wealth, it wasn't a problem ... and was actually a lot of fun. The effect was that during this vibrant period of our history we created a built environment that has become extremely inefficient, and terribly expensive to redo when the existing infrastructure gets to the end of its life cycle. These communal forms have become an excessive drain on the wealth of our nation, because the price for movement has gone up and our productive capacity has diminished due to foreign competition. These communal forms are costing us trillions of dollars in lost productivity through time and money. To compound the situation, we seem to now be caught in a system that doesn't add the same relative per capita degree of wealth to our economy as in the past. A situation which cannot be sustained under heightened levels of competition.

We will get to other community types and the creation of new communities in a minute. First I would like to note a couple of reasons why we have had increased productivity in our economy for the past 40 years and the effect that those factors have had on our ability to compete. Then we'll look at the effect those factors have had on the development and efficiency of the built environment. Those couple of reasons are the women's movement and computers.

The women's movement may have disrupted the social fabric and the corresponding institutions of the day, but the flood of new labor into the market over a couple of generations, from World War II to present, has helped to maintain or stabilize wages over the long run. Competition for jobs kept incomes from increasing too rapidly and held production prices down. It has also kept us as a nation competitive. This is one of those situations that if you want to thank someone for all that we have in this nation, you might want to thank God, but for sure thank women. Sometimes I think they are one in the same.

During the time period that our industrial economy was maturing, and the service sectors began to increase in influence, the influx of women in the workforce had the opposite effect on wages as what the labor unions had. It caused downward pressures on wages. I know there are still issues and vestiges of the male-dominated income disparity where everyone screams for parity. Just remember, the market wants parity as well, it just wants the base line to be that of the women's lower end of the salary scale, not the high end of the men's scale. Depending upon a variety of factors, this latest recession and the attending increase in unemployment can help to equalize this type of disparity.

That may seem heartless, but the reality is that our basic sector work-force has to compete with the rest of the world, and the service sectors have to be reflective of such. Wages will suffer if we don't get off our butts and do something about the many other factors that go into the price of all that we produce ... including the efficiency of our communities. That is what a sustainable community is all about, economically sustaining itself. This labor-force phenomena seemed problematic to some because as wages were stagnating, prices for production of food and housing and other things continued to grow due to increase in population and increase in demand. Some think this was terrible. Think what you want, the reality is that the women's movement made us more productive and more competitive. It gave the U.S. economy another 30 years of being able to effectively compete when the Japanese economy with its cheap labor was really heating up. The net result however, is that with the greater demands and greater expectations that exist, relative to 50 years prior, in some strata of our society it now takes two incomes to maintain a household. This trend along with birth rates and death rates and other factors have an effect on institutional behaviors, and therefore the decisions we make in developing our communities. Be aware of the impact of these issues on your decision making as you create your own sustainable community.

Here's the second factor that has affected productivity and lessened the pressure on us to create greater efficiency in the built environment: the infusion of the personal computer in all facets of our lives, particularly in our collective efficiency in producing the goods and services that make our economy run. Again, you can thank God for that ... or maybe Bill Gates.

Here's what is ultimately important in being aware of the women's movement and the use of computers: They represent the types of things in the world that cause us to take our eye off the ball. For 40+ years we haven't been addressing the efficiency of the built environment partly because the productivity of our workforce has been steadily increasing. Yes, there have been loads of groups proselytizing about everything green and trying to get the world to focus on a sustainable future, but the pressure for efficiency hasn't been consequential enough to get our collective attention. The current energy price crisis has got Mr. Pickens and us to briefly refocus, and to the credit of President Obama, he is trying to keep this issue in the forefront of our political and economic discussions. The past shocks in the price of energy have been cause for us to awaken to the issue and create some knee-jerk public policies. But the gradual loss of first- and second-wave jobs over many years hasn't been a shock enough, because we don't tend to connect those sorts of dots. Had the price and availability of petroleum remained as it had during the OPEC oil embargo, we would have been relentlessly driving towards greater efficiency in all that we do to maintain our economy. This type of focus will become more crucial if we are to sustain our economy and our communities in the future.

Now, community type 3. I'm sure you all have guessed what that is. A post industrial, communications-based model. Interestingly, it is a model that doesn't require any changes to take place to function. It does however allow us to create greater efficiency like never before in history. This we have discussed in previous chapters and will continue to discuss. As for community type 3b ... think about individuals that live in mobile homes or travel buses who create digital-form product and wealth in the third-wave basic sector of the economy anywhere they want to be. This model is nearly like the nomadic type zero, and has implications as to the efficiency of the communal forms that we select if we are to become more sustainable. The 3b scenario nearly brings us full circle in terms of communal human existence.

So, what does all this have to do with the efficiency of the built environment? Social changes and technological innovation have caused us to maintain and actually increase our productivity. This has lengthened the time we have had to build the inefficient communal forms that we enjoy today, and are cause for us to become less sustainable. Our increased productivity has obfuscated the fact that we were making poor decisions which would eventually catch up to us; decisions which have caused us to be less efficient, to lose jobs and our ability to create wealth; decisions which have caused capital to locate to other parts of the world; decisions which have caused many of our communities to be unsustainable; and decisions which have caused problems that we now have to turn around and solve.

Less efficiency in the environment and higher energy costs ... For your community to be sustainable and competitive, something has to give. If productivity of foreign labor continues to increase due to social and technological changes as it has done here, and we do nothing to create greater efficiency in our own built environment, then for us to produce enough basic-sector product to create enough wealth for us to sustain ourselves, our wage rates will begin to look more like those with whom we are competing. If you want jobs in a competitive global economy, and your produced goods and services to be competitive, and you want those jobs to pay a higher wage, then you have to cut some costs somewhere.

Demanding higher wages without creating greater production efficiency is folly at best. The point: your community has to be honest in dealing with income levels and quality of life issues NOW. If you wait, the future will be determined *for* you, and it won't be pretty. Let me put it this way, every time you get in your vehicle to drive twenty or thirty minutes to park at a super-store to buy diapers, that cost for energy eventually works its way into the price of everything we produce. All of this is in fact connected. What goes into the price of a loaf of bread is all the direct production costs, as well as the indirect costs that we think are just us as individuals making individual decisions about the car we drive, to the health care insurance we have. You need to be acutely aware of this as you develop your community into a sustainable community.

As each of you go about the process of creating your new communities, be cognizant of the history and rationale for the physical development of our built environment. It has always resulted from our demand for physical space to live and play and work; that is to say, physical space for the creation of wealth ... the basic sectors of the economy, and the physical space for servicing the basic sectors of the economy. We talked about the clumping or zoning or regulation of our use of land by way of laws and ordinances which have grown into an entire body of law here in the United States, and other parts of the world. Considering this, it is vitally important to significantly alter these ordinances to facilitate the post-industrial economy, because the rationale for those laws has changed radically with the third-wave sectors of the economy. If you don't alter these laws, you will continue to promote the terrible inefficiencies that have been part of the cause for us to be uncompetitive.

We have talked throughout this book about one of the components at the heart of why and how we create our new communities: a local Chamber of Commerce definition of growth. A definition where 95% (I made that number up to make a point) of local chambers define growth by physical expansion and increase in the numbers of people, not by the increased productivity of the economy. Productivity increase allows us to produce more per unit of labor so as to create greater wealth or, at minimum, compete more effectively in the world, thus not losing as many jobs to overseas competitors. As I have noted before, this institutional behavior at times works at odds with our goals, assuming our goals are to be more competitive, save jobs, work smart and create wealth for our citizens.

The questions for us should be: Are we creating these new communities in forms that will create greater efficiency? Are we developing these communities so they will help us become more competitive in an expanding, highly competitive global economy? The answers are, here in the US for the most part, NO and NO.

About 25 years ago, I was asked to make a presentation to a convention of planners. As an architect and a development consultant, my presentation was supposed to be about problems we experience with local planning commissions and planning staff while representing developers. As an aside, it is important to note that developers are for the most part the group of people, who by default, end up designing and building our communities. My presentation was to include obligatory bashing of the types of rules and regulations which make it difficult for developers to apply their trade in jurisdictions which have stringent rules and regulations. In my own mind, I wanted to discuss the nature of the institutions involved in the development of income-bearing real estate, and the institutional road blocks which make it difficult for a certain class of people ... in this case the developer. I had to do this without actually discussing the institutional conundrums or talking over everybody's heads, and without anyone actually knowing that that's what I was talking about. No one wanted me to discuss real institutional change necessary to alter outcomes, orthat we were entering the period where public input was a process of which many planners were unsure. I decided that I should come up with some hard and fast rules to follow rather than having a logical discussion of institutional changes necessary to create a sustainable community. I did all of this because the nature of the forum was not conducive to in-depth discussions as is A BOOK!

I'll mention these made-up rules quickly, then get back to the discussion of how each of you can create your own new communities and alter your existing communities. These rules were intended to spur some discussion. Boy, did they!

Rule 1. Don't confuse consensus-building with leadership.
The purpose of this rule is to distinguish between extracting ideas and information from the public versus the need to actually accomplish tasks. Without some leadership, the planning and development process can stagnate rapidly. I have to tell you that this rule was loved by those planners who didn't really want to embrace the public-input process, and was justification for some to not really take the demands of the citizenry into consideration.

Rule 2. Don't confuse those who follow trends with being leaders.
The world of planners, and politicians, is replete with followers. As discussed in Chapter 10, knowing what to think does not make a leader. This

rule doesn't mean understanding trends and capitalizing on certain trends is not helpful. It can be. Leadership in this respect does not consist of being a pontificating blowhard, but a thoughtful individual who can rally the troops and motivate others to get involved and stay involved: a vital behavior for a community involved in a community-based planning process.

Rule 3. Never allow a utility company to design your community.

It shouldn't be hard to figure out that our sewer lines should run down hill and that electricity is brought to you via a wire; beyond that, keep them away. Historically, we have by default allowed utilities to have too great an input in designing our communities. Create your goals and objectives and then have the utilities fit within your objectives. Remember, their objectives are to make a profit if they are in the private sector, and to install their utility at the least initial cost if they are in the public sector. Their objective is not to create a livable or sustainable community. That is your objective, so stay in charge and don't defer.

Rule 4. Never ever allow a traffic engineer to design your community.

This becomes a little more complex due to our land-use policies, or lack thereof. By default, traffic engineers have created land uses rather than the other way around. With all good intentions, they have tried to make our transportation systems more efficient, yet they have nearly single-handedly created one of the most inefficient communal systems to ever splotch the face of the earth; of which we are just now beginning to experience the horrors.

Rule 5. Never ever, ever allow a banker to design your community.

This may seem to be in conflict with what I said in an earlier chapter … ahh, but not so. What I have said is to *educate* those with the money, so they will support a model that will make them and others a return on their investments and will simultaneously accomplish your goals of creating a more competitive, sustainable community.

Rule 6. Never ever, ever, ever allow a developer to design your community.

Actually creating new sustainable communities and recreating existing communities to become sustainable entails a great deal more than designing a bunch of energy-efficient and "green" buildings that might be mandated through building codes and zoning ordinances, of which a builder or developer will sell as if its their idea and they are the experts in the market. I'm not saying this is bad. Quite to the contrary, this is important and can take us in the right direction. Remember that the whole is to the part as the part is to the whole. The developers are not in the market to create sustainable, competitive, efficient communities, but to get a return on investment in the short run. They will build green buildings and help you in the development of your own sustainable community if they can see a profit. There are many wonderful developers who in fact want to help. Your goal is to help guide them.

It is extremely important to note that up until about 10 or 12 years ago there was a great hope for the development of sustainable communities due to the long-term portfolio needs of insurance companies. Around that time, Congress allowed for greater merging of financial services, which has allowed lending institutions greater access to the capital and portfolios of insurance companies. For many years, and up until that time, a bright spot shown in the world of those of us involved in helping others understand the financial side of creating sustainable communities; a bright spot in which the link between the insurance companies' real-estate portfolios and the shift in actuaries as a result of an aging population could be seen. We began to discuss how health care could possibly be linked to financially underwriting the development of sustainable communities.

As discussed in Chapter 21, the increase in longevity has to be a part of the discussion as to the impact on an insurance company's portfolio. It mandates that the work force works longer. This implies the greater need for a healthier work force which would lose fewer days to sickness, so the risks are minimized for the work force to extend payments for real property to extend for longer periods of time … meaning getting more money out of the work force over the long run. That means that the workers can pay greater long-term debt. Such a scenario can help to finance projects with a long-term return, and projects able to show a long-term ability to create wealth and repay debt. This is the purpose of you developing a long-term comprehensive plan for the development and redevelopment of your community. It is to give those with capital who look for long-term investments a reason to look at you. An example of this you will see in the Centennial Chapter.

The unfortunate trend toward consolidation of financial services and short-term profits has unintentionally pushed real-estate portfolios into a more short-term focus, which helped crea e the current financial crisis. When the smoke clears, it will be n erestir ; to see how the insurance sectors of the financial services ind is ry fun tion relative to the use of actuaries as they relate to their portfol ⟩ long-term investments, aging population, and the long-term issuance o d :bt and its eventual repayment. Allowing the insurance industry's real-estate portfolios to receive significant returns on their long-term investments, without using high-risk

derivatives or the like, along with a healthier over-50 workforce are two
of the keys to the productivity of our nation. In some cases, it's also a key
to the creation of wealth, and justification for risk capital to be invested.
(Are any politicians paying attention?) This is at the heart of sustainable
investment strategies necessary to see investment take place in long-term
initiatives which can create healthy, sustainable communities. It's the key
to creating sustainable communities in a democratic capitalistic system.
That could be a book in and of itself.

You must begin to discuss the necessary changes in local, state and
federal legislation with your elected officials. This will be required to effect
such a change in investment trends which can aid you in developing your
own sustainable community.

Back to the basic needs that we humans have, along with the supply and
demand involved in creating new communities. Of course, the basic need
is food. Pouring more people onto the Petri globe means we need more
food. More people being born and more people living longer also means,
historically, that we need to consume more space for habitation. Humans
do take up space. This means competition for farmland, mainly because
the original locations of our cities were linked in proximity to some of the
most productive farmlands. What do we do? What is our response? We
continue to do the same as we always have: We use the farmland for our
expansionary needs and live on it. We strip away the long-term, sustainable, wealth-creating capacity of the community for short-term profit. This
horizontal expansion of communal living causes the price of surrounding
farmland to go up. We use more energy. The price of oil goes up. The price
of our petroleum-based fertilizer goes up. Farm production prices go up.
Speculators in the farm commodity markets, knowing this, try to extract
greater profits ... and you wonder why prices go up at the grocery store.

What is the response of the farmers? If they can't lease or buy land
and make a profit due to the increase in production costs and a squeeze
on prices at the market, then if you are lucky and you have land near the
fringe of a community, you cash out and hope that little nest egg will last
you the rest of your life. And if invested wisely, maybe you'll leave something for the kids, if the government doesn't take it away. If you don't live
near the fringe of an existing community, your best hope is that land prices
and commodity prices make a continual and steady rise in value, hopefully beyond inflation. It use to be that, if there was a continual increase in
returns beyond inflation, you could sell your farm to the real-estate portion
of an insurance company's investment portfolio; meaning someone with
cash that needs to invest in something long-term and something secure.

I mention all of this because the development of your own sustainable community is inexorably linked to all of these issues; issues dependent upon the composition of your economy and the future which you have selected; issues dependent upon technological changes and the beginnings of the communications revolution which have caused alterations in and diversification of the economies of many global city/states. Issues which affect how these and other factors will impact competition amongst your community and all of the other communities in an era of heightened global competition, and issues which affect the programs and policies which will be adopted by your community which are the underlying issues effecting the urban design concepts and urban design issues which we will see in the next chapter.

Just remember, you can change your land-use policies, zoning ordinances, laws that affect long-term investments, and set some criteria that disallow the same developmental models that have controlled the built environment for the past umpteen years. Then the communities that you will build every day, from now on, can in fact become sustainable.

23

Key Issues

In 1977, 13 years before the Eco-City Movement was established, I started a private foundation to deal with the issue of creating communications-based (post industrial) sustainable communities. I mention this because for all these many years there has been a difference in focus between myself and many of the wonderful groups working on educating others about developing sustainable communities. I have believed that the key issue involved in creating sustainable communities is that of economics, as we discussed in Chapter 4. The difference between my focus and many others' is that of allowing the economy to drive the planning and design process rather than the process driving or ignoring the economy. I'm not suggesting that either is wrong or bad, but merely a difference in focus. My opinion, and therefore my focus, is that many of the principles involved in creating sustainable communities, and most of the tools used to create efficiency in the various facets of human endeavor, are based on the functioning of the underlying economy. My specific economic focus has been on a post-industrial, third-wave, model and its implications on the evolution of old and new institutions as well as the built environment.

As noted in the previous chapter, we know that technological changes as well as the early stage implementation of the communications revolution have caused alterations in, and diversification of, the economies of many global city/states. How these and other factors will affect competition amongst these communities, and eventually the secondary and tertiary communities that most of us live in, is of issue. The efficiencies these communities will create in an era of heightened global competition, and the programs and policies which will be adopted by these communities, are additional underlying issues affecting some of the urban design concepts.

Understanding these issues and trends, and the paradigm shift which has begun to take place, are key to understanding and eventually developing applicable programs, policies and expenditures to facilitate the appropriate land usage. They must alsobring impetus to developing sustainable-built and natural environments for the next 50 to 100 plus years. Analyzing new and old trends and understanding the methods for altering trends are key to understanding these new models in this section. Additionally, we must also be aware of ICE industry potential causation and alteration in the physical constraints to the development of product. It is one of the main factors in developing the strategies for the development of the built environment. As discussed earlier, in a third-wave economy, and for the first time in human history, there are either little or no physical constraints to the development of product and the creation of wealth. Such a shift in the paradigm has extremely far-reaching implications as to the rationale for the development of the physical environment. It is the underlying foundation for the development for an altered model for the built environment.

Altering the form and efficiency of the physical environment, within the context of a more livable environment and eventually a more sustainable economy, is what is implied. It is suggested here, that once your community and other communities fully understand and begin implementation of this new model, an alteration of developmental form will take place. The rationale for investment in less-efficient forms will wane. And the sustainable, long-term investment strategies for major real-estate investment portfolios will follow the new trends from that point forward. The nudge, or lack of it, from the government or from enlightened corporate leadership will determine the speed at which this type of investment will take place.

Outside the issue of the economy, there are a number of key issues involved in developing efficient and sustainable third-wave communities which we have discussed throughout this book. In this section, I will recap these issues in a way to allow a community to evaluate itself and determine if it has the where-with-all to participate in this difficult process of recreating our nation to be more competitive.

The two big issues for me are: (1) the use of efficient forms in developing a community and (2) the process of identifying and selecting a future and the connection between the two.

Land-use forms that we utilize in the built environment can be lineal or concentric or some variation thereof. Always keep in mind that communities can take on a variety of forms due to topography, hydrology, the availability of energy, and the relative costs of the various forms of transportation. These land-use forms, if applied properly, can create much greater efficiency within the system. The underlying issue here is whether, within the context of the use of these forms, should we allow for land use to be the determinate for transportation, or should we allow for transportation to be the determinate for land use, or a combination of the two. A bastardized version of the second method has created much of the extreme inefficiency in the system over the past 60 to 80 years. The way we have allowed transportation be the determinate for land use has been cause for us as humans to constantly go through a trial–and-error process over long periods of time to hopefully, and maybe eventually, stumble on what could be a more efficient use of land. One of the problems with that process is that the constant redoing of the built environment, to facilitate the type of transportation networks which can create greater efficiency, tends to be more expensive than if it is done the most efficient way from the beginning. Such a scenario could negate some of the savings which comes from having efficient environments.

This experimentation that we have engaged in over the past hundred years has created what is referred to as a walking city, not a walkable city. A walking city is constantly developing new communities with the latest ideas on the outskirts of the existing community; it then allows the original to atrophy or die. Looking at it in plan, meaning looking down from above, it looks like it is walking away from its original core. There are thousands of examples of large and small communities which have done this all over the world, and many are continuing to do that.

Much of the development of the built environment today is a happening. I argue throughout this book for allowing the market place to run its course. But I have also argued that the use of rigorous zoning ordinances and land-use policies can play an extremely significant role in guiding fairness in the marketplace. I have learned from the good developers, in my thirty-plus years in this business, that stringent zoning ordinances and land-use policies applied fairly create a level playing field for all in the development business. It's seen as the most advantageous way to bring about the changes in the built environment. The question here is: Do we allow the marketplace to determine the forms of our built environment, or do we impose some standards? First off, let's dispel the myth that some developers use, that they are supplying what the consumer wants. Secondly, remember we have always imposed restrictions on land use as humans agglomerated into greater densities; more on that in Chapter 25.

Just remember, we don't allow for pig farms in urbanized areas for good reasons; and we don't allow for individuals to build nuclear reactors in the backyards of their gated communities. That's why we zone.

The development of real estate today has little or nothing to do with facilitating greater efficiency so that we can compete more effectively as communities or as a nation. Nor does it have anything to do with the built environment facilitating the expansion of basic sectors of the economy to facilitate the creation of wealth. It is a trial-and-error process in which all parties participating hope that something sticks. Here's how it is done in most communities: A developer looks around to see what the latest developmental trends look like in Dallas or Atlanta or Chicago. He brings that idea back to the local bank and shows how using that current trend, they will be able to repay a loan for a project. Typically, a pro forma goes along with it, but that is merely the justification for the idea which by this time is already set in stone. The banker looks into it and finds a high degree of probability that the developer is correct, which means lower risk, and consequently decides to fund the project. This trend in developmental form is reinforced until a new wrinkle is found. Until that new trend is developed, the development community tends to justify the sameness of what they do by saying that they are merely supplying what the consumer wants. In fact, due to the financial market forces, that's all that is offered to the consumer. The bright spot here is that consumers today are becoming more savvy, and their expectations are being heard by the enlightened developers. Continuing with the allegory, if the project is successful, then everyone is happy. The behavior is reinforced and repeated time and time again, and everyone believes that they are smart and wonderful because they put food on the table, clothed the kids, and participated in growing the community. Best of all for the participants, they can now be considered as the new experts on economic development, while creating an extremely inefficient community. It loses its ability over a period of time to be competitive due to the excessive amounts of time and energy necessary for the system to be maintained. They have, unbeknownst to them, help to create another unsustainable community.

The key urban concept under a paradigm shift is the rationale for and justification for efficient use of form. This can be derived from either past models, what some term as neo-traditional. But they may not be applicable for a third-wave-dominated economy, or a future model that I am suggesting in this section. The key urban design issues are the development of third-wave communal form, and the implication of that new form on the functioning of the existing physical environment. As an aside, I have noticed that planners and developers who work under the old model keep trying to find ways to attract artists to their community in the belief that it enhances a community and can bring people to an entertainment district, and so on. These folks are trying desperately to capitalize on those who are creative. You will recall that this is an agricultural and industrial model. It's a neat model that can work, but terribly inefficient. Unless these semi-entertainment districts are in a highly urbanized area, they will only survive by importing people and money. This has happened in city after city where planners try to save a deteriorating core by creating districts that have a financial incentive for the arts community to exist, which will attract patrons. The artists continue to be the monkeys on a string. Don't get me wrong, these can be wonderful projects that make the development community loads of money. But they tend not to create wealth for the community, and their focus is not to create wealth or a sustainable community. There are loads of examples where this has occurred and where we actually increase the need for transportation by creating a temporary demand for entertainment within urban entertainment districts and where the homes are in the suburbs. In an era of the automobile linked to an era of Mothers Against Drunk Driving it doesn't seem wise. It's actually a recipe for disaster. In any event, the development of the physical environment under the new paradigm shift can change your community forever. It will become the physical manifestation of the altered economy, if you so decide you want to alter your economy.

In 1976 or 1977 I wrote a paper in college called something like "The Oil Embargo and the Future of the Strip. Economic and Architectural alternatives. A contingency plan." This was the forerunner to the two cities of the future that I designed, Prodigy and Centennial. The premise was the redoing of the inefficient auto-laden forms so as to facilitate the efficient use of public transportation and the eventual use of mass transit, and to create greater efficiency in the future. The purpose was to allow us to retain our global competitiveness. Had we begun to redo those auto–dependent, land-use forms across our nation to facilitate greater efficiency 32 years ago as I had suggested, we would be saving lots of gas today. Over the years the savings would have been in the trillions of dollars. That money could have been spent here in the U.S. rather than overseas. Oh well, water under the bridge. This is why I advocate for a future with new and remodeled communities the likes of which we discuss in this section.

The issue of us chickens being in control takes on a lot of baggage. It rarely dawns on us that we are the cause of most, if not all, of our own problems. We as humans either create the problems we have to fix, or we define the world in a way that we have to fix whatever we defined as bad or wrong. If we are in control of our futures, institutionally it requires more competence and less faith. That means the new institutions which are replacing old ones tend to be more complex and potentially more bureaucratically burdened. For eons we have deferred to higher or maybe lower beings for the troubles, problems and solutions that we have. Flip Wilson used to say "the devil made me do it!" In our case, if we define the devil as stupidly following decision-making processes limited in their ability to solve multifaceted problems, rather than engaging in pursuit of the truth which requires greater engagement, greater complexity, and greater intellectual receptivity, then the definition is apropos. Point is that developing solutions to complex problems requires processes that take more into consideration rather than less. This is where we have been going and are continuing to go as a civilization. Rightfully so, this is the trend, and this is why functioning democracies which allow for free expression tend to see some of their most time-honored and beloved institutions eroded, and why there are a constant stream of new institutions being created. It is how we will institutionalize the development of new, efficient, sustainable communities.

To recreate your community or to develop a new community, you must develop the knowledge base, the strategies and the tools needed today and tomorrow to develop the initiatives to attract investment capital, and to compete more effectively in a more competitive global economy.

There are two things basic to making the changes within your own community if you are intent on laying a foundation for an altered future. First, changing your existing institutions and/or creating new ones, and second, changing the processes used to implement initiatives, if the ones you've used in the past haven't accomplished much. You should ask yourself if you are up for the task. It's a long arduous task, but it can be a lot of fun.

Changing the institutions begins by forming strategic partnerships between the public, private and nonprofit sectors at all levels for collaborative work and action. You should develop a broad base of leaders who see the big picture, and you should involve others in developing a shared vision. Along with that you should set up a process that will empower your community to shape its future.

After those type of housekeeping activities take place, you're ready to develop a strategic vision and an implementation plan that will prepare your community for the altered future. This is done by first identifying and building on the assets of your community, along with beginning to increase the capacity of the institutions, organizations, companies and individuals within them.

It is imperative that early in the process you begin to nourish sustainable development of the whole community by creating broad-based initiatives that address economic, educational, legal and political components of the community. You must also address the quality-of-life issues to include the livability and efficiency of the community under initiatives of the built and natural environment. As a helpful hint, don't discount the political and legal issues in the development of the third-wave sustainable sectors of your economy. Issues such as lien laws which are based in the concept of toil of the back must be equated to today's toil of the mind, and the protection of intellectual properties is critical. Your laws must address this forthrightly. From that, you begin to foster an entrepreneurial world that enables your private, public and non-profit sectors to be more productive. And you begin to use technology and information to enhance development within your community.

Key to all of this is allowing increased access to resources in your community, state, and around the world that supports the development of your community. You then focus on implementation and accountability, moving from good intentions to practical results, and from activities to real outcomes. You create incentives for innovation, and you reward activity that is desired.

As you proceed, focus on a variety of topics. As noted above, the issue of making use of decision making processes—which are more complex and holistic and don't rely on a "crossfire syndrome"—are foundational. Land use, transportation, the functioning of the local economy, and the desire for an altered future are pivotal.

Seems pretty simple, doesn't it? The easy part is saying that you are going to get started. The hard part is saying that you aren't going to quit, *and really mean it.*

24

A Planning Process

There are a variety of ways to go about planning your community, and there are a corresponding potpourri of planning processes which can be utilized. In colloquial terms, you could say that there's more than one way to skin that cat. Euw. That's one of those adages from the past that I still use without thinking.

We pick up on ways of expressing ourselves from a young age. Some of the expressions that I learned as a kid are still used today, and some have gone by the wayside. When expressions and behaviors are used consistently, we tend to pick up on them and integrate them into our own speech patterns and behaviors. As we noted earlier, the notion of doing what others did before you, because that's just the way things are done, is at the heart of how we can screw things up. We quit thinking and begin to defer to what we picked up along the way. That can be very good in some situations and very bad in others. The expression of skinning a cat does seem a little gruesome in context to utilizing various planning processes. But if we decide that the use of a repulsive archaic adage should no longer be used as an allegory, then likewise we can decide that using archaic planning methodologies, that have caused most of the gross inefficiencies in the built environment, can also be aborted.

As noted earlier, the democratization of many of our institutions has been going on for quite some time as a result of the changes in technology and the shift in the economy. Due to those factors and the intrinsic expectations which come from greater awareness and greater communication throughout our society, the democratization of our planning institutions and methodologies have been evolving and will continue to change and evolve and become more democratic.

The process we will discuss in this section, the Centennial Planning Process©, has its origins in this evolutionary trend in the democratization of the processes we use in planning our communities. There are underlying assumptions in this comprehensive process: the existing planning institutions and planning processes are either not serving the communities in their quest for an altered future, or they have been identified as the cause of current poor conditions or discontent. Of the total array of categories of a structured society, within which resides the various institutions and processes, there is one focal point requiring substantive change necessary to vary outcomes or to attain an altered future: those private, quasi-public, and governmental institutions involved in "Planning."

In the beginning, or maybe I should say when people began to plan their communities, it was just plain ole normal people that saw problems within their communities and decided to fix them. As communities developed and became larger and more complex, we began to rely on the expertise of a certain class of individuals driven by our political system. Planning concepts and ideas were discussed within a closed system of planners, designers and politicians, then decided on by "city hall."As representatives of the people, the politicians and city managers gave directives to the planners to implement what the politicians wanted, as long as they could find ways to fund the planning and design, as well as the eventual construction of the projects. Notice that in that scenario nowhere was the input of the public considered. Likewise, the big-picture concept of sustainability was never a driving force, rarely a part of the discussion, and probably not even an afterthought. The function of the citizenry was to just pay for whatever city hall wanted. This was the period that the public felt that it was useless in fighting what the powers wanted. "You can't fight city hall," was the mantra of the day in the U.S. It still is in many parts of the world. Today, here in the U.S., we know that not only can we fight city hall, we can beat it and we can control it.

As a result of the politicians needing the public to fund more and more of what they wanted, it became fashionable to engage with the public after the public projects were decided upon. This was the beginning of the democratization of the planning processes: The thought being that city hall would sell the projects to the citizens in hopes that the citizens would continue to fund the pet projects of the politicians. This was even if some of the projects work counter to each other, and even if the projects were detrimental to the long-term ability of the community to sustain itself. As a result of the perception and reality of abuses to this authoritarian process (you know, graft and corruption), and as a result of a free press and an unfettered legal system, the process of determining, planning, and funding public projects became more transparent.

The next shift in planning methodology is the one that many communities employ today. It is a more user-friendly and public-friendly community-based planning process. It involves the politicians and managers working in conjunction with the citizenry in coming up with ideas and projects. Then that assemblage of ideas drove the funding and selection of what needed to be done, again, even if some of the projects negated the effects of others, and even if the projects were guaranteeing that the community would not be able to sustain itself. In this scenario, the professional planners began to act more as conduits for the various parties and help the different factions express their ideas, They additionally helped to establish costs associated with the projects, as well as identify funding mechanisms for implementation.

The next stage in the evolutionary change to planning processes is one that necessitates even more public input. It's where the citizenry actually employs planners either through public or private funds, and where the planners work specifically for and directly for the community. The politicians, managers, public planners, private planners, and community, develops a plan driven by the community. The flipped piece: Instead of the public sector soliciting input and ideas from the community, under this community-based planning-process scenario, the community solicits input and ideas from the public sector through their hired guns. More of this is beginning to happen around the country. This is the continued democratization of our institutions caused by the institutional changes brought on by the communications revolution. This is part of the evolutionary trend in altering our planning institutions and methodologies necessary to alter outcomes or implement an identified future. You know, like creating a sustainable community.

The next stage in this evolutionary trend in planning methodologies was theoretical for many years, until we began to utilize it about 15 years ago. You will see it in more detail and in practice in the following chapters. It was my intent those many years ago to see what the future might hold if we were to design a process responsive to the essential elements of third-wave institutions. In this particular case, it meant a community-designed- and -driven process, where the community actually does the planning with technical help from professionals. It genuinely identifies a future based on the long-term ability of the community to sustain itself: a process that has at its core a de-evolved hierarchal system where information is shared more readily and more thoroughly. This is a more extreme version of the collaborative community-based planning process noted above. Should all communities use this process? Probably not to this drastic degree. But understand that the collaborative community-based planning processes are becoming not only more palatable to all parties, but they actually develop a better end product. They tend to develop a plan liked by more people and much easier to fund, not to mention it has the ability to consider the broader, more important issues. Remember what we talked about in Chapter 10: We have created a specialized simplistic profession, the planning profession, in a world that has become much more complex. This is one of the main reasons why we bring lots of community people together in a collaborative process where planners become facilitators: To facilitate more critical thinking and complex solutions to complex problems.

The intent in our case was to see if such a process would be able to develop conjunctive initiatives. Initiatives that would not run counter to each other. Initiatives that would connect dots and the big picture to the small; the whole to the part and the part to the whole.

Collaborative community-based planning processes rely on folks in the community being involved. How to create that involvement is discussed to a limited degree in some of the following chapters. What is important to remember: Community involvement has an ebb and flow to it. We must recognize the nature of community-based planning and the degree to which levels of engagement many times decrease as the quantity of data and work increases, as shown in the chart to the left. Many years ago I designed a process which takes advantage of this phenomenon. It uses it to advantage the group which is engaged in planning and design. It is impor-

tant to understand the development of and implementation of a sub process which can address the concerns over decreased engagement on the part of the community.

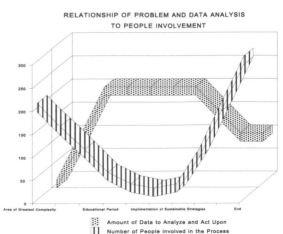

RELATIONSHIP OF PROBLEM AND DATA ANALYSIS
TO PEOPLE INVOLVEMENT

::: Amount of Data to Analyze and Act Upon
[] Number of People Involved in the Process

The graph shows the theoretical concept of designing a process which allows for the waning of community involvement and the subsequent re-involvement. This is significant to the evolution of community processes in which there is no government guidance and management or privately subsidized guidance and management.

Such a sub-process requires the alternation of institutions to facilitate the development of sustainable concepts in all areas of a community, thereby developing, over a long period of time, the institutionalizing of a more democratic methodology. The question for us at that time many years ago was: Can we design a process that will bring back into the planning process the number of people required to implement a complex strategic plan? The answer we came up with was, sure we can ... we're chickens!

This collaborative community-based planning process has as its underlying premise the development of institutions and processes that can accomplish the tasks brought forward by the development of a strategic plan with an identified future as its catalyst. The rationale for this altered collaborative community-design process, and its attended details, is fodder for an entire dissertation. That means we aren't going to discuss this in any great degree of specificity in this book. However, the intent of this exercise is to become familiar with the evolutionary, institutional and procedural changes required for the development of third-wave land-use patterns within existing communities, and altered land-use patterns for new communities which will eventually yield sustainable land-use patterns. Understanding the ups and downs of the democratic involvement of individuals in a planning process is key to developing the sustainable third-wave land-use patterns.

Now, on to the process we used for what you will see in Chapter 32. First thing involved in the process is identifying the problems within the community through a series of community-based meetings. Allowing everyone to bitch and moan and discuss everything imaginable from pot-holes in their streets to potheads selling drugs in the parks. Every bit of this is EXTREMELY important. Write it all down so that it can be categorized later. Next is educating ourselves through an additional series of community meetings. Here we discuss various trends and cycles and backgrounds and a bunch of other things. During this series of meetings, it is important to lay the groundwork for discussing "desired futures" and how to create an "identified future." Next, we develop multiple futures based on various scenarios. They result from projecting the various trends and cycles. Then we move on to the key component of selecting one of the futures. This selection of a specific identified future becomes the controlling component for decision making throughout. Remember the Wright/Jones Chapter. Then on to developing a process for the community to decide which of your goals will need to be accomplished and when.

During this time period, it is important to engage in a series of educational programs to teach the community about the various processes which can bring about change. It is also important to identify processes and institutions which require alteration and/or termination. You must also identify processes and institutions which will be required which presently do not exist. Subsequent to all of that, the community then can develop broad categories for cross-referencing purposes and implementation purposes.

During this process there should be additional large communal discussions about solutions and the mechanisms necessary to accomplish change; i.e., which components and trends must be altered to accomplish the goals. During our process, we thought it would be wise to take the time to educate ourselves about the history of and current trends in planning processes, the part we talked about in the earlier part of this chapter. From that discussion, the community can select a process right for them which allows for greater community involvement over a longer period of time.

At this point, a different type of work occurs which requires smaller groups. First is mapping the community's physical, institutional and human assets, then creating a composite map of all that has been discussed and decided: a comprehensive strategic plan. Then, from all of that, the easy part starts: creating a work plan based on the strategic plan. You determine the time frames for implementation of the various initiatives; you prioritize the initiatives; and finally you begin to implement the various initiatives.

Remember one thing: this plan is malleable. It is always in a state of flux. The process is considered to be never-ending and is in a continuous reevaluation. Also, the implementation of the work plan is a derivative of a number of factors: The identified nature of each of the initiatives as to the need for long-term or short-term implementation, and the relative degree of relationship to each of the other initiatives. In our case, this has resulted in a matrix of interrelationships for managerial purposes.

25

Land Use and the Fundamental Five

Land Use is one of the most critical issues which we must address to create truly sustainable communities. Without addressing land use and zoning within existing communities or within the new communities that we create, our ability to compete in an ever more competitive global economy will be severely limited. I can't overemphasize this: The issues of efficiency and competition are inexorably linked to sustainability in modern societies with so many people on the globe. Point is, don't whine about jobs going overseas if you are not willing to squeeze greater efficiency out of every system that exists within the built environment. That starts with land-use reform, zoning ordinances and building codes.

Here are the political and economic realities: It's tough to focus on much of anything when a constriction of the economy takes place, or when jobs go overseas, or when jobs are lost, or when incomes go down, or when prices for everything escalates, or any variety of reasons. If understood, all of these things can bode well for us in the long run. And if we plan properly for the future, we will become more competitive, which will allow for us to develop truly sustainable communities.

As discussed in earlier chapters, the basic sectors of the economy are the determining factors as to the land-use regulations which should be addressed. If your economy is totally service-oriented, then certain land uses and economic initiatives should take place. If your community is an agricultural-based economy, then certain land uses and zoning ordinances are appropriate. If your community is any one or more of the basic economic sectors, then land-use patterns will change to reflect that reality.

One basic thing to remember: The purpose of land-use policies and zoning ordinances is only partly about the buildings and structures. To a much greater degree it's about human activities, the reason for differing structures. It is the normal intent of such land-use policies and ordinances to civilly resolve or alleviate conflicting human activities before they occur. This laudable intent has been perverted so severely over the years that our land-use policies have reflected an overriding societal aversion to proximity. Instead, we require more and more energy for normal human commerce to take place. We have begun to see a radical shift in this human activity due to the communications revolution.

What's most bothersome is when planning commissions and community leaders think that one set of land-use rules fits every situation for every type of economy. If that situation fits your community, then it is proof that your leaders don't have a clue how the economy functions and how the world works.

Many of the problems that we experience today in the built and natural environment were created out of conflicts in human interaction or differing functions. These stem from what we think of as land-use and zoning issues developed in the past. In most urbanized and partially urbanized areas around the world, there are expectations for conflict between land uses or zoning categories which differ. That is the nature of human activity in the built environment. As simplistic as that may seem, the determination of use is ultimately based on these interpretations: (1) relative good or bad of the various activities, (2) appropriate location of those activities, (3) good and bad structures, and (4) appropriate location of those possible structures. These interpretations may vary slightly from community to community depending on two things: (1) either by established precedence brought on by decisions made by local governing officials with regard to the constituted legal documents that we call a city's Land Use Plan and Zoning Ordinance, or (2) by politics, decisions which have little or nothing to do with a city's established land-use policies or land-use plan. Such political decisions are made because an individual or group may sway the outcome because of who they are more than what they say. I mention this because many communities have a history of making decisions sometimes based on politics and sometimes based on rational judgment. This mixed bag of past land-use decisions can be cause for concern as to the enforceability of parts of a community's land-use plan. A greater level of professionalism, the results of some court cases along with greater community activism, can yield some positive results for enforcement over land-use and zoning concerns.

The attempt of segregating land uses and the purpose of creating zoning categories is an effort to minimize the potential conflicts which will naturally arise. Throughout the past five or six decades, there have been continuous attempts to further diminish these institutional and historical behavioral conflicts, which has been cause for communities to spread further apart. This minimizing of potential conflicts has been reinforced so consistently throughout our history around the United States and the world that it may now be considered as an expectation or a cultural or community norm. I mention that, because such basis has standing in land-use law. Such expectations are continuously validated and institutionalized every time a community annexes more property for expansion. This is in direct opposition to the fact that there may be enough available real property within their existing communities for much of their projected growth. The reinforcement of this type of institutional behavior is cause for us becoming less efficient and less able to sustain ourselves over the long run. This is an example of where a problem existed: human behavioral conflict; and in which we as communities implemented solutions: land-use and zoning regulations. We have *continually constructed before we designed*, or in more quaint terms, we have been getting the cart before the horse.

Before anyone gets a nose out of joint, this is not about the "taking" of land. It is not about the community taking your property to do as it wants. It is about the exact type of zoning regulations that have existed in 99% of communities in America. For those communities that don't have zoning regulations, they tend to have private developers impose various restrictive covenants. These are by default a regulation as to how you can utilize your property and how you are protected from others being allowed to do whatever they want with properties adjacent to yours. For those who live out in the country, remember you are still not allowed to put a terrorist camp or a nuclear reactor on your property just because you want to.

Creating a sustainable community starts with land-use regulation changes. I mean real reform which will facilitate efficient transportation and less reliance on fossil fuels. We'll talk about this in more detail in the following pages. Remember one thing: If you're not willing to squeeze all that you can from our public sector as it relates to efficiency in the physical environment, then you have relegated the entire burden for efficiency to your business community and to the individual. That doesn't make the public sector a very suitable partner. This is, among other reasons, why Wal-Mart and their competitors exist in the form that they do today. They are efficient and they continue to squeeze as much as they can from ALL of their systems. The land-use and infrastructure policies that most communities have throughout America is the reason why these types of businesses locate where they do and in the form that they do. If you don't like the footprint that Wal-Mart and others make in the physical environment, then change your land-use policies. They **WILL** change to reflect the new reality. That's what good businesses do. It doesn't mean you just make building code and zoning modifications that are inconsequential; that doesn't create the efficiencies necessary to create a sustainable community. It means you establish your goals and objectives based on an identified future, and you establish your zoning and codes to reflect such.

Again, the world has been in an economic paradigm shift. For the first time in human civilization, there is a basic sector of the economy with no physical constraint for the development of product and the creation of wealth. The implication of this on land-use patterns is staggering, and has not been explored or introduced by most communities.

Five factors lead us to the mind-set and the institutional changes which affect land use and the form of the physical environment for a post-industrial economy. I termed them a number of years ago as the "Fundamental Five." In simple terms, these are the things we do to dream before we design, and design before we construct. These factors affect the functioning of the system and the institutional behaviors. They allow us to extract from the human experience all that we can so we are able to sustain our economies and communities. You can call them whatever you want. The purpose of this chapter is to spur you and your community into discussions about the things necessary to change if you are to alter your economy and if you are to facilitate those alterations. Discussing the "fundamental five" begins your process of connecting the dots. The result of this process by the Central High Neighborhood you will see in the Centennial Chapter.

We have been talking about these five components in various ways in the previous chapters. The purpose of organizing these components is to help keep organized the myriad of initiatives necessary to make changes to your community. Addressing each of these components within your community can help to significantly alter the trends that have caused inefficiencies and degradation. These components include: (1) economic initiatives, so as to create opportunity and wealth for more citizens and the corresponding (2) educational initiatives—initiatives necessary to facilitate and supplement the economic initiatives. (3) Built and natural environment guidelines which deal with land-use and zoning issues. (4) Design guidelines for your community and the legal guidelines which are necessary to implement the design guidelines and land-use parameters. Last, (5) various political initiatives necessary to implement all of the above noted initiatives and guidelines. You can have as many or as few categories as you like. I have found that any aspect of human endeavor which needs to be addressed can be shoe-horned into one of these five categories.

As an example, the neighborhood noted in Chapter 32, the Central High Neighborhood, Inc., engaged in developing each of these five components specific to their own needs during their planning process. First they focused on the economic initiatives. The president of the neighborhood, Ethel Ambrose, and others continually note how it is difficult to do anything if you don't have a job making enough money on which to survive. Their intent under the economic initiatives is to increase income levels in the local economy and increase the numbers of people in the area creating opportunity and wealth for more citizens. They determined that their top priorities in altering the trend that had decimated their community, the trend of decreasing income levels and out-migration, would be accomplished through "job development and job interface through a multi-pronged approach to efficient product creation, product storage and retrieval, product distribution as well as the development of corresponding services by focusing on those identified basic sectors of the economy to enhance income levels." This was pretty amazing for a community that had been decimated by the effects of racism, white flight and economic disinvestment; a neighborhood that is not unlike many neighborhoods throughout the United States. They continued by stating that they would "retain existing neighbors and attract new home buyers to the community that have higher levels of income through various economic and educational initiatives, and that they would attract new home buyers and new neighbors of lower and moderate income levels through the development of affordable housing programs which are linked to continuous education programs which focus on income enhancement." Embodied within their statements is a harsh reality: They could no longer wait for the governing bodies to do right. For years, there was a continuous effort by the political powers to "dump" in the neighborhood. Because it was a poor neighborhood, it seemed that continuing to put housing for poor people in the area made sense. The neighbors realized that this was exacerbating the problem rather than solving the problem. It is still going on to this day.

They focused their attention on third-wave industrial development and the corresponding service-sector development and some minor second-wave industrial development. They realized that they would be hard pressed to compete as a first-wave farm community or as a service community to farmers. They decided to not pursue heavy industry for some obvious reasons, not least of which was the trend of foreign cheap labor forcing those industries to leapfrog over communities like theirs to go overseas. So, they decided to create the educational initiatives which would be necessary to facilitate and supplement the economic initiatives. These are the first two of the "fundamental five." As an aside, they have embraced urban farming as a viable component in developing a sustainable community. But they realized that they would be hard pressed to create wealth trying to compete in that market. There are some interesting concepts for creating competitive urban farms while allowing greater density; concepts that have been around for a couple of hundred years and which are more viable today than ever before. Call me if you want to know more about them and the implications to creating sustainable communities.

The Central High Neighborhood determined that the need for educating its citizens is of paramount importance if the community was to become successful at altering the trend of decreasing income levels, and eventually attracting others to live, work and play within their community. They focused on altering the educational outcomes by focusing on social skills necessary for a civil society to function, as well as for individuals to have the ability to interface socially and economically with others. They also focused on economic skills necessary for the neighborhood and the community to sustain any and all other facets of the community at large.

The Central High Neighborhood would determine which programs, policies and expenditures can be altered or created to help produce competent individuals who can create greater income levels by producing products marketed in the global marketplace. They would look at educational opportunities within the public educational setting, quasi-public educational settings as well as business, corporations and private educational settings. With a focus on education reform, they would develop the skills to produce ICE industry product and would develop career-oriented capabilities that would create wealth, affecting the ability for individuals to repay debt. This would eventually affect the built environment, another one of the five components. Before we get into that, the neighbors looked at various legal issues and guidelines necessary to implement design guidelines and land-use parameters. They identified numerous objectives which would require a greater understanding of legal constraints and legal opportunities that presently exist. They would identify those public and private groups and individuals that could help or hinder the development of the legal initiatives. They knew they needed to find a local attorney with the expertise to aid them in their endeavor, and who could work with the city as well as private groups. They also decided to locate a source of funding for legal counsel.

They noted that for certain economic, educational, social and physical changes to take place, they would need certain legal initiatives dealing with intellectual property law as well as land-use issues which would connect to State and Local financial incentives. How that would take place was a matter of politics.

These political initiatives would be necessary to implement all of the various initiatives and guidelines that had been identified. The politics of working with various governing agencies would allow the adoption of new local ordinances or the alteration of old local ordinances as well as state laws. This would facilitate the legal requirements to bring about the changes in the economic, educational, social and physical arenas.

The physical environment, this last component, is terribly important because it is what most people see. You may go about altering your economy and creating opportunity for more people in your community. But without some physical manifestation of what you are doing, there will be loads of people that will believe you have done nothing. As I noted earlier, these people can be important, but they are not big-picture people. Don't let them lead. They are the ones that tend to build before they design, and as noted, that is how we have painted ourselves into the corner we are in today: A corner of communities of extreme inefficiency that are unsustainable.

The Central High Neighborhood's built and natural environment guidelines focused on land-use regulations, zoning, and design guidelines to create a more livable and more efficient community. They created a "Livable Community" policy statement, along with attending details. It was actually derived from the brilliance of a bunch of architects from around the country who were members of the American Institute of Architects. The Central High Neighborhood noted that they were "dedicated to the principle that livable communities, whether in cities, towns, or suburbs, evolve over time, building by building, street by street, and neighborhood by neighborhood, to serve the diverse needs of their people." They continued to note that they also believe that "livable communities should reflect the many cultures and histories of the people who strive to make them beautiful, safe, healthy, affordable, and of a human scale, and that their success is linked to a sustainable local and regional economy and environment." Thus, the Central High Neighborhood would support actions, programs, and policies that emphasize the creation of human-scale neighborhoods and economic centers that incorporate a mix of uses as the basic building blocks of livable communities. They would coordinate efforts that link local neighborhood improvements to regional sustainability. They would place a priority on directing growth opportunities towards existing communities, where the vast majority of people already live. They would secure the participation of citizens throughout the planning, urban design, and implementation process. And they would promote the visualizing, synthesizing, and form-giving role that architecture and urban design can play in the decision-making process.

From those built and natural environment guidelines, they developed a series of supporting issues extracted from the best they could find from communities around the nation. They noted that they would focus on the development of human-scale neighborhoods and economic centers. Although communities are not the same nationwide, the Central High Neighborhood believed that good design can improve the human quality of places, and thus the activities of our daily lives. Well-designed neighborhoods and neighborhood centers, downtowns, and main streets that incorporate a mix of uses and are linked to both public and private transportation: these increase choices people have in housing, shopping, recreation, and job locations. Such places offer people convenience, create exciting and inviting environments, and add to a sense of community. A lack of good design, including land-use and zoning regulations that segregate uses, makes such places difficult to achieve.

From this they would support the creation of urban-design plans and regulations that result in multi-functional neighborhoods and economic centers. These would incorporate a mix of uses, building types, and choices in transportation. They would support a walkable public realm with trees, landscaped sidewalks, parks, and other places for public gatherings. They noted that a transportation infrastructure and building stock that supports neighborhood scale development could increase choices in the marketplace, and would build equity for all people.

The Central High neighbors supported neighborhood and regional sustainability. They believe that issues such as environmental health, jobs and employment distribution, housing costs and availability, traffic congestion, air quality, and open space development are regional. They all have a profound effect on individual communities and neighborhoods. Antiquated land-use and transportation policies, among others, that affect the shape of a region can directly affect the livability of communities. The lack of coordination among agencies and organizations at the regional level, can adversely affect all communities by allowing new growth in outlying areas apart from areas where the majority of people currently live. Thus, they would support the coordination between agencies and organizations at the neighborhood, community, municipal, metropolitan, county, and regional levels to develop multi-jurisdictional solutions to regional economic and environmental problems. They would also support urban growth limits and land development patterns that place a priority on directing new development toward the revitalization of existing areas, and secondarily towards the creation of new towns and peripheral areas only when growth cannot be accommodated in any other reasonable manner. They noted that the role of transportation routes and nodes in linking places regionally and fostering mixed-use centers and human-scale neighborhoods is important.

The Central High Neighborhood decided that in developing the physical environment, they would utilize citizen participation throughout the planning, urban design, and implementation process. They noted that livable communities are made by the people who inhabit them. Credible and effective citizen participation requires that people receive timely information sufficient for them to understand fully the issues. Such information often requires public education and technical assistance over a significant period of time to nurture democratic action fully.

From this, the Central High Neighborhood would support public education about the nature of neighborhoods and central places as an integral part of the citizen participation process. This includes a visioning and urban design program that would encourage people to consider what values they wish to further in their community and how to do so. They also noted the importance of architectural and urban design assistance that helps citizens to participate fully in the process of making communities livable. (Thank god for that, otherwise I wouldn't have had anything to do.)

With that recognition, they realized the role for architecture and urban design. They believed these two staples could offer their community powerful tools for developing a strategic vision for change. The design process results in a visual understanding of issues and development alternatives. These aid the public in making strategic planning decisions and help monitor results. By illustrating and synthesizing often conflicting ideas, visualizing alternative futures at the scale of the building, neighborhood, and region, the process results in a coherent plan of action that links issues. The Central High Neighborhood recognized that many neighborhoods within their own community, and many communities throughout the country, do not incorporate these tools in their community planning and citizen participation process. Therefore they would support the incorporation of architecture and urban design principles, along with processes within community planning efforts at all levels of decision making, from the neighborhood scale to the larger region.

Within each of these five categories, there can be numerous initiatives and projects. Each may require individual goals and objectives and corresponding work plans. The Central High Neighborhood developed over 100 interconnected initiatives divided among the "fundamental five." We will explore these in the Centennial Chapter.

To get to this point is a lot of work that takes a lot of time. It is fun work. It's not like the work that some have to do to survive in parts of the world, like walking five miles to get water for cooking and cleaning. This is time-consuming work which can result in altering your community so that your great-grand kids won't find themselves in a world unable to function in a civil and sustainable fashion. It is fun work that can make a difference in the lives of many individuals. It can make a difference in your own life.

26
Design Principles

The third component of the Fundamental Five, and the last one I would like to discuss in a fair amount of detail is the Built and Natural Environment Guidelines. The neighbors who participated in planning and articulating these five components decided that a succinct set of rules or guidelines should be developed to help guide those building or rebuilding within its boundaries. They surmised that this set of guidelines would be broad and sweeping enough to give an overall direction. Yet they should also be articulated with enough specificity to accomplish what they set out to do: create a civil, livable, and sustainable neighborhood. The neighborhood looked at a number of communities around the nation to see how they had developed goals and objectives regarding the built and natural environment. Below are thirteen Design Principles on which they decided. These principles, along with the overall vision for the neighborhood, guided the development of some of their most recent accomplishments. One of these was the adoption of a design overlay district for the neighborhood by the City of Little Rock in December of 2009.

The first principle was to provide housing diversity within the neighborhood. They noted that many communities throughout the U.S. tend to consist of uniform house sizes serving a particular economic and social constituency. They felt that this type of segregation was not healthy in the long run, and noted that, depending upon economic and political circumstances, such might not be able to be sustained. Lots of discussion involved this subject as well as the issue of gentrification. They noted that within our market area, the typical new subdivisions consist primarily of three-bedroom units, with attached two or three car garages. While this kind of residential development serves the needs of families with children, this household type represented less than 20 percent of American homes. The neighborhood extracted from certain demographic information the increase in age of the population as a mid-range trend. They also noted the existence of major medical facilities and a couple of small colleges within the district. All of these and other factors helped them decide on an increasing requirement for differing house types accommodating single persons, female-headed households, elderly individuals living in congregate facilities, and shared units, such as those used by university students. Rather than assign these various unit types to individual areas, it was proposed that the participating neighborhoods be redeveloped to accommodate the full range of residential needs.

This first design principle focused on creating a neighborhood with a range of house types: detached single-family units; attached single-family units; and apartments over garages. Incorporation of multi-family units, if carefully scaled and designed, could be included as well. They noted that rear alley parking access should be utilized where possible to keep sidewalks continuous. Where alleys were impractical, garages should be kept to the rear of the site, so that the houses will be more prominent.

The second design principle noted that landscaping and siteing were essential elements to the neighborhood. The placement of houses is often carried out in response to zoning regulations and concern for minimizing initial costs. Typically, placement on the land with respect to existing topography, vegetation, and natural surface run off are not fully considered. In order to help create their neighborhoods with the qualities which would survive over time, careful consideration of both siteing and landscaping should be undertaken. Landscaping design, in particular, needed to be treated as an intrinsic part of the neighborhood design, rather than as an afterthought. In addition to issues of initial appearance, thought needs to be given to long-term maintenance. The neighbors decided that this second design principle should state the importance of beautiful residential streets with tree-lined sidewalks and landscaped front yards. Add to this differing scales of ground cover and bushes which helps to create a comfortable and attractive transition from the public street to the private entrances of each residence.

You will see the result of this design principle in the creation of a botanical garden and expansion of some parks within the plan. More specifically, you should note the urban forestry within this neighborhood. Because of a tornado and the resultant hard work of a number of the neighbors, this neighborhood has one of the most successful urban forestry projects in the nation today.

The third design principle suggests that the inclusion of sidewalks and porches create functioning and livable neighborhoods. Within this discussion they noted certain detrimental developmental trends in which many newer neighborhoods include houses which place multi-car garages in front of the site, close to the street, while eliminating sidewalks and street lighting. These two factors, more than any other, have served to interfere with the creation of viable neighborhoods. They went on to note that the automobile has become so central to our daily activity, we have scarcely noticed its negative impact on our lives and communities. Many people who drive to work leave and arrive home through their garages. They seldom use their front doors or find a need to walk in their neighborhoods. They did note that the older neighborhoods in our community have lovely tree-lined streets with sidewalks, and that many of the houses include porches, which populated or not provide a sense of welcome. This design principle proposed that any new housing developed in the neighborhood should include both sidewalks and porches as fundamental components of neighborhood design. Also, traditional streets in older residential neighborhoods, the closely spaced homes, together with the shaded sidewalks and porches overlooking the street help to create a beautiful and safe neighborhood.

The fourth design principle specified that a priority should be given to rear access parking. They noted that subdivision development often includes house plans which place two, or even three-car garages closest to the street. This pattern creates public environments unfriendly for pedestrians. The many curb cuts needed for vehicular access interrupt sidewalks and pedestrian movement. They noted that one successful planning idea, incorporated in many new towns as well as some of the older neighborhoods, has been the use of rear-yard alleys for parking, service, and utility access. Typical street layout with parking access from the rear alley means the street in front of the houses is uninterrupted by curb cuts. This allows for closer spacing of residences, which increases neighborliness, and reduces costs of site work and utilities. Rear-yard garages do not necessarily have to be visually unacceptable.

Dealing with the conflicting land-use issues of proximity and privacy was the fifth design principle. They noted that around the country it had become commonplace to accept existing zoning patterns which create streets with considerable space between units in the form of side yards. The underlying premise for this legal requirement initially started out as a safety issue, fire prevention, but became a social issue to ensure privacy by creating minimum distances between houses. They saw that in practice, side yards were usually treated as spaces without practical use, representing a maintenance problem rather than an asset. In many of the older parts of our community, houses were closely spaced, with small front and side yards, reserving the major part of the site to back yards, where maximum practical use could be obtained. Although the setbacks within the neighborhood were less than certain other areas of the community, the neighbors recommended that residential zoning requirements be reviewed. The goal: Establishing rules which would encourage closer spacing of units, while establishing the basis for privacy and separation.

The sixth and seventh design principles focused on pedestrian activity and civic spaces respectively. The neighborhood committee observed that successful neighborhood centers in the older parts of the community, as well as other small cities throughout the U.S., supported development that was both compact and mixed. They saw that it was quite common for people to live close to shopping areas, government services, schools, and churches. Suburban development had dispersed people to the extent that most central city districts, including our own, had become places exclusively for downtown merchants. This trend, the neighbors noted, had seen some recent reversal. But in order to help re-establish the sense of community, the neighborhoods felt that they should create a core area as an active and vibrant place. Efforts had to be undertaken to create a safe and attractive pedestrian environment. The core business district within the neighborhood had need of an important civic square or plaza, identified in the public's mind as the community center. You will note on the plans those areas eventually identified and those areas which have already been developed. They felt that a civic square in conjunction with possible new community facilities, museums, and a business district represented a unique opportunity.

The neighbors also wanted to utilize these principles to create settings which would bring the community to the outdoors in hopes of decreasing the overuse of indoor energy. The two settings which they felt would speak to this: (1) pedestrian activity and comfort in and around tree-shaded outdoor dining places, where people can sit and watch other people strolling past; and (2) a market with pavilions in a designated public place which could attract additional visitors and add to the revenues of the neighborhood merchants. They noted that even though Little Rock's Central High School was one of the most visited historic sites in the state, the neighborhood merchants benefited little from the activity.

The eighth design principle: Creation and development of civic identity elements. The neighbors saw how many older towns in the U.S. were fortunate to have reminders of their historic past in the form of civic elements, such as fountains, markers, gates, arches, clocks, and other elements which lend character and distinction to their neighborhoods. Their efforts in the Central High neighborhood placed them in a unique position to establish a coherent and memorable district. This could occur through the construction of buildings compatible with older historic structures, as well as through the inclusion of selected civic items which would add to the richness and quality of the business and residential areas. They wanted to develop a plan that would help guide the city government, urging it to consider developing some thematic symbols or elements which would remind present and future residents of the redevelopment efforts and the history of the community. One of the most impressive projects that the neighborhood has taken on with respect to this design principle is that of the creation of gateways and boulevards. One of the projects completed through the conceptual and schematic design phase is a major gateway/ roundabout at the entrance to the neighborhood. It stands at the intersection of Martin Luther King and Daisy Gaston Bates: an intersection of two of the most important civil rights figures in history. The neighborhood is preparing to conduct an international design competition for a major sculpture at the location.

The neighbors also felt that encouraging the use of various types of civic elements would be warranted. As the redevelopment process continues, clocks and other distinctive elements would be integrated into building towers or treated as separate elements. Water features such as fountains would be welcome and provide additional attractions for the already large number of visitors to the community.

Design principle number nine focused on the diverse mix of buildings and the building types. The neighbors concluded that, in order to lend character and distinction to the neighborhood, efforts should be undertaken to create some uniform characteristics with respect to both materials and signage. In this respect, urban street improvements, including new sidewalk paving, pedestrian scale lighting, and street trees would be helpful. The value of a uniform design approach notwithstanding, it would be desirable to encourage a mix of building types and even some special elements within the overall business area. Reference had been made in earlier design principles to the value and importance of civic features, such as clock towers and fountains. The neighbors felt that the development of design guidelines based on these principles could encourage building owners to treat entrances or corners as the setting for a special architectural event, helping to enliven the area.

The tenth design principle: Consider increases in density at community/transit nodes. The neighborhood had some nodal areas, but was trying to encourage certain other areas to develop which would facilitate more efficient use of public transportation. They noted that older cities and towns in the U.S. could be distinguished from surrounding areas by compactness and somewhat higher density. Further, suburban development had created a uniform density sprawl environment. They felt that a vital and active community center needed to be denser than the adjacent residential districts. Also, a mix of uses including retail, offices, governmental and social services, entertainment and recreation, as well as residential and parking, all helps to create the kind of vigorous node attractive to residents and visitors.

In undertaking a redevelopment plan, the neighborhood is considering the benefits of encouraging higher density in designated nodal areas. A good prototype for accomplishing this within their community, they decided, would be a three-story unit in which retail stores would be on the ground floor, offices on the second level, with residential units above. They noted that real-estate development which incorporates a mix of business and ancillary uses, adjacent to a residential district, along with careful siteing and placement of landscape to create transition zones, would be needed to create visual and acoustic separations.

The focus of the eleventh design principle was parking considered in the aggregate. Meaning places where people can park and get out of their car. The neighbors noted that although core districts are usually assigned a zoning district classification, which does not require the same amount of adjacent parking as does suburban business zoning, local merchants usually insist on having as much adjacent parking as can be provided, for obvious reasons. The inevitable result, without aggregate parking, are core areas with a checkerboard of buildings and small parking lots. The neighbors thought that this pattern was not only visually unattractive but would work against pedestrian utilization, since the many curb cuts and vehicular activity interferes with the sidewalk system. In order to address this important factor, they recommended a parking authority be established for the neighborhood. This could develop a comprehensive parking policy for the district based on the land use and functional mapping that the neighborhood performed. The neighborhood noted that under ideal circumstances a number of designated common parking areas would exist within the nodal area. These would be sufficiently close so that visitors could park and then walk to all of their destinations without having to rely on automobiles between stops. They hastened to say that this also implied the need for having an attractive and safe pedestrian network from each parking area to shopping streets and civic areas.

The twelfth design principle: Landscaping and open space should be included in the business areas ... Street trees and landscaping were to be considered important not only for residential districts, but even more so in the shopping district. The establishment of a core area which would attract visitors and business would need to include a number of landscape and street improvements. All of the participating neighbors recognized the deficiencies with respect to handicapped access in the area, and had suggested that sidewalk improvements have a high priority. An integral part of this effort, they felt, should be a major urban tree planting program, coupled with the installation of pedestrian scale lighting, benches, street markets, trash containers and other civic elements. They also wanted to encourage building owners to invest in low plantings between sidewalks and their property.

Within this design principle, the neighbors strongly noted that a successful shopping street includes street trees, nicely scaled lighting standards, careful attention to shop signage, sidewalk treatment and landscaping. They stated that that all of these elements would add up to a comfortable, attractive, and prosperous setting which would aid in the neighborhoods economic vitality.

The thirteenth and last design principle noted that the creation of a vibrant neighborhood requires a community of houses. Because they were an older part of the community, they felt that the minimal standards utilized for housing of low and middle income residents, tended to be repetitive and monotonous, using one or two types, uniformly lined up along the street. Zoning requirements typically require front, rear, and side yards which result in equal spacing and large front street setbacks of houses: a pattern which does not encourage a strong sense of community. The neighbors noted that within this older part of town, a mix of housing types and scales should include differential spacing in certain designated areas which would create residential clusters. New buildings should utilize precedents found in this older part of the city. The neighbors also recognized development which incorporates land-use patterns placing houses close together in such a way as to create useful and attractive common open space between units. They stressed that this can be wonderful. To make this kind of physical organization possible, alterations to existing zoning restrictions may have to be considered. Consequently, discussions were begun to consider areas where zero lot line zoning could take place, and where innovative clustering of units might be possible. They also focused on the possible limitation of materials which might be employed in construction for compatibility purposes, as well as a consistent minimal standard roof pitch used on all the roofs within the district.

This and other design principles have been discussed with the community's federal Housing Authority. The federal agency has prepared plans for development of market-based housing which did not fit the physical context of the existing neighborhood. From what I understand, the results of these discussions were extremely fruitful. These discussions would not have occurred had the community not had a plan in place. But they did. And it has articulated succinct and intelligent design principles.

27
More Definitions

Muscoe Martin wrote in 1995, "The word sustainable has roots in the Latin subtenir, meaning 'to hold up' or 'to support from below.' A community must be supported from below—by its inhabitants, present and future. Certain places, through the peculiar combination of physical, cultural, and, perhaps, spiritual characteristics, inspire people to care for their community. These are the places where sustainability has the best chance of taking hold." He and others have defined the terms by which human civilization can live and prosper. If you want your kids and your community to prosper far into the future, begin to consider the following definitions for integration into your discussions and your lexicon. Help us as a society to think out loud by participating in the debate.

The chapter after the introduction to this book was a short piece called Definitions. That chapter showed in a broad sense the knowledge-base within the field of sustainability in which we would concentrate our attention. That chapter was to help us understand where in the myriad of subjects, within this field of study, this book would fit into the big picture. Having addressed much of the core of our subject, and having a better understanding of some of the whys and wherefores, I think it's time we can now dig deeper into the weeds.

The intent of this particular chapter: to see what this Centennial Model looks like in the eyes of the Central High community as it is being implemented. It is also to see some of the background information from which the community has been educated. This involves a wealth of knowledge from so many bright and wonderful individuals from around the world, and the wealth of knowledge housed within so many viable institutions. It's a knowledge base from which you and your community can also benefit.

A quote from the Central High Neighborhood's recently adopted Design Overlay District Requirements and Guidelines succinctly defines what they believe and intend. They say: "The Central High Neighborhood had determined that they will work toward the development of a sustainable community in which the livability of the neighborhood will be considered in all decisions made with regard to its short term and long term social and economic development. The neighborhood will also consider, as a top priority, the efficiency of the neighborhood and its various systems as it begins to redevelop a community that will be able to compete more effectively in global markets. Additionally, the neighborhood intends on focusing on the development of increased incomes for its citizens, as well as focusing on the development of multiple initiatives geared toward attracting others to live, work, and play within the area."

The Central High Neighborhood looked at multiple sources for their inspiration as they began this process. Among the great starting points in our research, and each of you could benefit from using, are the principles and definitions established from the Wingspread Conference. The federal government arranged this conference for many of us to think together about the future of how we go about developing and building the world around us. Having had the great honor of participating in Wingspread II, I obviously thought it was a good idea to reassess some of the conclusions of the conference with our neighbors.

The Wingspread Principles, to a great degree, dealt with disaster-prone communities. Yet it also focused on those principles which could be utilized by many communities in their efforts to build anew, which includes any community physically growing or rebuilding. Some of the applicable and extracted principles from the conference note that resources should be invested consistent with improving the quality of life in the areas of public health and safety, environmental stewardship, and social and economic security. It should also include plans designed to reduce the impact of disasters, and to encourage recovery by providing incentives to individuals, the private sector, and government to pursue sustainable development and redevelopment. It goes on to say that individual citizens, the private sector, and local, state, and federal governments should act as partners with shared goals and values to further the capacity of our communities to be self-sufficient. You might notice that the Central High Neighborhood is doing this. You might also see that, to the community, it matters not who accomplishes the various tasks or who gets the credit, as long as the tasks get done.

The Wingspread Conference also noted that decisions should be driven by a consensus-based, inclusive process that stakeholders use and trust. The process should identify local sustainability priorities, leading to the investment of resources that will meet those needs, emphasizing the need for local responsibility and self-sufficiency. Again, that is part of this Centennial process and part of the Central High plan.

The neighborhood began to embrace early in their educational process some of the various definitions of sustainability from the Wingspread Conference and other sources. These and other definitions can prove to be important to you and in your community's quest to develop in a more sustainable fashion. Write them down and either give them or quote them to your community leaders and to your neighbors. It can help you in your cause. Some of these definitions include the following noted below. I would give credit to the authors of some of these definitions, but I don't have a clue who wrote them. I wrote them down years ago so that I could refer to them just as I am asking you to do.

> *"Sustainable development is not a new concept. Rather, it is the latest expression of a long-standing ethic involving peoples' relationships with the environment and the current generation's responsibilities to future generations."*

> *"Sustainable development is a strategy by which communities seek economic development approaches that also benefit the local environment and quality of life. It has become an important guide to many communities that have discovered that traditional approaches to planning and development are creating, rather than solving, societal and environmental problems. Where traditional approaches can lead to congestion, sprawl, pollution and resource over-consumption, sustainable development offers real, lasting solutions that will strengthen our future."*

> *"Sustainable development provides a framework under which communities can use resources efficiently, create efficient infrastructures, protect and enhance quality of life, and create new businesses to strengthen their economies. It can help us create healthy communities that can sustain our generation, as well as those that follow ours."*

> *"For a community to be truly sustainable, it must adopt a three-pronged approach that considers economic, environmental and cultural resources. Communities must consider these needs in the short term as well as the long term."*

Robert Gilman once wrote, "Sustainability refers to the ability of a society, ecosystem, or any such ongoing system to continue functioning into the indefinite future without being forced into decline through exhaustion ... of key resources." And ... William Ruckelshaus, wrote over 20 years ago, "Sustainability is the [emerging] doctrine that economic growth and development must take place, and be maintained over time, within the limits set by ecology in the broadest sense—by the interrelations of human beings and their works, the biosphere and the physical and chemical laws that govern it ... It follows that environmental protection and economic development are complementary rather than antagonistic processes." This guy was really something. Re-read that a few times and you will see how brilliant he was.

If you want to research some position papers and principles developed by other individuals, groups and governments, I would suggest that you Google things like The Hannover Principles; The Natural Step Principles which emerged from an international movement that began in Sweden; Manatee County "Rediscovers"; Blueprint 2030 adopted in 2002 by the Twin Cities (Minnesota); City of Portland Sustainable City Principles; The Earth Charter; National Park Service's Principles for Sustainable Design; and of course the Wingspread Principles which were developed in 1998 and updated in 2003. There are loads more, but this can give you a good start. Be wary, there are jillions of governing bodies that have good position papers and laudable initiatives on sustainability, but most are eye wash that sit on shelves and are never implemented. No follow-through.

It is interesting to note how some communities and states have gone beyond position papers and have actually mandated through ordinances and acts that ongoing planning should embrace sustainable principles. The likes of New Pattonsburg, Missouri, Chattanooga, Tennessee, and Burlington, Vermont, and the states of Washington, Oregon and Minnesota. Also, there some publications like "What Are Sustainable Communities?" "What is Sustainability Anyway?", and "Coming To Terms With Sustainability" which can be useful to individuals in your community. Some other resources might include *About Planning* which is a clearinghouse for information on urban planning, smart growth, new urbanism, and growth management, and *EarthTrends*, the environmental information portal which makes key environmental and sustainable development information available not only to policy makers but also to the general public. Other resources include *the President's Council on Sustainable Development (PCSD)* which was formed in 1993. *Rebuild America* is a federal Department of Energy program that focuses on energy-savings solutions as community solutions. The last one that I will mention here is the great *Rocky Mountain Institute*, a nonprofit that focuses on energy, transportation, green development, water, economic renewal, corporate sustainability and security. Some of the individuals that have come from this organization are real experts on the subject and leaders in the industry.

As for books, there are loads of them. The likes of *Sustainable Communities: Guide for Grassroots Activists, Livable Cities: A Grass-Roots Guide to Rebuilding Urban America, Anthology of Sustainability, Building Healthy Communities*, and the Worldwatch Institute's *State of The World*.

This should get you started with definitions that you can use, just as it did with the Central High Neighborhood.

28

Goals and Objectives

About 19 years after I developed some of the citizen participation goals needed to create an efficient sustainable community for Prodigy, my city of the future, and about 11 years after I further refined the goals for the re-development of existing communities, guess what happened? The governments of the western hemisphere instructed the Organization of American States to give priority to the Formulation and Implementation of an Inter-American Strategy for the Promotion of Citizen Participation in Decision-Making for Sustainable Development. It was a good long title, but I'm not sure that many in our country or any of the participating members of the OAS know much about this. It is good, however, to see that the OAS is going in the right direction. When you read the OAS report on this, you will find an assumption: A level of democratic reform must take place for the strategy to work properly. You know ... citizen participation and all that kind of stuff. I don't think that all of the nations within the OAS are there yet, but it seems they and we are moving in the right direction. I mention this because the nature of the processes we have discussed does not actually require a federal or central government or any grouping of nations or a state to participate for them to be functional or viable. The functioning of new third-wave economic city-states requires motivated and efficient human capital, as well as a fair amount of post-industrial elbow grease. Most communities in North America possess the necessary ingredients to be successful, as do most every other community in the hemisphere. The communities around the world which are unfettered by bureaucratic B.S. and have the individual freedoms to assemble are light years ahead of those that are freedom-challenged. ALWAYS remember:

The creation of goals and objectives for your community does not require the blessing of the State nor does it require the participation of the State or any governing body for your initiatives to be validated.

The citizen participation model that I created—years before the OAS strategy was formulated—is one of the most extensive models ever developed for citizen participation. We used it in the Central High Neighborhood. It's the one we describe in this book. It's the process that I eventually termed as the Centennial Planning Process©.

We have noted in Chapter 27 where to locate certain information and initiatives which have emanated from federal, state, and local governments, as well as nonprofit and business groups; information and initiatives which can be helpful. Most of what these groups do is put together reports that all of us can read, hoping they will spur some type of sustainable development. A few of the governing authorities have actually created laws and ordinances which will hopefully guide sustainable developments. I mention this because some definitive goals could be set by governing authorities which could lead to redevelopment of our communities in much more rapid fashion.

The broad goals of the community should embrace the relationship between economic and educational equity, and the impact that such has on the economic viability and sustainability of the community. Where the federal government can come into play: it can lead in establishing a global Educational Doctrine setting the relationship amongst communities of the globe pertaining to the issue of economic and educational equity. This could be the precursor to creating a sustainable world just as the Monroe Doctrine, the Truman Doctrine, and Bush Doctrine did for defining our relationship with other countries around the world regarding national security. This type of leadership and foundational development would establish the ground rules by which nations and city-states would compete. After David Barlow conceived such a scenario, he prodded me incessantly until I wrote an educational doctrine about 13 or 14 years ago and sent it to President Clinton. It was the first time in civilization where the educational reforms of our nation, utilizing advanced technologies, were equated to the strength and security of our economy, and ergo to the strength and security of our nation. It was a national security doctrine. Such a doctrine is important to the development of substantive social and economic policy. It attaches, for the first time, explicit importance of education to the security of the world. It would have equated for the first time the education of our kids to that of bombs in our national security. Did it go anywhere? You tell me. The doctrine develops the necessary arguments for the global impetus of advanced telecommunications and real educational reform for all nations, and the necessity for the continued democratization of all institutions. This is a key to creating a sustainable world and a secure world, and is a leadership component that could set the ship on course.

Remember: The whole is to the part as the part is to the whole. Relative to this subject, the part on the doctrine was a piece of the whole, a piece of the big picture: Broad goals which can serve as guidelines for the development of public policy on which business and government can rely.

Let me back up for a minute. I guess it was about 18 years ago, or so, I met a brilliant engineer and software developer. This fella was going to be flying through my part of the country. A friend of mine that worked for the State convinced this software designer to delay his outgoing flight so that he could spend some time in our community. My buddy then called me and told me that I needed to take care of our new guest for a couple of days. Boy, was this a wonderful eye-opener. Our guest was one of the founding fathers of the videogame industry: Nolan Bushnell. He was then, and continued to be, one of the major players in the development of our post-industrial basic sectors of the economy; a leader of the computer and video game software industry that today grosses around $10 billion annually. As an architect and planner involved in the exercise of figuring out how to develop post-industrial sustainable communities of the future, I naturally wanted to talk with my new-found friend about the physical requirements for housing people that worked in companies he owned. This was one of those points in life where we develop greater understanding about the functioning of the world in which we live.

The discussions, with this wonderful, bright man, helped me to hone my model for the development of sustainable third-wave communities. Nolan gave very profound and succinct advice as it related to the development of local markets in the post-industrial economy. Part of his advice: I should set as a goal the development of the post-industrial economy within our local economy ... which I had already done. He continued to explain that I should figure out how to establish the objectives to attract the product providers of the future *to a specific place on earth,* which I then did. Meaning I set the goal and figured it out. Just as you can. From his advice I wrote what was, at the time, the first digital product incentive act in the nation. As its basis, I placed a component for issuance of financial rebates linked to specific places on earth: Digital Overlay Districts©. They were the first of their kind in the world which were land-use components based in current land-use law. This is a carrot that can help to drive the redevelopment process. It provides a greater chance for the repayment of debt, because it is an area where wealth is being created. This act is not intended for just any and all places on earth, but those places where a community engages in a strategic planning process. This process addresses the issues which can help create a post–industrial, sustainable economy and a civil and sustainable community. A process like the Centennial Planning Process©.

The implementation of the big picture into a community did not prove to be as difficult as I thought it would be. This was due to the aggressive nature of individuals like Mrs. Helen Tucker, Mrs. Mary Katherine Bew, Mrs. Wieke Benjamin, Mrs. Paulette Blevins, and many more of the neighbors of the Central High Neighborhood. During the planning process in the Central High Neighborhood, the neighbors discussed many of these big to small issues as they began to set their goals and objectives. They noted their goal to implement a model for third-wave redevelopment of urban form. It would be accomplished partially through the objective of a community-driven planning process, and through tax initiatives as a catalyst to create new third-wave form.

It was actually stated like this:

The **GOAL** *for implementation of this first third-wave model is to alter the form and efficiency of the physical environment within the context of a more livable environment and eventually a more sustainable economy.*

From that goal, they developed a series of broad objectives for implementation of this first third-wave model. First, they created a theoretical model for purposes of research into the *nature and manifestation of third-wave communal form.* They would also develop programs and policies as they relate to the functioning of multiple systems throughout the economic, social and physical environment. They recognized that being the first to do this was not the difficult part. Being aware of the recalcitrance of the existing governing and planning institutions to accept an altered way of planning and implementation could prove to be more challenging.

Their next objective was to create a guide for educating communities to the nature and functioning of communications-age communities in a more competitive diversified global economy. That's what this book is all about. Educating others about what you are doing is always important. As an added aspect of this educational objective, the neighborhood wanted to maintain a record of the project and the corresponding development and implementation of the model for purposes of educating others.

They also felt it important for others to be aware of the core "sustainable investment strategies" in a capitalistic economy and a democratic society which could cause land-use patterns to be altered. They should also promote awareness of greater efficiencies within the various "systems" of the urban environment which could be altered. The thought being that once others are enlightened, they may be more apt to help you, or maybe not interfere with you as much. That objective was the catalyst for the next objective: To educate governing bodies and investment managers on the implications of an altered economy on the nature of land use in the 21st Century, and how that altered economy impacts both short-term and long-term real estate investment decisions.

Once all of the objectives dealing with everybody outside the neighborhood were out of the way, the neighborhood then specifically focused on their own needs. They sighted the objective of altering the trends which have caused the degradation within the specific selected neighborhood. They wanted to break the governing cycle of social and economic deception by focusing on an altered future, rather than continuing to utilize the first- and second-wave models which had yielded extensive degradation.

These initial objectives were pretty broad in scope, but were developed to help keep the neighbors focused over the long run. This implementation of a model for the redevelopment of their existing community, based on the expansion of third-wave sectors of the economy were to be accomplished through a citizen-driven process. Another objective: Setting into motion the alteration of the local economy to that of post-industrial basic sectors. They also wanted evaluation and alteration of educational components which could help to develop the product providers and wealth creators of the future. It could also spur the resulting social, political, legal, educational, and physical manifestations necessary to accomplish the implementation of the model. This is partly where the Fundamental Five in Chapter 25 came from.

The neighbors understood that first- and second-wave economies and their corresponding service sectors gave rationale for the agglomeration of habitable structure and urban form. They surmised that, likewise, third-wave economies and the effects of heightened global competition could affect the built environment in new and radical ways. The community realized that this project would, in part, be an experiment and exploration. It would test the impact such an economic emphasis could have on the attraction and retention of those post-industrial industries based on their stated goal: Altering the form and efficiency of the physical environment within the context of a more livable environment, and eventually a more sustainable economy.

29

Run-up to the Plan

"In the global economy, knowledge is king. And those nations, and communities, that excel at creating new knowledge and transforming it into new technologies will prosper in years to come."- *Business Week*, June 6, 1992. Not many years after this was stated, the Central High Neighborhood decided to embrace this notion and integrate it into a plan for their future. Here we are now, nearly 19 years after the *Business Week* article to see how the neighborhood actually developed a plan which embraced this thought.

We have discussed a whole host of foundational issues as a run-up to the creation of a working plan for developing a sustainable community. Here's what's significant to the particular plan that the Central High Neighborhood is implementing: The integration of technological innovations and events, and how these have caused changes to our economy and the collective behaviors within society. This is a plan which looks into the future ... ceded from the various futures which exist for each of our communities.

Faiz Shakir, research director from the Center for American Progress, mentioned in a C-SPAN program that it is important to distinguish between "What is possible vs. what is necessary." He was talking about environmental policy in this particular case. But the neighborhood had seen that sentiment years before as the crux to developing a viable plan, along with significant public policy which can help to direct programs and expenditures when developing sustainable communities. A good plan needs to possess both components. The "necessary," which has a focus on the present needs, or what we termed earlier as pothole issues, and the "possible," with a focus on the future, what we termed as promises. This focus on the now and the future gives us an understanding of a functional plan's actual structure. Things that need to be done right away and things that can be done later. That doesn't mean things that affect the future can be put off for a later date. It means certain things need to be done first if you are to derive your desired future. Remember the example from earlier? I need to put my socks on before my shoes. Depending upon the severity of social and physical problems that exist within your community, certain things will need to be addressed immediately as you are simultaneously planning and implementing initiatives which will affect your future. Every community has a different, ordered set of needs. Having said all of this, it means that for managerial purposes the initiatives within your plan will need to be divided into short-range, medium-range, and long-range initiatives. Each will then be discussed and prioritize relative to the other. This will yield a matrix of items that need to be accomplished, and when they need to be accomplished. You will see a copy of this type of matrix in the Centennial Chapter.

In my business consulting, and in most businesses, we have various types of charts which help us organize scheduling and decision making. The matrix which the Central High Neighborhood developed is somewhat more complex and involved than most, but that is due to the scope and complexity of the undertaking. The more complex the undertaking, the more involved the charts can become.

Implementing this community-based process requires advanced planning to prepare individuals who participate in the earlier stages to re-engage in the later stages, as well as during the implementation of a work plan. This is accomplished with individuals identifying areas of interest which become a part of a managerial document of the work plan. A document that can be referenced as to who needs to be doing what, and when they need to be doing it.

In Chapter 24 we talked about the rationale for the development and utilization of the various planning methods. We focused on understanding the nature of the trend in democratizing our institutions to the development of third-wave systems. Here's one of the cornerstones to understanding third-wave economies and the corresponding institutions: The link of the de-evolved forms of governance to the development of institutions utilized for implementing community initiatives. The planning process the neighborhood employed is one of the most radical attempts to date to utilize a third-wave methodology. Such a method of community consensus building does not imply that leadership is not important or nonexistent. Although it is still required to engage with existing institutions, the nature of institutional leadership changes under this paradigm. What an institutional leadership model will look like in 20 to 50 years will depend on the nature of the financial models which emerge, a result of the incremental implementation of this decision-making model.

With no monetary support and no professional support from any governing body, the Central High Neighborhood embarked on developing and implementing what they believed would be the most comprehensive strategic plan of any neighborhood in America. Their methodology involved all citizens—men, women, young people, and children—in public-policy decisions.

The neighbors determined one of the important aspects required for institutional and procedural changes to take place, and for redeveloping their community into a third-wave community capable of sustaining long-term investments. This was the understanding of the democratic involvement of individuals in the planning process; i.e. understanding the upside and the downside of the community collaborative planning process. They realized this: It would be important to understand how developing and implementing processes could address the issue of decreased engagement on the part of the community over a period of time. The implementation process would also facilitate a subsequent re-involvement on the part of the community. They understood its significance in the evolution of their community process, in which there was not to be government guidance or management.

The neighborhood understood that the purpose of developing a long-term vision and the corresponding strategic plan: Lay a foundation for a community to create a stronger, more diverse economy, one able to expand opportunity and wealth for its businesses and citizens. That was very different than what many communities were doing around the nation. As others were looking to inculcate new communications infrastructure into their communities, the Central High neighborhood's goal was this: not to merely build a communications network to facilitate new industry, but to build a community more able to compete in the 21st Century through its ability to create wealth and repay debt.

They surmised that something akin to a communications age promotional plan could define the direction of the community's future economic growth. It could also describe a strategy for creation of a socio-economic environment necessary for specified growth to take place. From that, they felt that a community master plan would have to result from the process. It would help define the direction of future real estate and physical growth, and facilitate capital investment. This would amount to a blueprint for the development of a communications-based community of the 21st Century.

Understanding the nature of basic sector economic growth, the neighbors asked a thought provoking question which eventually guided much of what they have done. The question was: Are the people who utilize their neighborhood's telecommunications distribution infrastructure product suppliers or product consumers? Answering that question has had an extremely profound impact on the neighborhood planning. It was recognized that what they do to address that question will affect their ability to attract capital investment and pay off debt. It would be at the heart of the programmatic requirements for determining the infrastructure needs, design and cost. They recognized that the developing a strategic master plan which emphasizes a third-wave sustainable global community is one major need that their community had for attracting future long-term investments. Such a plan would be the rationale for developing a networked community concept and any possible telecommunications master plan.

Most interestingly, the neighborhood understood that they needed to accept that greater competition is an opportunity rather than a burden, and recognize that changes taking place all over the world would open possibilities for those prepared to take advantage of them. Then they would be further down the road to recognizing that corrective action taken now could lay a foundation for a brighter future. They realized that preparing their local economy and lowering the risks for telecommunications investment is far and away the most advantageous scenario for any community. This included their own community, because it creates an environment which attracts additional investments in many other areas of the economy ... sustainable investments.

As for their own planning process, the neighbors believed that it should have this underlying premise: the development of institutions and processes able to accomplish the tasks that they would eventually set forward in a strategic plan with an identified future as its catalyst. The underlying assumptions here: (1) The existing institutions and processes were not serving their community in their desire for a better or altered future, or (2) the existing institutions and processes had caused their then discontent or conditions; conditions which were pretty abysmal.

The Central High Neighborhood had determined, in essence, that they would work toward the development of a sustainable community.

30
Developing a Plan

The Central High Neighborhood determined, in their early discussions, that the urban design processes utilized for the past 40 years had not benefited them or the community at large. They, like many other communities throughout the country, had experienced both public and private disinvestment due to any number of factors. They negated the practice of focusing on one project at a time, in isolation to both the community's objectives and the overall development of the physical environment with little or no regard to the broader issues. They felt these were the underlying causes of the social and physical degradation within their community. They considered these, at best, naive on the part of planners and city administrators. The neighbors therefore determined it incumbent upon them to take over the process of planning their neighborhood for their future and the future of their kids. They decided that they should plan for a much different future than what the trends had in store for them. They knew that, if they were to continue down the same path as the previous forty years, their future would be pretty bleak. They knew that implementing a plan for a different future, one that would be historically outside the domain of mere physical planning on the part of community planners, would be difficult; but they had nothing to lose, and plenty to gain.

Developing the physical environment based on an altered economy and heightened competition: this became the foundation for developing their decisions for programs, policies and expenditures. It eventually proved the determinate for developing the built and natural environment. Altering the form and efficiency of the physical environment, within the context of a more livable space and eventually a more sustainable economy, became the underlying focus of the community's redevelopment.

These were key to the development of the planning process: Analyzing the new and old trends, understanding the methods for altering trends, and understanding the machinations involved in selecting a definitive future appropriate for the community. Awareness of third-wave industries' potential causation and alteration in the physical constraints to the development of product became one of the main factors in developing the strategies for the development of the built environment. Those strategies we noted in previous chapters.

Considering all of this, their next step seemed pretty obvious. Develop a plan, but not just any plan, a plan that was community-driven. They discovered certain things needed to be done: Their plan needed specifics if they were to change the world around them. They wanted to identify both large-scale and small-scale problems in both the long term and short term. They knew that they should educate themselves. That is to say, explore the real reasons why many of their problems existed. Subsequently they knew they must determine some viable solutions based on the best information they had learned. From all that they would learn, they then could develop a set of guidelines and initiatives, including a specific set of items on which to work. This could help direct them over the long run in implementing any possible solutions. Below is the simple version of what the neighbors set out to do, and subsequently accomplished. These are the core components to their plan:

- They needed to identify the neighborhoods' problems through a series of community-based meetings where the community was not constrained by limitations of any governing institutions or past planning methodology.
- Next, they needed to educate themselves about the various problems, as well as their history and other background, through a series of community meetings.
- They then would have discussions about past and current trends, and how to determine the differences between trends and cycles. That difference is critical in making long-term decisions.
- Next they would discuss what they thought might be the most desirous futures from multiple, possible futures, and then discuss how to create that identified future.
- From that identified future, they would need to develop the vision and goals which could guide them in their decision making.

- Next they would need to educate themselves on how to bring about change.
- Next, discussions about various processes and institutions which would require alteration to accomplish their goals. They would also identify possible new processes and institutions which might not exist, yet which could help to accomplish their goals.
- They next needed to develop some broad categories based on the many problems and solutions identified in the early stages. This was for cross-referencing purposes and for eventual implementation purposes.
- They then would discuss solutions to the various problems. A critical stage in the planning process. At this juncture it would be important to not allow historical constraints to control outcomes.
- Next the neighbors needed to identify the mechanisms to accomplish change. That is to say, which components or institutions must be altered, and which trends must be altered to accomplish the desired future.
- Next the folks in the community would educate themselves about the history of planning processes and the current trends in the processes.
- They then would develop a planning process specifically for their needs so as to assure greater community involvement over a longer period of time.
- Next would be the mapping the community's human, institutional, and physical assets.
- Creation of a comprehensive plan that could be continually referenced, a strategic plan would follow.
- Then the creation of a detailed work plan. A plan that would give specific initiatives a place relative to other initiatives.
- Next would be to determine a time frame for implementation of the various initiatives in the work plan.
- Then, prioritize the initiatives within the work plan.
- Assign the work-plan tasks to individuals within the community for coordination and implementation.
- The final component would be the implementation phase, which is never ending.

31

The Prodigy Model
creating new

This chapter is not about the Central High Plan directly. It is about how I got to the stage of working with a community to redevelop their little piece of the world. This chapter was thrown in as a reminder that building communities is like building homes. I may have mentioned this earlier, but you can either build a new home or you can remodel an existing home, or some combination of the two. The same with your community. As I noted in the Acknowledgments, nearly 30 years ago I designed Prodigy, the first sustainable "Third Wave City of the Future" in history; the model on how to build a new community based on a post-industrial economy. How this came about was fascinating. A lesson from which I hope some of the younger generations can benefit. Hanging out and exchanging ideas can lead to some good things, if you don't try to dumb down everything.

After I moved away to go to college in 1969, I would go home to Miami every year for Christmas and New Year's to be with my mom, dad, brothers and friends; 1979 was no exception. The one thing I tried to always do while home was to get together with one of my best friends, Rod Glaubman. Rod and I had been best buddies since seventh grade. Like my brothers, he and I talked about anything and everything as we just hung out. The fun part of hanging out with Rod was not just the catching up with him, and the comradery, but we liked to sail. This particular Miami winter day we decided to sail out on Biscayne Bay in Rod's catamaran. It was an easy and enjoyable way that we could just talk and catch up on each other's life. We launched from one of the small islands off of Rickenbacker Causeway leading to Key Biscayne ... near the Miami Marine stadium.

We were doing just fine on our sail until we got around the end of Key Biscayne near the lighthouse when the wind died. We sat on the boat for what seemed like an eternity, trying to get back while we talked and baked in the winter sun. In the hours we were out, one of our discussions revolved around music and the arts in and around the Dade and Broward County areas. Mainly because Rod had started, along with Steve Parsons, a community-based musical outreach program in Miami called P.A.C.E., an organization which eventually grew into the largest musical outreach program in U.S. history; taking music to every community venue imaginable. At its peak, Rod was producing 1,500 concerts a year. Oh yeah, another part of the fun of hanging out with Rod was getting to get into all of the best music venues in South Florida, because every musician and every bouncer knew him. There was no waiting in line, and a lot of times no paying a cover charge. Anyway, the discussion focused on the future of the arts and the eventual delivery systems that music would take. A future of music delivery that I have seen come to fruition 30 years later.

We finally made it back to land and to the ice chest. While refreshing ourselves, the discussion continued about the future of the arts and the pivotal role that creativity would play in our emerging post-industrial, communications-based economy. Being an artist, an architect, and an economist, I was really into the subject. Because we were in the shadows of the Marine Stadium, figuratively speaking that is, Rod began to discuss the need for more venues for music and entertainment that could function better than the Marine Stadium: one of the many venues that he used. At that point, we began to sculpt into the sand the type of venue that would be ideal. From that original sand sculpture, I began to focus on the various other functions that this facility of the future might be able to handle. Understanding the changing components of our economy, I started from that model in the sand to show the arts' functional interdependence on the development of a local and regional economy. I began to explore the physical ramifications of this altered economy on the built environment and land-use patterns.

When I got back to Little Rock, and over the next couple of months, my focus began to turn towards the possibility of changes in human interaction and human behavior as a result of the forecasted changes in technology. I looked at what that meant to the physical environment and eventually to our zoning and land-use policies in the world of the future. I developed the concept further, and then designed "Prodigy," the first sustainable, post-industrial city of the future. It wasn't until my local Congressman, Ed Bethune, told me to read Toffler's Third Wave did I realize I could attach an actual label to the project. I was calling it a post-industrial sustainable city of the future; it was in fact a third wave city of the future. The first exploration of the physical manifestation of what Alvin and Heidi Toffler had so eloquently described. It was like somebody could see into my mind and describe what I was seeing. I have been forever grateful to Congressman Bethune not just for his understanding, but more-so for his thoughtfulness in guiding a young guy who was trying to explore the workings of the world. It wasn't until after Congressman Bethune took the concept to the White House, and received a response, did I realize that he understood the ramifications of what I was doing as well as I did.

In the future, more and more people who reside within a more diversified economy, an economy with a preponderance of ICE industries, will be living digitally. Not just moving the informational and entertainment product that they create, but they will be digitally commuting—telecommuting—in greater numbers. This reality will have a huge impact, as we are beginning to now see, on shopping patterns, living patterns, transportation patterns, and patterns of human interaction. Human interaction—that's a euphemism for a variety of forms of human expression and behaviors, including sex.

Rod Glaubman and I didn't have cell phones with cameras back then, and I'm not sure if either one of us had brought a camera. Having grown up in Miami, going back wasn't typically considered by my wife—girl-

Original 1981 concept / pencil sketch

friend at the time—and myself as a vacation in which we needed to take pictures. I'm not sure either one of the girl friends thought that taking a photo of Rod and me doing what we always did since we were eleven years old was worthwhile. Anyway, we don't have a photo of what we created in the sand. But as the concept began to develop and questions began to be asked about what it looked like, I sat down and did a quick 10-minute sketch of what I was seeing in my mind's eye. The original concept sketch from early 1981, shown here, is just that, a conceptual sketch. The design is important to some because it becomes real to them; but what it looks like is much less important than how it functions, and the process by which it is accomplished.

After discussing the process and how the post-industrial functions merged into the existing institutional structures, and then into the new communal form, Rod said that it was like J.C. Penney comes to Arcosanti. For those who are not familiar, Arcosanti was a city of the future that Paolo Soleri had designed and eventually tried to build in the desert of Arizona. Actually, there was some great insight and truth to what Rod had said.

In 1974, I had met Paolo Soleri and had a chance to engage with him. He was at the University of Arkansas lecturing and trying to get young architectural students to pay him to come work for him in the desert. (I won't get into that.) Soleri was one of the bright young students who had studied under Frank Lloyd Wright at Taliesin in the late '40s just as Fay Jones had done. At the time that Soleri came to espouse his philosophy at the University, Fay was dean of the architectural school that now bears his name. Fay brought in some of the most engaging architects from around the world during that period, Soleri being one of many.

Soleri's Arcosanti was based on his concept of "arcology." What he described as architecture linked with ecology; a wonderfully brilliant concept. He advocated that communities should become more urban to maximize interaction and accessibility and to minimize the use of energy; a somewhat different, rougher, less-utopian thesis than Frank Lloyd Wright's Broadacre City which was a magnificent dissertation on the modern movement. Soleri championed the lessening use of raw materials and land. He proselytized for the need to reduce waste and environmental pollution, all important issues in creating sustainable communities. All this while creating greater interaction for the individual with the surrounding natural environment. This was important for me to hear at the time. It was a foundation for me eventually designing Prodigy. Soleri academically explored many of the important components involved in developing the built environment in a sustainable fashion. But I never got his physical leap to a place on earth that didn't have enough water to sustain plant life, much less humans. Building in the desert was antithetical to the issue of sustainability. That, along with a lack of focus on a functional economy gave me reason to pause. I thought then, as well as now, it is vitally important when discussing sustainability to consider the ramifications of the basic sectors of the economy on the design, development, and functioning of the built environment we humans create, and the impact such has on our ability to sustain ourselves. I realized then that cheap land and tight budgets can cause developers to do weird things, and Soleri was no different at this juncture as a developer. You have to credit him, however. He wanted to show that, if humans could survive sustainably in the desert, then some of the principles which he espoused might be applied elsewhere. He was absolutely right.

Prodigy is a de facto model for developing communities of the future. It is not an Arcosanti-type model which failed to focus on much beyond the physical manifestations, but a model which focuses on the underlying elements and systems which are the determinates of and manifestation of the physical. The Prodigy model assumes further democratization of institutions and assumes all of the things we have discussed in the previous sections. Prodigy supposes that human interaction is a historically important component in the continued evolution of our society, where the trends and technology tell us that such is not a necessity for the continued existence of our species. The rationale for Prodigy assumed, then as well as now, that heightened levels of competition would occur on a global scale. That technology would allow for peoples of the world to become more educated and competitive. Those components have proven to be true in the ensuing 30 years.

The Prodigy process was and is an attempt to create community-outreach models based on my understanding, at the time, of various trends and of the institutional paradigm shift which would take place with maturation of the economy's third-wave sectors. Understanding that creativity would be the foundation of the post-industrial economy, Prodigy attempted to define the functional interaction between the "Creatives" as the wealth creators and the rest of the functioning economy and the physical manifestations of this paradigm shift. Prodigy recognized that art would no longer be a luxury, but a human necessity for the functioning of the economy. Also, that understanding the scope of that necessity in a global third-wave economy, which consumes ICE Industry product, would be at the core of understanding this: Individuals, corporations and communities would have future needs for altering existing programs, policies, expenditures, institutions and methodologies. This is the foundation for the next chapter as well.

Prodigy embraced the origins of influence of a third-wave economy. It recognized the path to wealth creation in the 21st Century and beyond, and how that wealth creation would facilitate and manifest itself in the built environment. Prodigy was the conceptual and philosophical manifestation of the paradigm shift discussed by Alvin and Heidi Toffler. It utilized a comprehensive nascentistic philosophy discussed by Fay Jones and Frank Lloyd Wright. Prodigy is the precursor to the model that the Central High Neighborhood is implementing. The Centennial model. Next Chapter.

32

The Centennial Model
remodeling old

In 1976 or '77, I wrote a paper in college on the future of strip developments in the United States as a result of the oil embargo. Then, in 1977 I created one of the first community development corporations in the nation to focus attention on the inexorable changes which would take place to the built environment. These changes would be due to emerging technologies and the implications those technologies would have on the economy. That private foundation was called the Architectural Educational Corporation for Community Development. At the time, it was told to me by the law school student who handled the incorporation that I had to have three people involved in the incorporation process. So I got my girlfriend, now my wife, and a wonderful bright architectural student, Nelson Hodges, to sign on the dotted line so I could get started. I would go around to various civic organizations throughout Northwest Arkansas, when I was supposed to be in school, with my handy-dandy slide presentation. I had developed it for what seemed like a fortune at the time: $21. I was educating people about green and sustainable design based on the changes in technology and the eventual changes in the economy. I must admit that those slides are still relevant today. Then, as noted in the last chapter, in 1980 I designed Prodigy along with the corresponding third-wave methodology necessary to implement the design. All of this was the origin for me to develop in 1986 a much more important and complex model for recreating urban form within existing communities. Both this redevelopment model and the Prodigy model were based on the development of third-wave sectors of the economy and the diversification of a local economy within that basic sector. This more complex model for redevelopment began implementation in 1996. It was subsequently termed as the Centennial Planning Process©, named after the geographic area in which the implementation of this process began.

Speaking of the geographic area, the original area selected for implementation of this planning process encompassed nearly one square mile, or approximately 600 acres, and housed about 9,000 people. That area was scaled down somewhat over the years as the participating neighborhoods got closer to implementing a design overlay district, and as local politics came into play. The original area of community participation was the first suburban development of our greater community which took place at the turn of the 19th Century, and was platted as the Centennial Addition those many years ago. The Central High Neighborhood is located within the Centennial Addition. You can probably guess the reason why the neighborhood is called what it is. There's a school in the neighborhood called Central High. It happens to be the famous high school integrated in 1957 that made international news. Governor Orville Faubus, used the National Guard to keep nine black students from entering the school, and the President of the United States, Dwight Eisenhower, used the Regular Army to let the students in and to keep order.

The background and history of what was once called the most beautiful school in the nation is a must read. You can get information about the civil rights history through the Department of Interior's National Park Service, because the school is now a part of the Parks Service. I know that living here might make me a bit biased, but it would be worth a trip to come and visit one of the most significant historical civil rights locations in U.S. history. As a quick aside, this specific national park exists because of a community-based initiative begun by a wonderful man named Mark Abernathy. The initiative did not emanate from the business community, the existing political structure, city hall, state government, the feds, the Parks Service, the Department of Interior, or any other established entity. It came from concerned citizens within the surrounding neighborhoods. A bunch of neighbors got together and decided on making it happen over the objections of some of the existing power structure within the community(who, by the way, eventually got in the middle of it when they knew it wouldn't go away, and then helped to take credit.) Regardless of the machinations, this was a good example of a bunch of motivated people (some chickens) deciding what needed to be done, and doing it. It didn't necessitate convincing any governing body as to the need or value, and it didn't require a politician to take it on as a pet project to justify the need for additional tax revenues, to justify moving forward. It merely took the vision and desire on the part of some motivated citizens. Like you.

The selection of the Central High Neighborhood for implementation of this model was partly serendipitous, and partly due to the strong and enlightened leadership within the neighborhood. A little over 20 years ago I got involved in the early development of a neighborhood movement in our community. A grouping of neighborhoods from around the city decided, for political reasons that they should coalesce. Then their individual voices would be stronger, knowing there was strength in numbers. I initially got involved because of my curiosity and to observe what was happening within the neighborhoods. Architects are not just designers, we're observers as well. After about a year of observation and some minor participation, I realized that there was some real substance in the movement, and that the individuals involved were passionate, motivated, intelligent and above all, fearless. One of the neighborhood leaders who I met was the president of the Central High Neighborhood, Mrs. Ethel Ambrose. That was the serendipitous part. This larger group discussed the problems that our community faced and the possible solutions which could be implemented. Over the years, the respect and admiration each of us had for one another and our friendships flourished. Mrs. Ambrose and I began to discuss things we could do together to help each others' individual neighborhoods. This is where the strong and enlightened leadership comes into play. Or maybe I should say this is where I got roped into working with the Central High Neighborhood: Something she wanted me to do, and I guess something that I wanted to do.

After some discussion about collaborative community-planning processes, Mrs. Ambrose decided that her neighborhood should bring together the neighbors in her community with city leaders, city staff, businesses, and institutions. In addition to those individuals noted in Chapter 28: Mrs. Tucker, Mrs. Bew, Mrs. Benjamin, and Mrs. Blevins there were other neighbors who became significant players in the process. Cliff Riggs, Perrilyn Floyd, and Joyce Van de Grift, are but a few of the scores who participated. They also include business leaders within the community, individuals from the local utility companies, representatives from the school district, and representatives from the University of Arkansas at Little Rock and Arkansas Baptist College. Also represented at the early community meetings were developers and bankers. One of the most important groups represented was Arkansas Children's Hospital: A major employer in the neighborhood. Scott Gordon and Scott Allen from the hospital were then and continue to be active and helpful neighbors and partners. From the initial discussion that she and I had, to the finish of the first large-scale community meeting with the many people and groups involved, took about a year of preparation and implementation. That was the easy part.

The neighborhood embarked on creating a model for third-wave redevelopment of urban form. It included creation and implementation of a planning process designed by them for their specific situation. This would be a monumental undertaking, and the core group that began the process knew it. After another couple of years of work, the neighborhood had composed a strategic plan and a corresponding work plan which included a physical master plan for the neighborhood. Some might consider this one of the most comprehensive plans devised by any neighborhood in the nation today. This work in progress has around 120 identified initiatives, of which over 50 are in various stages of discussion or implementation. Some are merely in the talking stage and some have been completed.

The neighbors realized that an undertaking of this scope would require organizing. They would have to categorize the many initiatives identified in their community planning sessions for managerial purposes. You've seen this in previous chapters. Arranging the initiatives into common groupings would allow them to identify and combine resources more readily. For managerial and implementation purposes, the original discussions in the first set of meetings were divided into seven groups which are discussed below. These eventually were placed into five categories, "the Fundamental Five" as noted in Chapter 25.

As a quick digression, I would like to note what I think is the biggest void in this particular plan; a component that I would suggest be created by any community wanting to develop third-wave sectors of the economy within their community; a Communications Age Promotional Plan (CAPP) which would link with a physical master plan. Such a plan would give the political and business leaders a blueprint as to the types and levels of expenditures necessary to turn the economy towards those new basic sectors that can generate greater long-term sustainable revenues. The Central High Neighborhood is doing this to a certain degree with maps which identify both public-investment and private-investment opportunities. Their decision to focus their resources, as they have, excluded a definitive CAPP. They have not precluded developing or having such a plan, but as of yet it is not one of their initiatives. Bill Williamson, Dave Barlow, and I did develop a plan of that sort many years ago. We delivered it, by request, to our State Economic Development Agency. I'm not sure anyone has actually read it outside of the agency director that received it at the time, but that's okay.

The Centennial Model is a composite of all that you have read so far. The manifestation of the process which we've discussed is a series of short-term and long-term initiatives developed by the neighborhood and shown on the following pages. If your community were to engage in this process, the resulting initiatives would legitimately be different than what you will see below. The physical, economic, and social composition of your community and every community is somewhat different. Having said this, great similarities run consistent through all communities.

Within this chapter will be a shortened version of what was produced by the neighborhood. It will be loosely based on the outline noted in Chapter 30: Developing a Plan.

We began the community involvement process with a large-scale community meeting, the first "Charrette," in which we **Identified the Problems** that existed within the neighborhood and the community at large. This type of session some might term a bitch session. It is the type of engagement that allows the participants to get off their chest whatever they want, and allows others to see the scope of the undertaking. The early sessions can be terribly frustrating for some and liberating for others. Starting with the early phases and running throughout the process (which runs forever) it is wise to explain to the group as a whole how messy the process may seem at first, but not to distress over it. They will eventually see results. This type of meeting was the first of its kind to be used in the planning process for a Little Rock *neighborhood*. Stakeholders in the community were brought together for an intensive two-day session. They not only talked about the problems, but additionally identified the strengths and weakness within the neighborhood. Stakeholders included neighborhood residents, business owners, and public and private institutions with a direct interest in the area. The likes of Winthrop Rockefeller Foundation, Volunteers of America, Philander Smith College, The National Trust for Historic Preservation, 11 different departments from the City as well as the City Manager's office and the Mayor's office. We also had representatives from the Coalition of Little Rock Neighborhoods, the Transit Authority, Boatman's Bank (which is now Bank of America), Comcast, AT&T, State Representatives from the local district and many other groups and lots of neighbors.

Some of the subjects discussed during the first Charrette included historic preservation, existing and new infrastructure needs and limitations, the environment, land use and zoning, various business opportunities, cultural needs, housing, public safety, human capital, and transportation.

From those early discussions resulted a focus in seven original interest areas: housing, economic development, infrastructure and development, historic preservation, community pride, education, and civic involvement.

The second Charrette was a one-day event held about six weeks later. The intent was to encapsulate what was learned in the earlier meeting, and to begin educating ourselves about important trends and cycles. Once again, the community stakeholders were brought together. Representatives from different public and private organizations shared their plans and projects taking place throughout the neighborhood. This time, after some discussion, the participants split into five groups to vocalize things that needed to occur to revitalize the neighborhood. Each group categorized their points under the "fundamental five" topics: Economic Initiatives, Educational Initiatives, Built and Natural Environment Guidelines, Legal Guidelines, and Political Initiatives.

The group educated themselves about the particulars of the neighborhood. They decided on an initial study boundary (shown on the map below). The area initially selected was from Interstate 630 on the north, (the right side of the map) south to Roosevelt Road (the left side of the map) and Martin Luther King Jr. Drive on the east, (bottom of the map) west to the Union Pacific Rail Road tracks (top). That initial study area changed over a period of time.

You will notice on the map that the neighborhood is laid out in a basic grid pattern. It was primarily residential, though some small commercial establishments did prosper along a former streetcar line.

THE CENTENNIAL NEIGHBORHOODS

Neighborhood Boundaries

Map 1

Many of the neighborhoods' early developers and residents were the elite of the community at the time; the neighborhood remained a stable single-family environment until the mid 1950s when expansion to the west began, and many residents migrated to the new subdivisions. Race relations and integration of the schools hastened movement from the neighborhood in the form of "white flight." Gradually the neighborhood changed from single-family homeowners to single-family renters, and eventually to apartment units within what were converted single-family homes. The neighborhood was eventually separated from the downtown and State Capitol Complex by a six-lane interstate highway with four vehicular bridges which cross the interstate, and allow access into and out of the neighborhood.

Despite the sizable population, there are only a handful of retail businesses in the area. There are no fast-food establishments, and the only grocery store located in the Central High Neighborhood was closed in early 1997. The area has several large public/institutional uses. The Arkansas Children's Hospital draws patients from nationwide. Central High School has been in use since 1927. It is one of the most dominate buildings in the neighborhood.

The Central High area accounts for approximately three percent of the city's population, and the residents in the area are predominantly black: 92 percent. About 7 1/2 percent are white, and about .5 percent are considered other races. Hispanics, at the beginning of the study, accounted for about .2 percent of the population. The population of Little Rock is about 65 percent white and 35 percent black. The Central High area is about 93 percent black. Overall the Central High Neighborhood has a higher percentage of children than found throughout Little Rock. The over-65 population is the same for the Central High area as for the remainder of the city. The adult working population is a smaller percentage than that of Little Rock overall: 56 percent compared with 63 percent citywide; that is before the latest downturn (2008) in the economy. At the time we began our work in the neighborhood, 33 percent of families in the neighborhood fell below the poverty line.

A great deal of additional information was shared during the time that the neighborhood educated itself, information that we have discussed in some of the previous chapters: trends and politics and land-use law and more. What resulted from informing ourselves about a myriad of subjects was the categorization of all of the things to do, into those fundamental five. They included the economic initiatives which would create opportunity and wealth for more of the neighbors, various educational initiatives

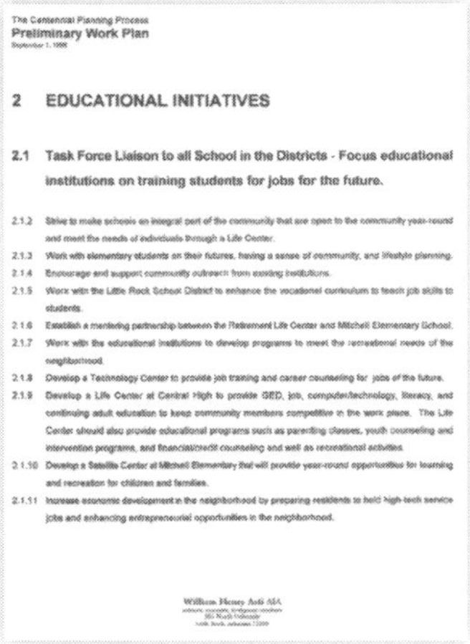

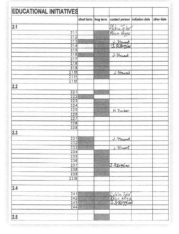

Figure 32.1

Figure 32.2

necessary to facilitate and supplement the economic initiatives, and the guidelines necessary to help develop the built and natural environment: those land use, zoning, and design guidelines. Additionally, to-do initiatives were put into the areas. They dealt with the legal initiatives necessary to implement design guidelines and land-use parameters, and political initiatives which might be required to implement all of the above components.

Each of the initiatives identified by the neighborhood were categorized into the five categories, numbered, and put in a work plan as shown to the left. Each of the initiatives were then evaluated as to whether they were long-term or short-term, shown in figure 32.2.

From that chart, individuals from within the neighborhood would then select the various initiatives on which they wanted to work. Then, each of the initiatives was evaluated as to its relevance to every other initiative. This was made in the form of a matrix. It determined where resources could be saved or utilized in better ways, and where additional help was required for implementation. That matrix is not shown, but here's an example: If an individual in the neighborhood was working on developing a design overlay district within the Built Environment Initiatives she could reference other relevant legal or political initiatives to help implement her own initiative.

As implementation of the various initiatives from the work plan began, we noticed certain more substantive initiatives either developed by the neighborhood or by me that were deemed significant enough to assign individuals to press for further development and implementation. Due to the proprietary nature of some of these initiatives, the scope of undertaking, and the voluminous nature of some of these reports, they will not be included in this book. These initiatives involved changes to institutions and process, various macro and micro initiatives, and the planning of the physical environment.

Some of the macro and micro initiatives that we worked on would ultimately alter the form of the built environment. They included an ICE Report for the State of Arkansas. It articulates two major initiatives to develop the foundation for third-wave industries within the state. This report created links to existing economic development programs for the Central High Neighborhood, as well as communities throughout the state. It also focused on the development of community strategic plans that would link to Digital Overlay Districts ©—the first one in the U.S. being in the Central High Neighborhood—and various tax-incentive programs. Additionally, this initiative was linked to third-wave industries in other states, and linked to additional initiatives in retirement-community housing and to the redevelopment efforts in other existing communities. This strategic plan was additionally linked to a Digital Product Incentive Act, which linked tax incentives to a physical location where creation, distribution and investment in digital form product could take place: the Digital Overlay Districts.©

Another initiative I mentioned earlier in this chapter was a Communications Age Promotional Plan for the State. It defines the direction of future economic growth, and describes a strategy for creation of the socioeconomic environment for specified post-industrial economic growth to take place. Here are additional initiatives in which the neighborhood either helped or has tried to further develop within the neighborhood: The alteration of intellectual property/lien laws, the EAST Initiative, a Central High technology committee, Inner City FutureNet, Property Pride Program, the saving of historic structures within the neighborhood, an urban forestry program linked to botanical educational initiatives and to the Property Pride Program, and the Central High National Park and Central High Museum and Visitors Center. The neighborhood was also involved with initiatives which focused on high-tech utilities placement, the locating of sources of investment capital, business recruitment, the creation of multiple tourism initiatives, the creation of multiple basic sector initiatives, the creation of multiple service sector initiatives, the development of public investment maps to help guide the city in making capital improvements linked to private investment maps, a means to help private investment in decisions on investment.

Within the various initiatives, the neighborhood created a parks initiative which links to educational initiatives and private initiatives and beautification of the community, as well as the expansion of the Centennial Park. They created a green space initiative, neighborhood image creators, a public relations brochure and neighborhood marketing plan. They also created an initiative for future educational initiatives in the neighborhood high school and local university, focusing on digital product training, and one of the most recent initiatives adopted by the city Board of Directors was a Design Overlay District.

As we focused on the physical environment, there were a number of the initiatives on which the neighborhood focused their attention. First was a Community Master Plan which would help direct implementation of the many initiatives related to the built environment. This Community Master Plan defined the direction of physical development and growth so as to facilitate capital investment. Based on an identified future selected by the neighborhood, the Community Master Plan was manifested in a series of maps. They described certain physical initiatives which are intended to either facilitate or augment other initiatives or fulfill certain goals or objectives. Maps were developed as guides for development of the physical world, and for focusing programs, policies and expenditures. These maps help to define the direction of physical development and growth to facilitate public and private investment, and to direct capital to facilitate returns to investors.

The maps that were developed included: Neighborhood Boundaries map, Existing Land Use map, Public Facilities/Quasi Public Facilities map, Constraints map, Land Use Alterations map, US National Parks Service Overlay map, Historic District map, Tourism Initiatives map, Green Space/Parks/Urban Forestry map, Transportation map, Image Creators/Entries to Neighborhood map, Design Overlay District map, Digital Overlay District © map, Public Investment Strategies map, Private Investment Opportunities map, Combined Investments map, A Multiple Overlay map, and a Comprehensive map.

I have included examples of a few of these maps. Significant to the process was the level of engagement on the part of the community. Although it is easier today to have maps developed on computers, we printed out maps and had individuals from the neighborhood either draw on or write on the maps we brought to the community meetings. After discussing the types of things that needed to be included on the maps, we asked that the maps be taken home and distributed around the neighborhood for direct input. The maps eventually came back marked up and ready for further discussion. The mark-ups and discussions pertained to the goals and objectives developed by the neighborhood. They were based on a common future developed and selected by the neighborhood, producing this series of maps. These maps were created right in front of the neighbors with markers in hand, not on the computer at the office. Those maps were subsequently digitally entered into the City's computer system for future land-use and zoning decisions.

A description of the maps is shown on the remaining pages of this chapter along with examples of a few of the maps.

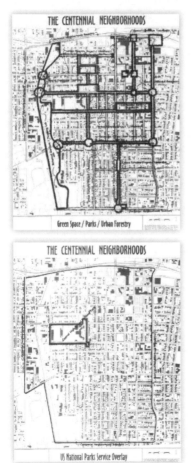

Map 2

Green Space/Parks/ Urban Forestry Map

This is a major initiative within the community based on programmatic requirements for educational space, entertainment space and recreational space. Additionally, the beautification and livability of the community are key components for the long-term development of the community. This map links to the transportation initiatives and to the public and private investment map as well as to the educational initiatives of the Property Pride Program developed by Inner City FutureNet, linking botany and landscaping initiatives to the schools and to sustainable land-use initiatives on the part of Heifer International.

Map 3

US National Parks Service Overlay Map

This map is part of a long-term initiative on the part of the neighborhood to develop a human rights institute linked to the 1957 Central High Crisis. The U.S. government finally made the school and surrounding area a national park in late 1999. This is significant for further implementation of the neighborhood goals and the numerous tourism initiatives developed by the neighborhood.

Existing Land Use—not included
This map shows the existing uses of individual buildings (created by the City).

Land Use Alterations—not included
This map is used to begin the political and legal initiatives necessary in making specific land-use changes to the City's land use map. It is also the origin for discussions pertaining to the land-use implications of a Design Overlay District. It also identifies the significant implications of the Digital Overlay District© and the multiple business incubator concept as a derivative of the ICE industry initiatives.

Map 4
Tourism Initiatives Map
This map is utilized to help the State and City Tourism officials develop a resource allocation initiative and program initiative. This is linked to the neighborhood public relations brochures and eventual videos. Additionally, the development of the tourism initiatives is linked to ICE industry development, and to service business development within the neighborhood.

Map 5
Historic District Map
This map shows the physical area of the neighborhood historic district, an area that the community has identified as necessary in disallowing any further loss of housing stock. This area is important to the development of the strategic plan for the development of a tour of historic homes and connecting the preservation initiatives with tourism initiatives.

Map 6
Transportation Map

This map shows the major throughways and transportation initiatives necessary to accomplish the neighborhood goals. It is additionally used by the neighborhood in regional transportation planning and linking to other initiatives throughout the city. This plan helps the community direct the city in their transportation expenditures and transportation enhancement expenditures within the neighborhood. It also helps to prioritize local projects on the regional network and provide intermodal connections to other initiatives in the city.

Constraints Map—not included

This map is a combination of concerns of the neighborhood. The intent is to identify physical areas which pose possible impediments to the physical and economic development of the area. These impediments can include either the physical degradation, physical constraints, crime or just activity which may be deemed as detrimental. This map is significant to the implementation of the community initiatives because it identifies physical locations of problems that the community wants to fix.

Multiple Overlays Map—not included

This map shows the relationship of the various overlays and shows a visual image of concentration of initiatives.

Comprehensive Plan Map—not included

This map shows a visual image of many of the various initiatives and the agglomeration of resources for public and private investment.

Combined Investments Map—not included

This map shows the combined public and private possibilities for investment decision making.

Map 7
Design Overlay District Map
Due to the City's developmental pressures to continue to economically segregate the city, the neighborhood intends to raise standards to attract long-term investments. The neighborhood intends on deflecting any degradation in imagery which could impede long-term economic growth, and to help guide development within certain areas of the neighborhood as pressures begin to arise due to the speculative nature of real property surrounding the new National Park.

Along with the DOD Map is the city ordinance adopted along with suggested guidelines for design and construction within the DOD. This is a 100-page booklet used by the neighborhood to aid developers and contractors build within the neighborhood.

Image Creators/Entries to Neighborhood
and Sign Locator Map—*not included*
This is a location map for directing people throughout the neighborhood, identifying significant locations for self-guided tours and defining the edges of and the entries to the neighborhood.

Public Facilities/Quasi Public Facilities Map—*not included*
A visual image of those facilities which the community felt could work as resources for the educational, social and economic development initiatives. This map helps the community to make decisions as to the possibilities of concentration of initiatives.

Map 8
Public Investment Strategies Map
This map shows where concentration of resources can cause the greatest benefit, and helps to prioritize public expenditures and attract private investment.

Map 9
Private Investment Opportunities Map
This map is one of the most important to the neighborhoods. An aberration for most communities, this map is a catalyst for discussions with private investors, inviting them to see the potential returns within certain areas of the community.

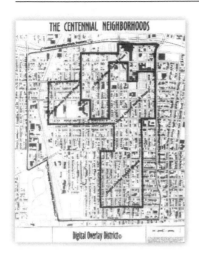

Map 10
Digital Overlay District© Map
This is the first of a kind in the U.S. This type of overlay district, if linked to appropriate tax law has the ability to alter land use. This map additionally helps to direct private investment dollars in telecommunications infrastructure.

33

Creating your own Sustainable Community

Assuming your community would like to become truly sustainable, you can do a number of things to prepare yourself for stepping into this new era. You can become one of the many economically vibrant global communities, which will help the United States and the world become sustainable. First, acknowledge that you and your community have the ability and the where-with-all to make it happen. Remember that you are the chicken. Secondly, recognize that you don't need the existing power structure to get started. Quite honestly, your activism takes the burden off the existing governing institutions to perform. Their dilemma has been, and will continue to be, that they have to deal with special interests and politics differently than do you. Most local governments are burdened with trying to manage what is already on their plate. This brings us to a third thing for which you should be aware and put into practice: institutional and procedural changes. We have talked about this throughout this book. Being cognizant of it and integrating it into all that you do is difficult and important. Never kid yourself about the functional limitations of governing institutions. And always be aware of the differences between your local governing structures and state and federal structures. The locals are those with whom you want to foster a relationship, and with whom you want to work, and who you want to help. You shouldn't waste your time with the state and federal structures. They can be useful in accomplishing certain tasks down the road, but they are not important to developing your plans for your future sustainable community.

Here's the issue in dealing with any governing body: Most, if not all, who work for governing agencies want to help. That's different than being compelled to help. If we, meaning citizens, the media, and our politicians—those who define the world using the crossfire syndrome— continue to blame the governing institutions and bureaucrats for all that's wrongs in the world, then understand this: They will be compelled to take over those tasks and take responsibility for everything we're blaming them for. If the political structure thrusts at them additional work, then they will over a period of time define the work that they will have to accomplish, and they will define it so that they will be successful. Do you see the folly in that? That is a much different institutional goal and institutional function than what you should be trying to accomplish. Try not to fall into that trap.

As an aside, let me give you a couple of examples, one on a federal level and another on a local level. This deals with functional limitations of certain institutions, and specifically with the issue of developing new local institutions to focus on creating sustainable communities.

From 1952 till about 2000, I had been through every hurricane that grazed or hit Miami, with exception of Hurricane Andrew, one of the most powerful and devastating hurricanes in history. If I wasn't living in Miami, I would always fly down to be with my parents for all the major storms. The reason I wasn't there for Andrew was because I was sailing with my daughter from Martha's Vineyard to Maine with our dear friends Sandy Schlicker and Bill Renfro. As an aside to the aside, my sailing vacation would have been considered as one of those eco-friendly carbon footprint forms of entertainment ... had it not been for my daughter and me taking airplanes, rental cars, cabs, ferries and other forms of transportation to get to the boat. Anyway, during our trip we would listen to the marine radio, following the whereabouts and strength of the hurricane, because we were concerned about our family in Miami.

As soon we got home from the sail, I turned around to go to Miami to be with mom and dad and my friends. What I saw in South Florida was overwhelming. The shear devastation from the winds was incomprehensible. As far as you could see in all directions, Florida City was gone. Every house destroyed. Devastation that displaced hundreds of thousands of people. Individual lives that needed help because we weren't prepared to deal with a storm of that magnitude. I mention this because over the many years leading up to the Andrew disaster, and eventually the Katrina disaster in New Orleans, we had been gradually moving towards creating communities less and less able to fend for themselves. Less sustainable communities. And we have been gradually developing institutions compelled to help due to our individual inabilities to help ourselves. Should it be that way? Probably not, but that's not the point if you want to develop a sustainable community. It is a trend for which you need to be aware, and you need to address these types of shortcomings in your future plans.

When Hurricane Donna hit us in the '60s many of us actually lived in a more sustainable fashion. I mentioned earlier that, when I was young, I didn't know that there was any other way of heating domestic hot water than with a flat-plate collector on the roof. That's what we had, and that's all I knew. Likewise, if we thought or knew a hurricane was coming, we would fill our bathtubs with water for flushing our toilets—with well water and no power there was no pressure for moving the water through the pipes. The old Miami house that I grew up in had been built in the first decade of the 1900s. No air-conditioning and plenty of screened porches to live in when the temperature got too high. It had gas for cooking and boiling water in the event the power was out due to a hurricane, and we had a big storage closet with all of the canned goods and necessities for a month. One of the big deals after a hurricane hit was that no one, and I mean no one, was allowed to open the refrigerator or freezer except mom for fear that we would ruin what was being kept cold. She knew exactly where everything was located.

After my parents moved into a smaller house with all electricity in the mid-'70s, they made sure that they always had enough propane gas available for cooking on a Coleman stove, and plenty of canned food and bottled water on hand in the event of a hurricane. The city government back then did their best to pick up the debris as fast as they could. Florida Power and Light tried to get the electricity on as quickly as they could. You might be without power for as much as two weeks. You could listen to a local radio station on your portable radio to find out what was going on, if you had plenty of batteries, and you and your neighbors helped each other. Within a few days or so, the Red Cross and some others would show up to help those who were in real need.

When a disaster confronts us, the issue of sustaining one's self really hits home. The issue of developing sustainable communities able to withstand natural disasters becomes even more apparent in those areas and communities that are prone to disasters. This is why I had suggested in an earlier chapter that reviewing the principles from the Wingspread Conference could be advantageous to your own initiative. This was a conference which focused on the development of sustainable communities in disaster-prone areas. You know, like all the coastal areas and earthquake areas and tornado areas of the world.

Building in the desert where there isn't any water to sustain life may seem perplexing to me, but to build complex, man-made environmental systems that are in disaster prone areas isn't folly. It's just not real bright. The cost for replacement after a disaster doesn't make us more competitive, it makes us less competitive. Especially when we rebuild the same inefficient forms that existed before, which means it makes us less sustainable over the long run. It means that everything we produce to create wealth to sustain a complex economy is more expensive than it needs to be, especially to be competitive. It means insurance goes up, it means investments will go down. It means over the long run capital will find its way to those places where returns have less risks or can be guaranteed. Creating sustainable communities under this model means to link all of this to the issue of your community's defined sustainable investment strategies. One caveat here: The federal government will have to, at some point in time, pass legislation that will allow for long-term investment portfolios to benefit over the short-term portfolios. That's in contrast to what has happened in the past 10 to 15 years and to what has caused the 2008 financial meltdown.

My friend Rod, from Miami, had been through all of the same hurricanes I had been through, including Andrew. At the time Katrina hit, he was living in New Orleans. Being sensitive to the devastation of hurricanes and knowing what hurricane preparedness was all about, he knew that he wasn't properly prepared. He also knew that New Orleans was below sea level, prone to having a major disaster. So, he got out of there. He left New Orleans two full days before the hurricane hit, and a day before the mass exodus occurred. It seems odd that he was able to see this and act upon it, but those that knew New Orleans the best and those who lived in one of the most susceptible areas on earth to a natural disaster were oblivious. This isn't about people not knowing what to do, but is a good example of the egg coming first. This is an example of institutional incompetence, where we have allowed ourselves to defer to the decision making of the institutions that surround us. This is one of those examples of the institutions having been in control of the lives of the individuals for such a long period of time, the individual succumbed to the will of the institutions. This ought to be a really good example as to why you don't want existing governing institutions to control the process for developing your future sustainable community.

Continuing on this train of thought, the Federal Emergency Management Agency came to New Orleans to help a community that was institutionally dysfunctional with respect to living and developing in a sustainable fashion. FEMA and other federal agencies got blamed for causing the misery in a community that was intellectually dishonest about the nature of sustainability. As we noted in earlier chapters, having a scapegoat is much easier than understanding that you are part of a problem, and that the institutions surrounding you are doing what they were set up to do. Due to numerous generations deferring to the surrounding institutions, it was actually a given that many in New Orleans would react the way that they did, just as it would be for many other communities around the world. I will hasten to note that, as understandable as were the behaviors exhibited after the Katrina disaster, it is equally understandable to note the vehemently negative reactions from those not supported by the same types of institutions. Recognizing this is foundational in developing the needed institutional changes if you are to create your own sustainable community: Altering institutions, processes and behaviors, these are the keys to creating sustainable communities.

The function of FEMA, that is to say the Congressional mandate for FEMA, was not to preempt and give money to those who have been damaged as a result of a natural disaster. Its function is to help coordinate relief efforts after a disaster occurs. As a result of the crossfire syndrome in our media and in our politicians, FEMA has become another bastardized institution. An institution that 15 years ago could engage in honest policy-making about disallowing the rebuilding of communities in disaster-prone areas to that of now participating in the allocation of massive amounts of aid to perpetuate unsustainable communities … at the risk of being crucified.

Knowing that these are the type of institutional problems which well up from within governing institutions and other existing institutions, the question for you in developing a sustainable community is this: Is that the type of institution or governing body that you want helping you develop a sustainable community, where the essence of sustainability is that of rational decision making and honesty?

After the Central High Neighborhood had finished its first round of community meetings, they initiated and conducted a follow-up meeting with all of the many interest groups from within the community to discuss the outcomes of the early charrettes. During the follow-up meeting, the City folks said that they would take over and continue the planning process for the neighborhood, and would implement the processes they were using in all of the other neighborhoods around the city. Their generous offer was met with a rebuke from the neighborhood. The excoriation on the part of the neighborhood didn't settle real well at first. It was a source of some conflict for a period of time, but that was to be expected. That is the nature of institutional conflict. Be prepared for it.

The neighborhood did not want to be pre-empted by the same institutions that had created some of the most inefficient built environments in the city's history. Besides, the neighborhood had as its overall goal that of becoming a sustainable community, whereas the city had no such goal. This inherent conflict many times manifests itself in institutional and personal battles. Be careful that you don't let that happen to you. We were lucky because we happened to have kind and bright planners. Regardless of the method of interface and the underlying institutional conflict, they were always available to help. It also helped to have a city manager and a mayor that understood that this process would not be easy, and would require patience from all parties.

What does this have to do with creating your own sustainable community? Everything! Be responsible, think ahead, and don't depend on institutions that may not be functional for your specific purpose. Remember, if the existing institutions were functioning to create sustainable communities ... it already would have been done. Don't follow them and don't let them lead. Get out front.

Part of that which many times overwhelms our governing systems, and part of the source of frustration for many of our governing agencies, and part of what causes certain governing institutions to function in an intractable fashion is this: the prospect of or reality of more work outside the definition of what they already do. That's why we tend to create new agencies that seem redundant, and that don't work with existing agencies. Do you think that existing governing bureaucracies want more work or want to take on a greater part of the economy? Well, you're in part wrong and part right. On the one hand, more work is an additional burden. Yet on the other hand, to the professional bureaucrat it means job security: the expansion of work activities as well as an increased chance for advancement along with a retirement that beats anything. That's as good as it gets for those few that don't do anything, or don't know what is going on around them. Having said this, always keep in the back of your mind that the bureaucrats are, in fact, your friends. There are brilliant planners in communities all over this nation that know what to do and how to do it. I've found over the years that they want to be helpful. They would love to participate in making their own communities more sustainable, but coordinating a massive undertaking is typically not part of their job description. The question for you is: Do you want this to be part of their job description? If you do, you will be burdened with a bureaucracy that may not function in the ways that you want. So don't press your politicians too hard. They may want to help by getting involved; which means more ego and possibly more bureaucrats.

Remember, the politicians typically follow trends. Once they realize the trend, they will want to get in front. They will require results differently than you. Their results are short–term, so they can look good for the next election. Your results are to create a sustainable community which might require some political help. You may have to walk a very tight rope.

What to do next? Once you get started, you should organize a core group of individuals. When forming your community's core group, I might suggest that you start with individuals who are knowledgeable about your community and care about its future. Then ask the following questions: What do you want to accomplish in your community through this process? Who can help you accomplish that? What critical issues are most likely to surface as you discuss this in your community and group? What organizations, companies, and institutions need to be involved to address these issues and legitimize this effort in your community? What organizations, companies, and institutions need to be involved who have a real stake in your community and make key decisions that affect its future? What organizations, companies, and institutions need to be involved which could contribute financial or in-kind resources to this effort?(Have them send a real functioning representative to serve on your group.) What organizations, companies, and institutions need to be involved to insure a broad-based representation of your entire community? Which individuals care about these issues and can be spark plugs to address them? Which individuals know how to organize and get things done? Which individuals are respected by particular groups or parts of your community? Which individuals are willing to commit the time and energy for this to be successful in your community?

Another bit of advice, don't just talk about these things. Make sure you write down your questions and your answers so that you can revisit them periodically.

It is important to extract from this core group, as well as those that come along in the interim, an admission that your community needs to possess or develop the knowledge, strategies and tools needed today and tomorrow to develop these initiatives: efforts that will attract long-term sustained investment capital and aid your community in competing in a global economy. This minimum level of acknowledgment will signify to others the willingness to engage in selecting a specific future which will be the controlling mechanism by which **ALL** decisions will be made. This allows for your community to be proactive rather than waiting for decisions made beyond your geographic boundaries to impact your destiny. It also helps those in the investment community know that you will be developing a long–term plan which will focus on the ability of the private sector, and the public sector as well, to repay debt. Hopefully that doesn't need to be explained. If it does, give me a call.

What some call a visioning process is a good starting point. I must warn you, 98% of what communities do in these processes are worthless, unless a definitive future is selected and there is an overriding focus on repayment of debt. If there is not that controlling mechanism, you will assure yourself of repeating the same political mistakes which have made most of our communities so terribly inefficient, and made your own community desirous of trying to figure out what to do.

After you and your committee have decided that your community is capable of competing and is worth living in, then you need to develop certain operating principles. These might include forming strategic partnerships between the public, private and nonprofit sectors at all levels. This will lead to collaborative work and action, as well as developing a broad base of leaders who see the big picture. It will also involve others in developing a shared vision and empowering your community to shape its future. Additional operating principles might include the development of a strategic vision and an implementation plan that can prepare your community for the future. You can build on the assets of your community and increase the capacity of the institutions, organizations, companies and individuals within it. One necessary operating principle would be to nourish sustainable development of the whole community. You do this by creating broad-based initiatives that address economic, educational, legal and political components of the community, as well as quality-of-life issues to include the livability and efficiency of the community under initiatives of the built and natural environment.

Operating principles which focus on fostering an entrepreneurial world that enables your private, public and nonprofit sectors to be more productive in the global economy would be helpful. Along with this, explore the use of technology and communication product to enhance development within your community; and increase access to resources in your community, your state, your nation and the world that support the development of your community. A focus on implementation and accountability, moving from good intentions to practical results, and from activities to real outcomes are the type of operating principles which can guide your process Add to this the principle of creating incentives for innovation and rewarding activity that's desired.

After developing your Operating Principles, it is vital that you build leadership capability from those within your community. Some advice ...

you've got to get past the ego model of leadership. Develop the new leaders from motivated individuals. Having bright leaders helps, but it shouldn't supersede motivated individuals who never give up and are tenacious. Egos can play a vital role, but they should not be the pivotal role. Many times they are fragile, and if they break, the ego-laden individuals may take their ball and go home.

Develop a community training and implementation program designed to launch your community into the future: Year one for training and planning, and year two for implementation to see new technologies, acquire vital skills and learn about resources. Seminars should be held around the community at large to address strategic visioning, economic development, education and workforce preparation, health and safety, natural resources and local government, to name a few. Try to connect these subjects. Dot connecting is important from the beginning. It can be overwhelming to some early on, but once it becomes a part of the thought process, you will find that these individuals are the best advocates.

The purpose in building your leadership capability is so you develop visionary leaders who understand this new era. They must have the knowledge, tools and access to information that will enable them to weave the fabric of your community's future. Special training sessions should be provided for a few individuals from each identified community sector, who could serve as designated facilitators. They'll help lead a strategic visioning process that involves your community in identifying critical issues, creating a strategic vision and action plan to address these issues and implementing that plan. For communities that already have a strategic plan, there are mechanisms to update their plan for the communications age in a global economy, and to truly define a future which the community can get behind. An understanding of technology and the ICE Age products, and product creators and providers, will enable you to accomplish your community's goals more effectively.

To really create a strategic planning process, your community must be realistic about the time frame involved. You must think about the process required leading up to a start date. Your community needs to define itself and its geographic boundaries by neighborhoods, city limits, school districts, trade area, county lines, half of a county, multi-communities or some other configuration. It needs to gain the formal commitment of a broad-based group of key organizations, institutions and companies from within the identified area, including your appropriate local unit(s) of government. Another necessary component in creating a viable strategic planning process would be for your group to form a broad-based steering committee, differentiated from the original core group. I would suggest an odd number of somewhere between nine to 15 members that represent various organizations and are willing to commit to the planning process for at least a two-year period. With this group in place, select a leadership team of five individuals and two alternates from the steering committee. They will participate in the seminars and return to lead the strategic visioning process in your identified area. Also select two individuals from the leadership team who are willing to serve as designated facilitators for the entire process. We did that in the Central High Neighborhood, with me and the president of the neighborhood group.

If this is a larger community-wide undertaking, it is important to raise adequate funding to cover the expenses of the leadership team, and other expenses incurred in the planning process. You must also fund an implementation period in your community and pay a facilitator that knows something about implementing futures. Also, make sure you have a designated outside organization to be the fiscal agent for the steering committee. Don't get into the trap of the steering committee handling the money. There are too many occasions where perception can override reality. And don't allow any governing bodies to control the purse strings. There will be politics enough involved in the process without allowing the agenda of some politician, who could conceivably control funding, to get in the middle of the process.

The fun begins when you have your initial community meetings. Your community should actually host these meetings. Hosting meetings for itself and the facilitator give a chance for the facilitator to engage directly with citizens. This process is unencumbered by filters and proves to the community the willingness to participate in the visioning and planning process. These community meetings give an opportunity to identify the most critical issues facing your community, those things that are holding your community back, or those with the potential to move your community forward.

As for your preparation going into the community meetings, start by answering some of the following questions, and be prepared to change your answers depending on the community responses. What is the name of your community, county or area? What geographic area does it cover? What boundaries did you select for your plan? Why did you choose these boundaries? What is the population of the area, and how would you describe the population?

Describe current activities: What is going on in your community as it relates to technology, Internet access, use of computers and other technology by companies, organizations and institutions. Has your community (or a part of your community) undertaken a strategic planning process within the past five years? If so, for what purpose? How would your community's participation in a new planning process relate to that process?

Describe possible community involvement and support: The critical issues facing your community. How did you arrive at these issues? Describe the organizations that have agreed to co-sponsor a planning process and to serve on your steering committee, including local units of government. Explain how they represent the people and issues in your community.

Provide a list of your possible steering committee members, their occupations and involvement in community organizations. Provide a list of your leadership team members and alternates, and how they reflect the critical issues identified in your community. Who might be chosen to be your designated facilitators? What background and experience do they bring into the vision and planning process? Which organization is your fiscal agent? Who will perform the necessary staffing functions?

As for financial support for the process: Describe the funds you have available, or will have available for the implementation of the visioning and the planning process, and the source of these funds. What other resources can you leverage through your community's involvement in the process?

Finally, you need to articulate the desire of the community in participating in a visioning and planning process: Why do you need to participate in this process, and why do you need to participate in the process now? Describe what degree of importance your community would place on this effort, and describe how other communities or neighboring communities could benefit from your community participating in a visioning and planning process.

Be prepared to discuss the nature of the "new economy" and how to compete more effectively in a global economy. Helping your community better understand the functioning of the basic sectors of the economy is crucial. If the development of new sectors within your existing economy is desired, or the diversification of the existing economy is desired, it will be necessary to develop a "Communications Age Promotional Plan" (CAPP) or something equivalent. Should this be the will of the citizens, such a plan can be created by the cooperative efforts of the business community, local government or other governing entity, and the educational community working toward common goals, with the help from people like me. This type of plan should be discussed in the community meetings, and how such a plan can move business and government to focus on educational preparedness for the postindustrial jobs, and developing long-term substantive jobs that create wealth for the community and its citizens. If the generation of a CAPP is decided upon, the integration of such into your community's master plan (what your community will be in the future) should be conducted to direct future capital investment into the built and natural environment, thereby helping to secure long-term returns on investment. This should be done in concert with the design of a promotional package, and the development of a master plan which will appeal to targeted industry groups and individual companies, inviting their participation in the effort.

Here's a simple outline of what has been discussed above:

- Form Strategic Partnerships.

- Develop a broad base of leaders through community training.

- Understand the Components by forecasting and understanding trends.

- Create a Plan
  - Develop a Strategic Vision
  - Develop precise Goals and Objectives for Implementation.
  - Develop a Strategic / Implementation Plan
  - Develop Policy Recommendations
  - Develop a Communications Age Promotional Plan (if a post industrial economy is selected)
  - Design a Promotional Package
  - Create a Community Master Plan
  - Identify Investment opportunities for the Private & Public Sectors
  - Develop an Investment Matrix
  - Develop a Private Investment Strategy
  - Develop a Public Investment Strategy

- Implement the Plan
  - Create a decisive Action Plan
  - Supervise the Implementation

Now you are ready to enter the future ... a future which allows your community to participate in a global movement to create sustainable communities. A future which allows you and your community to develop and implement a planning model to help you further the development of local, state and national objectives of creating efficient and livable communities: Communities able to sustain their economies, as well as their natural and built environments, in a more competitive global economy. Communities which will assure a promising future for our kids. A future which will show your respect for your environs, and your love and respect for those around you—present and future.

34

THE END

I try to have a pen and paper in fairly close proximity when I listen to radio programs or watch TV. That's just in case I need to jot down some notes, or maybe buy one of those only-on-TV special doo-wop music collections from some terribly interesting 3 a.m. infomercial; nothing worse than a telephone number on the TV screen that you need to write down and not having anything to write with. I try to scribble what I think are interesting thoughts so I can go back and revisit them periodically. I normally put these notes in my To-Do file so I have to actually look at them. After about two or three years I clean out the file to make room for other notes. If it is a real good thought, it might make it through a couple of clean-outs.

Sometime in mid-to-late 1993, I was listening to National Public Radio. The particular program was a presentation by Michael Crichton, an extremely brilliant guy with whose talents I had been fascinated for many years. My interest was piqued and my pen was in hand. This particular day and for this particular presentation, I found myself frantically writing down as much as I could and in a particular form because Mr. Crichton's presentation was so compelling … To this day, I'm not sure if I can tell you what the presentation was about; but I remember that the structure of his presentation and his logic was so believable and meticulous that I found myself wanting to write everything down so I could emulate it. I mention this because the first time I referred to those notes was later that same year. I was preparing a presentation on governance to a local chapter of the Daughters of the American Revolution. I tried desperately then, as I still do today, to remember Michael Crichton's thought process and poetic rhythm.

I revisited the lecture that I gave to the DAR as I began this book, because I believe the content is as relevant today as it was 17 years ago. I believe it encapsulates much of what we have talked about and, in a not so concise manner, brings our discussion to some form of closure.

The presentation was titled: "Governance, Politicians and How We Physically Develop Our Society OR the Course of Capitalism in a Truly Democratic World." (I like to give long titles to my paintings and sculptures as well.) Some of what is written below came from that presentation. Hopefully in a compelling way, it's similar to what I learned from Michael Crichton.

As noted throughout this book, about 30years ago I designed a city of the future that dealt with issues of transportation, security and safety, image, leisure, the arts, recreation, education, economic development, politics, legal issues, revitalization, housing, the built and natural environment and governance. Those are many of the crucial initiatives established by most communities which try to plan for their future. How all of these issues agglomerate to create policies and programs, how all of these subjects merge to create an overall direction that allows for programmed societal development, and how all of these areas come together to allow us to physically develop our cities is what we have discussed throughout this book, and what I hope to recap.

We see certain types of real-estate developments which can affect our communities and are opposed prior to their completion. We see developments which are picketed or opposed prior to conception, or in some cases find extreme opposition once an idea is floated. What we are seeing in these cases is a populace that believes this: The powers that be are indifferent to what really matters. They believe that the politicians and developers are not solving our neighborhoods' problems, our city's problems, our state's problems, or our country's problems, but they are part of the problem. The populace sees no difference between the narcissistic self-serving developer who tries to push through another short sighted non-sustainable project and the narcissistic self-serving politicians who don't ask the key questions on how we as a society want to develop. Nor do they seek concrete, creative solutions.

There are a number of responses that politicians and developers have to opposition. The classic one is: "We're just trying to do what's best for the community, but there's this vocal minority that opposes everything that we try to do." Then there's this: "Why are people against growth? ... Everybody should be for growth." This deflects from the real issue. Then the politicians respond with: "This is a time for reflection." Or the best one of all: "We should bring in some experts and have a study made." Then they get an expert with a focus on solutions which best represents the politicians' point of view. These types of responses show that the politicians and developers may not understand cause and effect. They're idiots: the Jay Leno type of idiots. What causes this type of behavior? Many times we believe something may not be true, so therefore we won't try it or we won't discuss it. Politicians and developers are no different. They, and us, tend to see the way the world is, and then surmise that's how it is supposed to be. It's hard for an enlightened populace to sympathize with that.

As we discuss the peculiarities of developing the built environment, the question for us should be: Why should we as the consumer or constituent be unhappy with the same junk that every other American city has? Why shouldn't every city look and be the same as a hundred or a thousand other cities? Why should we as the consumer or constituent be unhappy with developments that don't distinguish one place from any other place in the United States, and eventually—watch out!—every other place on earth? This is what the French have been complaining about for 15 or 20 years, and what other parts of the world are beginning to complain about today. Where do we get off thinking that each of our communities can be different and even better than other parts of the world; and maybe even reflective of our specific environs: sympathetic to our topography, responsive to our local flora and fauna, and to the weather patterns? Oh yeah ... that's what we use to do before cheap energy and developers took over the building of our communities. Based on this trend, just think, one day we will be able to go to Afghanistan and find a community that looks just like one in which we live in America. How fun is that?

The agglomeration and globalization of our banking industries has exacerbated this trend. If local communities and governments don't take action to counter such efforts and to mandate green buildings and sustainable land-use patterns, the problem will get worse. The hope is that the people with the power—the financial institutions, not the politicians—will alter their lending requirements. This will have every developer becoming an expert in sustainability overnight, and then politicians will lead by following the trend.

Now, let's shift to our current concept of urban development and planning: It is out-moded. And it's what I have hopefully correlated with the trends in democracy in the world, in the United States, and yes in our own communities and neighborhoods. Set aside the typical platitudes for a moment of developers, politicians, developments, planning, economic models, and projections on growth. Let's just talk about quality. Real-estate development as it relates to the development of a community is an industry. Their product is space for human habitation with all of its implications and manifestations. Along with many other American industries, the real estate development community in most parts of the country creates a product of very poor quality. Flashy but basically junk, because their focus is to do the minimum they can get by with to make a buck. Their focus, because of their appropriate need to repay their loans, has not been on creating green buildings or sustainable communities or high quality buildings—structures which last for five hundred years, or magnificent spaces which elevate the human spirit.

Poor product quality as well as lousy politicians stem in part from the American educational system. It graduates individuals and workers too poorly educated to generate high-quality developments or, for that matter, high-quality politicians. It's a problem of short-sighted management. In part, it's a failure to respond to changes in the world and changes in technology. In a larger part, it's a failure to respond to changes in demographics and changes with the consumer.

Instead of focusing on quality, developers have tried to be engaging, selling the sizzle and not the steak, the amenities and not the total design. Or like in television: Selling the talk show host, not the quality of talk; the format not the subject. Which form in this panorama of government, planning, developing, will be the next GM, an institution that finds itself obsolete and outmoded with a labor force that refuses to change?

We know we have failed to respond to the change in consumer demand and consumer behavior. Here's an example: I had a client that lived in an upper-income part of town who indignantly questioned why Wal-Mart had to rape the land where they intended to build. This wasn't your radical conservationist. This was a conservative housewife married to a doctor. She will in fact be shopping at the store she berated for not being sensitive to the environment, because all other alternatives are just the same. Why? Because our community, like most communities, believes that the "system" won't allow them to make changes. They are responsive to the governing institutions and to the ordinances created for the perseveration of the institution. They don't realize that we are the Chickens and we can change the outcomes. We, in fact, can create sustainable and humane environments. We are in charge in a democracy, but that's a lot of work … and bureaucrats are like every other couch potato out there. Why exert ourselves and create all this change when everything is rocking along just fine? Why shouldn't we continue to be oblivious to the fact that our collective actions are creating extreme inefficiencies which will severely impede our ability to compete in the next 50 years or to sustain ourselves. Answer: It's like my friend Roger Armbrust said ... "Because we have to quit poisoning our earth, our water, our air, and oh yeah ... ourselves."

Do you want to survive in a more competitive global economy? Do you want to maintain a decent standard of living for your kids and grandkids as well as for people around the world? Then you and I need to set the ground rules (laws and ordinances) that will allow individuals and companies involved in real-estate development to compete equitably. Laws that allow boards of financial institutions to establish loan standards for development which directs funding only to those communities with real long-term strategic plans in place. And these plans must be based on an identified future which will help secure long-term sustainable investments. Those communities that don't want such strategic plans combined with corresponding work plans and ordinances should be allowed to dry up and blow away. The communities that create the efficiencies allowing us to compete more effectively over a longer period of time, exacerbated by focused investments from the financial community, will flourish. They will be able to repay debt over a longer period of time. This is part of what we termed throughout this book as "Sustainable Investment Strategies," the key to creating sustainable communities. The other communities won't actually dry up and blow away. They will eventually come around. If they don't, they're idiots: the Jay Leno type.

The financial community has massive power in developing sustainable economies and sustainable communities ... they either just don't know it or haven't figured out how to make it happen. Banks and other financial institutions, in this current national and global financial crisis, have the opportunity like many other companies have had over the past couple of decades. They can go though the painful restructuring to produce high quality products: flattening the corporate hierarchy, moving critical information from the bottom up instead of from the top down, empowering workers, localizing decision making and problem solving. Changing the system, not just the focus of the corporation, and relentlessly driving toward a quality product produced at a better price. This chance to restructure investment portfolios, which reflect long-term sustainable investment strategies, can move the nation towards real sustainability. A radical change like that could have happened with the large financial institutions under the government bailout. Will it happen? Probably not, but we can have "hope" and we the people, not just the politicians, can say "yes we can."

Is that type of institutional alteration happening with our governance or with our developments, or for that matter, with our educational system?

No. Improved quality requires a change in the existing structure and the existing institutions.

Is any of what is happening to our economy good or bad? And, what does all this mean to us? Well, the good part is that it can change all of our lives. The bad part is that it can change all of our lives. Because of just that, politicians that talk about change, and the electorate that vote for change, tend to get scared of what they can't see. Change for change sake tends not to solve problems. Unless all the changes in programs, policies, and expenditures, in both the public sector and private, are focused on driving towards the same identified future. Good luck getting a politician to actually quit squirming long enough to articulate a future without equivocating. This is why the hope for creating sustainable communities lies at the feet of our financial institutions in a democratic capitalistic system.

We can only hope that our governing institutions will morph into a form that is responsive. That it will be a catalyst for the relationship between developers, banks, and the communities to change so that the risks are lowered over the long run for bank investments. So that bankers and developers engage consumers in a process that allows the buyer to get a product that has greater longevity, and is a part of a community that is efficient … remembering that all of our inefficiencies in the built environment go into the price of all of the goods and services that we produce. It's to the bank's long-term interest that communities become efficient and sustainable. They have a real financial stake in the outcomes. Politicians and developers don't have the same financial stake, due to the nature of what they do.

We spend more for our environs than we do for basic sustenance. We don't pay because we think we get good developments. We pay because that is what's available. What if somebody offered developments of extremely high quality NOT High Price? … where transportation was taken into consideration; where security and safety, image, leisure and the arts were taken into consideration; where recreation, education and economic development were taken into consideration; where revitalization, housing, the environment, governance, cultural diversity, public service and health and human services were taken into consideration; a sustainable community able to attract long-term investments, sustainable investments. What would that be worth to a community trying to "grow" or trying to manage a rapidly growing environment? A lot.

Good quality sustainable developments in a community and in a city have great value. This notion—that developments created in every other city are good enough for you and your own community—is an outmoded idea. It does not take our country into the future. It does not create the sustainable environments able to repay debt over the long run. It puts your community where others have been for the past 40 to 50 years. And your problems will mirror theirs as you emulate the past. We see this all over the country.

Another trend exists that we as consumers want: direct input and access to government and how our communities develop. Increasingly, the people expect to get it. Because of technology our expectations have changed. Once upon a time we would pick up a phone and an operator would come on and make a call for us. Now, if you ever had the experience of being in a situation where someone else has to make the call for you, you know how exasperating it can be. We can all do it faster and better ourselves. Increasingly the consumer wants to remove the layers of bureaucracy of government and developers, so their own input is heard and acted upon. It is becoming the expectation. We are beginning to see the restructuring of, if not the end of, the individual type developer that just takes without inputs from the users or the populous. Once the masses are exposed to alternative methods, the monopoly ends. The banks will follow the investments where they will make money, and the trend of sameness and mediocrity will end … assuming a few significant things come to pass.

This may be 10 years or 50 years away. Regardless, we have seen the start. We are at the crossroads of creating sustainable communities. The question for us is: Do we want to recognize it and embrace it, or do we want to fight it?

There is an acceptance that superficiality is the norm, and everybody knows it. Our response is not to act to solve problems, but to endlessly debate. As noted earlier, how we frame our debates is of critical importance. *We ask Mr. Developer: Aren't you ruining the inner city… raping the land and causing misery in our neighborhoods? Mr. Neighborhood activists: aren't you against growth?* The same types of questions are being asked, and in the same manner, in reference to the Gulf of Mexico oil debacle.

Two points need to be made. First, the structure of the question dictates the answer. No one will say they are bad, mean, or against growth. Secondly, the most important point: such questions assume a simplified either/or version of reality to which no one subscribes. We don't want simplistic questions and simplistic answers. This is an anomaly. We go about our lives which are specific and complex. Then we go to our community meetings to discuss urban policy issues and hopefully issues of sustainability; but interactions are general and simplified. Why? Michael Crichton had said it's because it is easy to behave this way. He said it doesn't take a lot to answer questions such as: Are we doing enough? Are we doing too much? Is it fair? Is it really the best way of going about it? He said that this procedure is a way of hiding institutional incompetence.

Let's say I'm a city board member. I don't know much about current trends in city and urban development, or issues on planning or sustainability; but we are going to have a meeting dealing with these issues. I've got one hour to prepare. I'll ask questions about what the consultants found out. The questions then look something like this. *Are our policies for growth fair as they exist today? Is expansion happening too fast? Are we doing enough? Is it happening too slow? Are our expenditures in the inner city enough? Is it fair? Can we compete with other cities of the same size with our current budget? Should we add more staff?* That should just about do it. These generalities create a fundamental asymmetry between subject matter and politician, and politician and constituent or consumer. The politician justifies the questions by saying the constituent just wants the basics. They don't want details. The politician can blame his or her own poor behavior on the constituents, AND if they complain you are merely the bearer of bad news.

The question for us should be: Do we need a city board or a group of developers to act as filters? Answer … Yes and no. But this idea—that I don't have time for those things that interest me or are important to me—is an incorrect notion. What the constituents are saying is that the questions are poorly researched, often uninteresting and in all likelihood irrelevant. The insistence to be general rather than specific has many unhappy consequences. It is inherently superficial and it is also inherently speculative. It focuses on attitude and what people think, not on what they do; which may be contradictory.

We are expected to reside at one extreme of the opinion spectrum or the other: Pro-abortion or anti-abortion and nothing in between. We are for growth or against growth and nothing in between. In the real world, few of us hold these extreme views. There exists a spectrum of opinion. The extreme positions of the Crossfire Syndrome require extreme simplification, which requires framing the debate to ignore the real issues. The real issue IS NOT growth in your city … does it make sense? The real issue IS NOT should your city have an urban policy. It is whether the one you have (which in most cases is not adhered to, because no policy is a policy) serves you well. The real issue IS NOT whether the growth in your city is appropriate? It IS how your area should respond to domestic and foreign competition, and how the issue of sustainability can impact your long-term ability to compete.

The fundamental question or notion of how to control our developments, or what some want to categorize as growth, must address the nature of growth. The beliefs that developers have—that someone is going to do it, so I might as well before they do—is the core of the problem that cities and communities must address.

Polarization may be useful in getting people to cross the line, but the world isn't always black or white. We're presented with extremes, even though the majority of humans are somewhere in the middle. If my choices are for abortion without limitations or for no abortions regardless of consequences, I don't like either one; same thing with the debate about community growth. First off it is the wrong debate. Secondly, it is framed with extremes which have nothing to do with resolution of the problems that exist in most communities around the world.

Do we want to lead the world in creating forms in the built environment? Forms which can lead us in becoming more sustainable? Then we need now, more than ever, to experiment with new ideas and different viewpoints. We need to be vigilant in rejecting familiar ideas repeated long past their demonstrated validity. We need to be vigilant in our quest for answers and to not frame our questions that generalize, polarize and characterize our opponents as well as distort the issues. We need to be vigilant in our duty to be civil and to not participate in the decline of civility. We need to be vigilant in protecting the principles of our Constitution. And we need to be vigilant in nourishing the principles of the modern project, for that is the foundation in our quest for the truth.

Most of all, to create sustainable communities, a sustainable nation and a sustainable world, we need to seek truth, and we need to keep the spirit of the American Revolution alive.

Index

U

V

W